T0244313

Praise for *Binding the Ghost*

"Ed Simon's incantatory book conjures up a world where literature and mysticism meet—where prayer is poetry and poetry is prayer. Delving joyously into centuries of texts, it promises nothing less than to reenchant our relationship with reading."

—Briallen Hopper, author of *Hard to Love*

"All truly perceptive writers and readers of literature know that they are engaged in something uncanny—call it magic, sacrament, theurgy, communion with things unseen, or what have you—and that to enter into the depths of language is to practice conjuration and enchantment, or to be possessed and addressed by divine powers. Apparently, Ed Simon was practicing 'Orphic criticism' long before he found a name for it. There is a luminous quality to all of these essays that shows he has long been aware that the true experience of literature is an initiation into mysteries, and a glimpse beyond what nature alone can reveal."

—David Bentley Hart, author of *That All Shall Be Saved*

"Ed Simon's writing is bold, norm defying, and refreshingly heretical. 'All poetry is incantation' and 'all prose is conjuration,' he writes in this book. And for good measure, he adds: 'Between those two poles lies the entirety of literature.' With frightening intelligence, a true polymath's breadth of knowledge, and a prophet's pathos, Simon shows in *Binding the Ghost* that the genuine work of art is a gesture toward transcendence. The best literature always takes you 'out of this world.'"

—Costica Bradatan, professor of humanities, Texas Tech University

BINDING THE GHOST

binding
the
ghost

Theology, Mystery, and the Transcendence of Literature

ED SIMON

FORTRESS PRESS
MINNEAPOLIS

BINDING THE GHOST
Theology, Mystery, and the Transcendence of Literature

All Scripture quotations are from the King James Version.

Image: Close up of spray water on black background
Credit: iStock, user Paperkites, ID number 1207523029
Cover design: Kristin Miller

Print ISBN: 978-1-5064-7877-7
eBook ISBN: 978-1-5064-7878-4

For my son, Finn, in the hopes that you forever
find the beauty in imagined worlds and the
truth in artful words carefully arranged

Contents

Part Three: Greatest of Characters

Introduction

Attend Muse to Our Sacred Song

Giordano Bruno didn't like England. The occultist and itinerant lecturer had arrived in London in 1583, having already called Naples, Venice, Rome, Lyon, Tours, and Paris home. Only a year later, and he'd write in his dialogue *The Ash Wednesday Supper* that English scholars, such as those he disputed with at Oxford, were a "constellation of the most pedantic, obstinate ignorance and presumption, mixed with a kind of rustic incivility, which would try the patience of Job." Despite his disdain, the Italian would have a productive two years in the country, producing six books, including *On the Infinite Universe and Worlds* and *On the Heroic Frenzies*, arguably conceiving the earliest hypotheses that consider the possibility of extraterrestrial life and of cosmological infinity. Bruno was an audacious thinker, part astronomer and part mystic, whose embrace of pagan occultism promised a new intellectual vitality

1

and threatened the established order. The sixteenth century was an era marked by tumultuousness in matters doctrinal, philosophical, and scientific, and Bruno was at the nexus of all three, a pugnacious man who was part Copernicus and part Martin Luther, though irreconcilably himself. At the core of his vision was the acknowledgment of reality's uncanny nature. "Divinity reveals herself in all things," wrote Bruno in the 1584 tract *The Expulsion of the Triumphant Beast*, "everything has Divinity latent within itself." Such enthusiasms are why Bruno found himself strapped to green kindling in Rome's Campo de' Fiori in the first year of the new century, immolated by the Inquisition for his heresies.

More than any other English thinker, Bruno would find a sympathetic spirit in the great statesman, poet, and critic Philip Sidney. Bruno dedicated two books to Sidney, evidence of deference afforded to the poet by many throughout his career. After Sidney was killed during the Battle of Zutphen in 1586, the steadfast Protestant enlisting alongside the Dutch in their war of independence from Spain, Fulke Greville, memorialized the great man, writing that "knowledge her light hath lost, valor hath slain her knight, / Sidney is dead, dead is my friend, dead is the world's delight." Celebrated for his immaculate verse, such as the sonnet cycle *Astrophel and Stella* and the romance *The Countess of Pembroke's Arcadia*, perhaps Sidney's greatest achievement was his slim book of literary criticism, *An Apology for Poesy*. Most likely written in 1580, though only published posthumously fifteen years later, Sidney's defense was for why cunning lies artfully organized should be countenanced by a Christian society. Philosophers and theologians had, since Plato, viewed literature with a suspicious and critical eye, often understanding it as being at best diversionary and at worst idolatrous. Sidney, by contrast, valorized poetry as "a speaking picture . . . to teach and to delight."

Much of the opprobrium directed at writers was that they invented truths, that they lied. Plato wrote in *The Republic*, as translated by Allan Bloom, that that "imitation is surely far from the truth . . . because it lays hold of a certain small part of each thing, and that part is itself only a phantom . . . those who take up tragic poetry in iambics and in epics are all imitators in the highest possible degree." By contrast, where Plato saw writing as a "kind of play and not serious," Sidney affirmed the intrinsic value of that very same play. *An Apology for Poesy* defends poetry by complicating Plato's claims about imitation. According to Sidney, Plato's central suspicion was entirely wrong, for "the poet, he nothing affirmeth, and therefore never lieth." Sidney allows that other people who manipulate words are capable of duplicity, or error, such as the historian who "affirming many things, can, in the cloudy knowledge of mankind, hardly escape from many lies." But the postulates of poetry are not like that of history; they do not correspond to reality in the same way. For that matter, neither does fiction, for when an author explores a world, they are not lying about something in our reality—they are creating a new reality.

An Apology for Poesy doesn't claim to be a book about magic—but it is. Any kind of hermetic basis for the book has been unexplored, and yet it's tremendously evocative to imagine what Sidney and Bruno might have conversed about at that Ash Wednesday supper. Sidney claims not that fiction and poetry aren't false or true but rather that literature is almost truer than true, realer than real. By positioning "words set in delightful proportion," the poet can generate entirely new worlds, all through the manipulation of letters and punctuation. Sidney's and Bruno's theories of language are thus similar, for the latter was an adept kabbalist, hermetist, and occultist, adhering to that Neoplatonist understanding of the significance of language that was so popular in the Renaissance.

Frances Yates explains in *The Occult Philosophy in the Elizabethan Age* how Italian thinkers like Marsilio Ficino and Giovanni Pico della Mirandola embraced a "theosophical mystique, nourished on elaborate search for hidden meaning in the scriptures, and on elaborate manipulation" of the alphabet. Drawing inspiration from Jewish kabbalah, these figures emphasized the ways in which letters, words, and punctuation didn't just describe reality but generated it, and Bruno was in the direct stead of those earlier scholars.

As with Sidney, literature didn't just correspond to truth or falsehood, which existed independently; rather, it created its own being—the end result was a new creation. Poets don't lie because they've created an entirely new universe, and their statements and claims now no longer have anything to do with the mundane reality that we all exist in. Positing that sentences can transcend the dichotomy beyond truth and falsehood intimates being able to do something with words that's almost supernatural. The text, for Sidney, is a thing-in-itself, a singularity, a null point, a metaphysical concept that's almost godlike. Furthermore, what makes the implications of his aesthetics so fascinating is that the writer affectively becomes a mage. What evocations might Sidney and Bruno have discovered during conversation, this poet and literary critic in conversation with a kabbalist, both committed to a faith in the transforming power of placing symbols in a particular order? "This space we declare to be infinite," Bruno wrote in 1584's *On the Infinite Universe and Worlds*, "since neither reason, convenience, possibility, sense-perception nor nature assign to it a limit. In it are an infinity of worlds of the same kind as our own." Not just an infinity of worlds but an infinity of words as well. Bruno's is almost a description of some sort of boundless library.

A specter is strangely not haunting literary criticism. The specter of, well, *specters.* Literature—it must be affirmed, admitted, understood, experienced—is fundamentally spooky. This often goes unremarked upon, unnoticed, or ignored, interpreted either as so obvious as to be unimportant or as sentimental obfuscation. But literature *is* spooky, for the mere uttering of words affects the world. And not just that, but literature with all of its mimesis and exposition is able to create entirely new worlds. Literature preserves characters and voices that seem as real to us as our own families, there are histories and narratives that seem as tangible as our own lives, there are lines of poetry that read as if they were spells. Undeniably, uncannily, unnervingly, deeply weird. Sidney is not blatant on that score, but the idea that there is language that is free of the need to be either true or false has its own implications. All of literary criticism, from Aristotle onward, eschews engaging with just how odd poetry, fiction, and drama actually are, preferring rather to dwell on the orthodoxy or aesthetics, the formalism of structure, or the historicism of biography. But all of these approaches are dogged by a shadow tradition, or at least an alternate sentiment, the ineffable feeling that when we approach the experience of literature, in all of its paradoxical grandeur, we are engaging with something that is a bit otherworldly.

To that end, I'm suggesting a new literary theory, not to supplant or replace, but to supplement. There are several potential names for such an approach; I entertained "supernatural criticism" but rejected this, since the prefix implies a neat division in our reality that I don't recognize. For a while, I called it "Fortean criticism" after the turn-of-the-twentieth-century folklorist Charles Fort, who collected accounts of all manner of anomalous phenomena, but with its connotations of conspiratorialism and the paranormal, that too I rejected. Finally, in honor of that mythic poet who harrowed hell, I decided to call it Orphic criticism, finding in the figure of Orpheus somebody deeply resonant with the mystery of this thing called literature. A theoretical orientation that asks "Attend muse to our sacred song." A literary theory negotiated between Sidney and Bruno. More than an approach, a methodology, or even a style, Orphic criticism is defined by a sentiment. Its operative position will be that the written word has historically been endowed with magic, and we'd do well to keep that in mind when we produce interpretations of texts. The aforementioned shadow approach has always lingered about the edges of our pages; whether kabbalah, exegesis, or hermeneutics, reality has been defined by the Logos—by the Word. Charged, enchanted, and numinous, literature is a practice commensurate, on some level, with mystery. Admitting it as such doesn't supplant traditional methods of analysis. Formalists can still examine grammar, syntax, and diction; historicists can still look at biography and cultural context. Nor does an approach that understands that literary analysis can benefit from a *magical* perspective need find formalism or historicism unhelpful. What such an approach does offer is grandeur, wonder, and ecstasy; it is a practice that fully embraces the inherent weirdness of literature—and if not offering explanation, hopefully supplying revelry.

As you read through *Binding the Ghost*, there are two motivating principles that structure Orphic criticism and, even if not explicitly stated, have motivated my approach to literary analysis. My first axiom is that *all poetry is incantation*; my second axiom is that *all prose is conjuration*. Between those two poles lies the entirety of literature. An admittedly (and purposefully) hermetic set of definitions, meriting a bit of elaboration. As regards the first principle, the purpose of verse—however it's written and structured—is to affect some sort of alteration in our reality, even if only in the mind of the reader, in a manner that's equivalent to how a magical spell is intended to have a spiritual consequence. Poetry is defined not by meter and rhythm, rhyme and alliteration, but rather by its purpose being to enchant, possess, and enrapture so that any trope that helps in that (including all I've mentioned) constitutes the form. By contrast, when I say that all prose is conjuration—whether fiction or nonfiction—what I'm saying is that the purpose is not necessarily to alter our reality but to create an entirely new one, where any similarity to our own experience is superficial. Prose uses all of the tools of narrative, plot, and story—regardless of the factuality of what's being written about—so that whole new universes can be invented. Poetry alters reality; prose creates it. As a caveat, something can be both incantation and conjuration, for in fact, no text can ever be entirely either, as absolute poetry and prose are abstractions pushed to the extreme. This distinction between poetry and prose is concerned less with generic definitions than with their transcendent functions.

Most of the pieces assembled here weren't composed with those principles of Orphic criticism explicitly in mind, though in the half decade from 2015 to 2020 when they were written, a general sense of my approach began to coalesce. As a scholar of literature, my own training is entirely more conventional—I didn't focus on the occult import of punctuation in my master's program, and my doctoral training didn't include bibliomancy. Orphic criticism is, however, something that I've intuited throughout my career, a general sense that literature is haunted by unspoken strangeness and that we'd do well to develop a critical vocabulary worthy of that oddity. Because economic considerations within academe are now so poor, there is now little need to play the game of adhering to critical orthodoxy for professional reasons, and so to that end, it's become much more enjoyable for me to write the bizarre little things that I want to write. Despite preferring to be both correct and interesting, if forced to choose a side, I'd rather be a partisan of the latter. It's what Bruno always did until it got him into trouble.

Part One

The Incantations of Poetry

Part One

The Implications of Poverty

1

Moved the Universe

Imagination here the Power so called. . . . That
awful Power rose from the mind's abyss.
—William Wordsworth, *The Prelude* (1798)

I call to the mysterious one who yet
Shall walk the wet sands by the edge of the stream.
—W. B. Yeats, "Ego Dominus Tuus" (1915)

More contemporary writers need to invoke the muse. I sing not of
the mundane human muse, the problematically feminized variety
configured as a vessel for male artistic inspiration: Beatrice Portinari
atop Paradise's mount, neglected Amelia Lanyer with almond eyes
remembered only as Shakespeare's Dark Lady, or Fanny Brawne,
whose beauty inspired truth in melancholic, tubercular Keats—all
muses depicted as seemingly devoid of agency. Nor do I envision

this invocation of the muse as being that of the nine listed by Hesiod: among them, Calliope with her tales of brave Ulysses, Erato whispering in Sappho's ear, and Euterpe scattering her lyrical fragments in the form of frayed Mediterranean papyrus.

At least that's not exactly what I envision, though if there is a sense of the sacred, occult, or even superstitious in that model of the muse, then I thoroughly embrace that. Rather, what I call for is a bit of that old magic, that incantatory whiff of incense that ritually signaled the beginning of ancient epics, that acknowledged that a poem is first and foremost a type of spell. "Tell me, O Muse, of the man of many devices, who wandered full many ways after he had sacked the sacred citadel of Troy," supposedly plucked out on lyre strings either by that blind poet Homer or by a whole bevy of bards (depending on your critical inclination) collaboratively conjuring the *Odyssey*, as rendered by Samuel Butler. Virgil spinning a yarn of imperial propaganda and chanting, as translated by Edward Fairfax Taylor, "O Muse! The causes and the crimes relate; What goddess was provok'd, and whence her hate." Or another poet eyeless in London millennia later, John Milton, who dictated *Paradise Lost* to his daughters so as to "Sing Heav'nly Muse, that on the secret top / Or Oreb, or of Sinai, didst inspire / That shepherd, who first taught the chosen seed, / In the beginning how the heavens and earth / Rose out of chaos" (appropriately enough, order out of chaos is the precise topic of this essay). Even after epic poetry had long been supplanted in popularity by the novel, there is a late appearance of that "American muse, whose strong and diverse heart / So many men have tried to understand," evoked over the pyres of Manassas, Antietam, and Gettysburg, burying our hearts at Wounded Knee, by Stephen Vincent Benét in *John Brown's Body*.

The invocation of the muse is a conceit that's been sadly neglected for a few centuries. Sadly neglected because it has more significance than just a rhetorical flourish, more importance than just a performance of mytho-cultural-superstitious peacocking and hedge betting. I should clarify that my desire to hear the muse accorded her due respect in contemporary letters is more of a conceit than it is an actual proposal. Imagining contemporary literature making an invocation leads to some cringeworthy hypotheticals, from "Sing, Fresh Green Breast of the New World, about a hero from the land of dusk, a man named Gatsby who searched for emerald hues on long islands" to "O Ducks of Central Park! Relate to me the tale of one who had no patience for phoniness." Rather, when I wish to let the muse back into the machine, I mean the significance of those prayers to her; I'm speaking of literature's sense of the ineffable, the numinous, the transcendent, the ecstatic. For in evoking the muse, scholars can draw attention to one of the rarely spoken scandals of literature: the perennial mysteriousness of inspiration that neither formalist New Critical scalpels have been able to cut away nor historicist analysis has been able to ever fully explain. Academic literary study can illuminate much, but when it comes to the true bundle of strangeness that is this thing called literature, criticism's light is feeble, and as the Spanish writer Federico García Lorca wrote in his *Sonnets of Dark Love*, "Only mystery enables us to live. . . . Only mystery." The dismissal of the muse must, thankfully, always be incomplete, for all the reductionist and disenchanted theories of how and why poetry is ultimately written can't completely silence her call. Better to be forthright in the manner that Johann Wolfgang von Goethe was in approaching the sublime artistry of the Italian violinist Niccolò Paganini, describing in an 1831 letter to an associate the musician's sublimity as "a mysterious power which everyone senses and no philosopher explains."

The pre-Socratic aphorist Democritus claimed that his fragments were composed "with inspiration and holy breath," which the Irish classicist E. R. Dodds in his consummate *The Greeks and the Irrational* understood to mean that "the Muse is actually inside the poet." Whether the voice is within or without is of no accounting to the voice's register, as the voice exists in a different state of consciousness than the lucky vessel who gets to hear and transcribe her words. In such a model, literature can be understood as conscious, both fiction and poetry as beings with awareness and agency, and the characters that are described can be understood as also being real. In the *Symposium*, translated by Lane Cooper, Plato describes the concept of the "daemon"—the inner muse, if you will—which inspires the creation of poetry, claiming that it is "a very powerful spirit . . . halfway between god and man . . . flying upward with our worship and prayers, and descending with the heavenly answers and commandments." This schema has a certain utility, but I'd ask to complicate the model a bit, for the identity of the daemon—internal to the author, external, or the text itself—must be ambiguous. The daemon can be read metaphorically or literally. Of course, we must understand it as the former, but don't see this as dismissive, for metaphors are all that humans have.

Because in conjuring the muse, or taking literally Lorca's admonition that "the first thing one must do is invoke the *duende*," we are neither casting lots nor engaging astrological divination but rather embracing the mysterious weirdness of literature—its prophetic import in the classical sense of that word. Literature is always collaborative, a process negotiated between the writer and the reader so that the muse transmigrates from the former to the latter. After all, who narrates the voice that you are currently reading in your head? Who is the speaker in omniscient narratives? Perhaps Sophia, that Platonist concept of wisdom that was the original word that was with God. The classical corollary to the Hebrew concept of Shekinah, God's indwelling presence that was grammatically feminine and is perhaps a bit of the reason why there have traditionally been nine female muses. In the apocryphal Wisdom of Solomon, the anonymous author describes Sophia as "the breath of the power of God, and a pure influence flowing from the glory of the Almighty . . . she is the brightness of the everlasting light, the unspotted mirror of the power of God, and the image of his goodness." Let's not literalize a metaphor no matter how good, for we must admit that contingencies of grammar tricked some into believing that the muse must always be a woman and the creator a man, but such reductionist binaries have no reality in the actual transcendent realm. Better to admit that though it's a metaphor, it's a powerful one, and critics can generate new and more powerful ones as well, for whatever its gender, the muse is a generative spirit. Metaphors are the thoughts of God, which past wisdom saw fit to call angels.

It's less the metaphor of the muse that I desire than that glowing kernel of inexplicability that defines this strange thing called literature, this weird theurgy that sees the creation of complete worlds and conscious characters, of poems that bottle the present, and of drama that lets the actress be possessed by the soul of someone who was invented. Don't mistake my exuberance here—I've no desire to return to some version of Arnoldian criticism, of Harold Bloom taxonomies and baseball card collecting. I've no need of a critical apparatus that trades in anything as mundane as quality, and if I want to rank works based on greatness, I'm fine with reading entertainment magazines over anything by the partisans of theoretical traditionalism, because in the former, at least the reviews are witty. And while I do appreciate the positivist impulses of that first critical revolution in the 1920s, the vagaries of the formalists who at least applied some rigor to the analysis of literature, and the multiplicity of approaches that were created in their wake (in either inspiration or reaction), I ultimately still find their approach to be like trying to weigh a soul or measure God's beard.

As a student and inheritor of theory as it was inaugurated in American universities with Jacques Derrida's 1966 Johns Hopkins lecture, and then as it filtered through the panoply of schools like deconstruction, post-structuralism, New Historicism, gender theory, postcolonial theory, critical race studies, queer theory, eco-criticism, and so on, and so on, and so on, I can no more fully reject those who taught me than my own birthright. Like all literary scholars, especially in this era of culture wars détente in the academy (as everyone is too busy worrying about finding a job), I tend to cautiously hew between formalist and historicist impulses, and when it comes to writing criticism, I find that such an approach is estimably pragmatic. But when it comes to really answering the sorts of questions I want answered (ones not just about inspiration)—Where do characters go when I close the book's covers? Can a poem think? Can it speak to other poems? Can it alter my very consciousness, make me into a completely different individual?—when it comes to Uncle Walt's promise that "you shall possess the origin of all poems," I find that theory is lacking.

In the *Tractatus*, Ludwig Wittgenstein writes that "even when all the possible scientific questions have been answered, the problems of life remain completely untouched." A mystic after my own heart, for I'd claim that even when all the possible literary critical questions have been answered—all the questions of form and biography, ideology and reception—the problems of literature remain completely untouched. As poet Edward Hirsch writes in his invaluable *The Demon and the Angel: Searching for the Source of Artistic Inspiration* (which supplied much in the way of my secondary examples in this essay), "Art is inexplicable and has a dream-power that radiates from the night mind. It unleashes something ancient, dark, and mysterious into the world." Again, do not mistake this as a call for some kind of conservative return to prelapsarian aesthetic considerations—I've no need of someone in tweed with elbow patches tut-tutting and telling me what's great; I can tell what's great on my own, *thankyouverymuch*. My purpose is the opposite, for I've no interest in taste, discernment, or style but rather only in communion, ecstasy, and transcendence (and if that makes me a neo-Romantic, so be it, save for the fact that I've no interest in genius). Rather, I want to understand whether chanting Emily Dickinson alters the fabric of space and time, I want to know what happened to Ishmael after he survived the *Pequod*, I want to know if *Paradise Lost* can hear me when I write marginalia in her margins. In short, I want to possess the origin of all poems. And while criticism and theory can illuminate any number of important and interesting questions, I find that the cosmic, astral, metaphysical alphabet that composes all of reality must be a bit beyond their grasp.

To that end, I propose the inauguration of a new approach to reading literature, or perhaps a very, very old one. So much of the discourse surrounding the academic study of literature is indebted to fashion in one way or another. Since the explosion of isms a generation ago, the *Chronicle of Higher Education* profiles any number of ingenious new ways to read, from the digital humanities and distance reading to Darwinian criticism, hoping that one or the other might stick. What's one more school to inaugurate, then? I propose that we need a hermetic means of approaching literature—the interpretive pose of the mystic, the magician, the mage. An occult method of analysis, one that offers less in the manner of explanation and more in the manner of reverence and awe, for as Hirsch writes in *The Demon and the Angel*, "Awe bears traces of the holy." This reverence is not to be inculcated as a means of bolstering particular power arrangements; it is not the cultivation of a particular aesthetic so as to advertise one's cultivation (in the Pierre Bourdieu sense of habitus). Instead, such reverence should be understood as an engagement with that profound Other that we call the divine, that we call the sacred. It's reading poems not as texts but as prayers, novels as liturgy, drama as ritual. And in the process, it's acknowledging the fundamental mysteriousness that accompanies the paradoxical truth status of fiction, that in the construction of visceral realities that contain such people in them, reader and author are collectively implicated in a manner of profound magic.

I envision such criticism as being less engaged with answers than with avoiding evasions about literature's fundamental strangeness, a methodology defined not by the results it generates but by the questions it's willing to be honest about. These would include "Where does literature come from?" the most fundamental of issues, which can in part be explicated by recourse to culture, craft, form, and history but against which any totalizing explanation must come up short when confronted by the sheer enormity of how real the sailors of *Moby-Dick* are or how conscious Jane Eyre is. Better to consider the origins of poetry with William Blake's declaration in *Songs of Innocence and Experience*, "I write when commanded by the spirits and the moment I have written I see the words fly about the room in all directions." These would also include rumination on how literature corresponds to reality. That is, how we're to understand the odd function of fiction, halfway between lie and truth yet seemingly neither—albeit at its most crucial, in the service of the latter.

How must it be incontrovertible truth that Sherlock Holmes always lives at 221B Baker Street and yet there is no real man? That there is an eternity to Mrs. Dalloway's existence, a perennialism to Dean Moriarty and Sal Paradise's perambulations? If these characters are not real, what act of conjuration makes these characters appear so? And if the kiss given to Helen of Troy is actually imparted to some demonic automaton, what, then, is precisely the difference? Furthermore, can we speak of literature itself as conscious, as understood psychologically not as a matter of interpretation but as one would approach a distinct individual with a mind, agency, and the ability to react and change? Asked about the sources of his inspiration, as recorded by Richard Garnett in *William Blake, Painter and Poet*, the prophet responded that "the Authors are in Eternity," but what if we take texts as the authors of themselves or from some Platonic realm where they are as the very breaths of God?

These questions, so central to our own experience of literature when we're moved by a novel, ecstatic from a poem, or enraptured by a drama, relate to the fundamental strangeness of writing, which is the rapturous hallucination triggered by staring at bits of inky stain on crushed wood pulp. That old hash eater and consummate kabbalist Walter Benjamin phrased it perfectly when he claimed that "the reader, the thinkers, the loiterer . . . are types of illuminati just as much as the opium-eater, the dreamer, the ecstatic," for in making that Orphic harrowing into the symbolic realm, we discover "that most terrible drug—ourselves—which we take in solitude." Ultimately, it is that which gives this new criticism its name: Orphic criticism. For as that mythopoeic father of poetry descended unto that which was the origin of all poems, we too must become cosmonauts in the weirdness and strangeness that is literature, but unlike Orpheus, we must endeavor to return, rather being like Rabbi Akiva, who was the only one of four to return from the Garden of Paradise intact.

Orphic criticism doesn't have its origin with me; merely, like any greedy academic, I just choose to apply some terminology to a thing that already exists. For there are brilliant Orphic critics writing this very hour, from Hirsch and the consummate George Steiner to the Argentinean student of Borges, Alberto Manguel. There are precursors too, not just critics like Benjamin and Lorca but all those who divined literature with an understanding of the sweet magic that animates phoneme and possesses word, sentence, and paragraph. An unseen vein of Orphic criticism runs from the moment that baboon-faced Thoth first invented the alphabet to when Enoch of the seventh generation "walked with God: and he was no more; for God took him," becoming that archangel voice of Adonai whom we know as Metatron (and who is the rightful narrator of all third-person omniscient narratives). Because what defines the Orphic approach is never necessarily analytical acumen (certainly not that) nor adept close readings but rather an ecstatic, enchanted, enraptured sense of the numinous at literature's core. Orphic criticism is neither method nor approach but rather attitude and perspective. It does not elucidate so much as it serves to befuddle; it trades not in falsifiable positivities but rather in smudged scraps of papyrus with spells written upon them. No exact method can be explicated, for that is part of the point.

Orphic criticism is that which is sympathetic, even metaphorically, to the sentiment of Blake when he sat for the painter Thomas Phillips and simply told the artist "that angels descended to painters of old, and sat for their portraits," as recorded by Allan Cunningham in *The Cabinet Gallery of Pictures*. Orphic criticism does not shun from the implications of Hirsch's description of Blake's "habitual way of conversing with angels, spirits, and demons." Orphic criticism tries to re-create the conversations between the Romantic poet and "my demon poesy" for three weeks in the spring of 1819. Orphic criticism is that which takes seriously Blake's visionary account of a "shape dilated more and more" where "the roof of my study opened" and a figure "ascended into heaven . . . stood in the sun, and beckoning to me, moved the universe," for such a figure "was the arch-angel Gabriel." Orphic criticism does not reduce Gabriel to neurological ephemera or to historically contingent metaphor. It reads Blake neither as insane nor as lying; rather, it takes the great prophet at his word and duly tries to move the universe alongside his angel. For what Orphic criticism finally offers are not answers but questions. What Orphic criticism does is take literature on its own terms. Finally.

2

Prayer Is Poetry

Attention, taken to its highest degree, is the same
thing as prayer. It presupposes faith and love.

—Simone Weil, "Attention and Will" (1942)

I do not mean to deny the traditional prayers I have said all
my life; but I have been saying them and not feeling them.

—Flannery O'Connor, private prayer journal (1946)

Murmuring fills the stone halls of Mount Athos's monasteries, exhaling like breath into a cold and clear morning. With its
thousands of monks, there is not silence—there is the opposite of
silence. Excluding the sounds of nature—the cooing of turtledoves
and the swooping of Dalmatian pelicans, the sound of rain hitting
the granite paths of the isle, the lapping of the ocean upon the jag-
ged rocks—there is the omnipresent shudder of thousands of men's

faintly mumbled devotions, called to prayer by one of their brothers hitting the metal of a semantron with a wooden mallet. Like chill dew condensed on green leaves still black before the dawn, prayer clings in the atmosphere of this place. Prayer is the ether of Athos through which light must travel; the din of monks chanting at every hour of the day and for all days is like holy cosmic background radiation.

At the tip of that rocky peninsula, jutting like a limb into the wine-dark Aegean, are the twenty communities of the Orthodox Monastic Republic of Athos, an outcropping that has been continuously home to ascetic, celibate, reverential monks for eighteen centuries. There, overlooking the Greek sea, sit buildings like the blue onion-domed mirage of Saint Panteleimon Monastery, filled with Russian monks keeping their liturgy, and the Byzantine castle that constitutes the Stavronikita Monastery in honor of Saint Nicholas. That holy bishop looks down on his novices with black eye from gold icon; Saint Nicholas is joined by companions such as Saint Gregory, Saint Nektarios, and the gentle Virgin of Theotokos, as painted by the great artist Theophanes the Cretan. In their otherworldly position, what do the icons see? There they watch scores of dark-robed monks, who with lips covered by black and gray and white beards repeat the same prayer as if breathing, over and over: "Lord Jesus Christ, Son of God, have mercy on me, a sinner."

Such a process, the continual repetition of the Jesus Prayer until it begins to lose coherence, in the same way that a continually uttered word begins to sound like nothing if you do it long enough, lends the words a different sort of significance. Any true hearing of the prayer has to consider the words beyond the words, gesturing toward that which exists beyond literal statement. Meaning is sacrificed for mystery, and in the process, an infinity is gained. Many who use this approach, known as Hesychasm, do so "not just as a philosophical device for indicating God's utter transcendence, but also, and much more fundamentally, as a means for attaining union with Him through prayer," notes Timothy Ware in his classic introduction *The Orthodox Church*. The spiritual cosmonauts who are Hesychasts engage in this extreme repetitive prayer, chasing the literal semantic meanings out of words like souls departing from dead flesh, because such "negations . . . act[s] as a springboard or trampoline whereby the mystical theologian [seeks] to leap up with all the fullness of his or her being in the living mystery of God," as Ware explains.

As superficial attributes are burnt away, the sinner is to encounter the noble silence that is at the core of all of us, the ineffable utterances of prayer. A process whereby those enraptured in the liturgy will subtract that which defines their externalities—a prayer so fervent that it will blind your eyes, mute your mouth, and deafen your ears. This is prayer at its most extreme—absolute, indomitable, and unceasing. Philip and Carol Zaleski explain in *Prayer: A History* that the "roots of the Jesus Prayer lie in the traditional belief that names contain power . . . and that repetition of a name concentrates and focuses this power." The famed utterance is based on these contemplative principles of Hesychasm formulated within Eastern Orthodox Christianity, whereby the individual empties her soul out so as to make room for those defusing molecules of holiness. In such a space, it is not just the spirit, mind, heart, and mouth that utter the anchorite's prayer, but indeed the elbow and ankle, the eyelash and earlobe, the knuckle and wrist also. Writing in the fourth century, the Church Father John Cassian said that the Jesus Prayer is to be one that you think upon "as you sleep, as you eat, as you submit to the most basic demands of nature. . . . You will write it upon the threshold and gateway of your mouth, you will place it on the walls of your house and in the inner sanctum of your heart." For if the Jesus Prayer is a narrative, it is one into which those who pray must descend; if it is a poem, it is one where the words themselves become indistinguishable from the reader, where the recitation becomes life.

The Jesus Prayer is not mere supplication; rather, it's a variation on what Walt Whitman intoned in *Leaves of Grass*, whereby "your very flesh shall be a great poem." When one transforms themselves into an evocation, it matters not whether we're speaking of "prayer" or "poetry," for in heaven, those categories are the same thing. Prayer is like poetry in that the greatest examples of both take as their greatest subjects themselves. All true prayers are about prayer; all beautiful poetry is really about poetry. Like all divine utterances, the Jesus Prayer is also narrative and rhetoric, capable of being read critically. This is not to diminish the import of this celebrated Orthodox prayer; we must avoid collapsing the liturgical into the aesthetic, the profundity of ritual into the mere marketplace of art. But the Jesus Prayer—all twelve words, four clauses, three commas, and one period that constitute it—wouldn't be as effective were it not also poetry, if it did not also have an endlessly regenerative story at its center. A script into which any penitent could imagine themselves.

For those who aren't Orthodox but are familiar with the Jesus Prayer, it's perhaps read less as literature itself and more a concept that may have been encountered in literature. The prayer plays a large part in the plot of J. D. Salinger's novel *Franny and Zooey*, whereby the former of the two Upper East Side Glass sisters becomes obsessed with the Jesus Prayer after reading an account of it in the nineteenth-century anonymous Russian tract called *The Way of a Pilgrim*. As Franny recounts to her college boyfriend, when considering unceasing prayer as is practiced on Athos, one must emphatically ask if they had ever heard "anything so fascinating in your *life*, in a way?" Far from mere neurotic scrupulosity, the Jesus Prayer is a melding of the person with the poem, whereby the author of *The Way of a Pilgrim* could say, "Sometimes my heart would feel as though it were bubbling with joy; such lightness, freedom, and consolation were in it." The repetition of prayer is like wheels turning in the wind, equally dispelling meaning and its malignant sibling, worry. Franny was right to be fascinated.

So let's close read the Jesus Prayer as poetry. It begins with that invocation, a calling upon Christ as if Homer entreating the muse; it transitions into the statement of identity for the Son of God, whose majesty is contrasted with the narrator of the lyric, who is in need of saving grace. The plaintiveness of requesting mercy has the weighted heaviness of its simple declaration. So much is held in those last two words; the indefinite article indicating the universality of sin, the confession of that condition the material for all great drama. The Jesus Prayer is a microfiction written in the present tense, where the main character is whoever should be speaking it. The great tale it tells is that of unearned salvation. The peroration is inconclusive, the ending yet to be written.

God will hear any prayer as poetry—even the recitation of the alphabet or guttural nonsense syllables may be recognized by the Lord as prayer—but humans require prosody to stick in the brain. Too often, prayer is dismissed by the secular because it's reduced to a mere plea for intercession; it's slurred as being a cosmic gift card and not recognized for what it actually is—the only poetic genre defined by its intended audience being the divine. Not enough attention is paid to the poetic aspects of prayer; scarcely more attention is paid to the prayerful qualities of poetry. Prayer is just as deserving of critical analysis, of close reading and interpretation through the methods of literary interpretation as any verse is. Such is the position of the *New Yorker*'s esteemed book critic James

Wood, who in his introduction to the Penguin Deluxe edition of the archbishop of Canterbury Thomas Cranmer's 1549 the *Book of Common Prayer* argued that the Church of England missal marked "one of the great, abiding works of English literature." There are a handful of anthologies that treat prayer with the literary interest expressed by Wood. The *Oxford Book of Prayer* is an ecumenical anthology compiled by a group of scholars that goes beyond Christianity to explore the varieties of the poetic numinous, with the committee member George Appleton explaining that their desire was to express admiration for "all who value the religious experience of mankind, and are seeking the Eternal Mystery and Transcendence." Religion popularizer Karen Armstrong offered her own selection of prayers as poems in the collection *Tongues of Fire: An Anthology of Religious and Poetic Experience*, which is sadly out of print. But for the most part, there is an endemic critical fallacy separating prayer and poetry.

Theologians frequently divide prayers into five categories: adoration, petition, thanksgiving, contrition, and confession; in an act of Episcopalian parsimony, the essayist Anne Lamott collapses those categories in her New Age guide *Help, Thanks, Wow: The Three Essential Prayers*. Certainly prayer as a genre has multiple uses, with petition for the Lord to redress our needs and desires being but the least of these. That's not to diminish the importance of supplication; there are few things more understandable, universal, and human than the individual crying out to God in helplessness. Even God himself supposedly does it as he dies upon the cross. If poetry is to be an expression of the breadth of humanity in its full experience, then the various purposes of prayer represent a helpful encapsulation of what it means to be a person, running the gamut from ecstatic wonder to humble gratitude, desperation to guilt. The most powerful of prayers arguably embody all of those reasons for praying in the first place, because it's not always easy to separate the terrible wonder toward God from our desire for redemption or our cries for help.

Filmmakers often understand the innate dramatic potential of a prayer, whether it be calmly spoken by John Cazale's stoic Fredo in the seconds before his brother Michael, as played with reptilian efficacy by Al Pacino, has an associate shoot him in the back of the head during an ill-fated fishing trip in Francis Ford Coppola's *The Godfather: Part II*; bellowed out in horror and sadness like Harvey Keitel's tortured scream within a cathedral at the conclusion of Abel Ferrara's gritty noir depiction of a corrupt cop in *Bad Lieutenant*; or recited by Samuel L. Jackson's character Jules Winnfield before executing someone who has run afoul of him in Quentin Tarantino's *Pulp Fiction* (the bit of scripture was rather hubristically invented by the director). If crime drama seems heavy on prayer, then it's because prayer isn't only for quiet meditation but exists at those places where sin and the sacred must by necessity occupy the same space. Such is the explanation as memorably delivered by Jackson, who reflects that when it comes to his scriptwriter's pseudoscriptural inflection, "I been saying that shit for years. And if you heard it, that meant your ass. I never gave much thought to what it meant. I just thought it was some cold-blooded shit to say to a motherfucker. . . . But I saw some shit this morning that made me think twice. . . . The truth is . . . you're the weak, and I am the tyranny of evil men. But I'm trying."

Prayer must, by definition, be extreme; to make oneself a conduit for the transcendent by words artfully arranged is, in a materialistic culture dominated by ruthless pragmatism, a transgressive practice. For those who reject prayer as maudlin affectation, more Thomas Kinkade than Caravaggio, know that the latter has been at the forefront of the sacred a lot longer than the former. Not surprisingly, but strangely, underremarked on is the understandable facility that poets themselves have in composing prayers. The nineteenth-century novelist Anne Brontë wrote her own subversive supplication in 1844, asking in a poem titled after her first line, "My God! O let me call Thee mine! / Weak, wretched sinner though I be, / My trembling soul would fain be Thine, / My feeble faith still clings to Thee." The poem is perfectly orthodox (lowercase *o* emphasized), for there would be nobody in the Church of England at the time who would look askance at a confession of their faith's fallibility. Yet there is also an eroticism in Brontë's lyric, the romantic connotations of asking the beloved to be the speaker's, the desire to cling to the beloved. In her language, she calls back to the seventeenth-century Metaphysical tradition of George Herbert or especially John Donne; in her punctuation, she calls forward to Whitman. The forwardness of her confession that "not only for the past I grieve, / The future fills me with dismay" is Brontë's alone, however—the universality of such an observation paradoxically belying its personal nature.

Some of our greatest modernists have penned prayers as captivating as anything written in a patrist's cell or jotted in the margins of a Puritan's notebook, and not even necessarily the obvious figures who had religious fascinations like T. S. Eliot or Ezra Pound. Broad-shouldered Carl Sandburg of that hog-butchery capital of the world, Chicago, wrote an unlikely prayer, appropriately enough for his proletariat subject matter entitled "Prayers of Steel." In a manner that evokes the Holy Sonnets of Donne, Sandburg asks the Lord to "lay me on an anvil, O God. / Beat me and hammer me into a crowbar. / Let me pry loose old walls. / Let me lift and loosen old foundations." If prayer is erotic, then it's also violent—it's instrumental. Such a practice is to be a technology for transformation, and Sandburg's desire is to be made into something with all of the heft, energy, and grit of sheer matter so that God would "beat me and hammer me into a steel spike. / Drive me into the girders that hold a skyscraper together. / Take red-hot rivets and fasten me into the central girders." For such is a fundamental tension, a beautiful paradox of prayer—that it requires a profound humility but is based on the belief that a simple human can casually compose verse for the infinite so that he who is in repose may "be the great nail holding a skyscraper through blue nights into white stars."

Another modernist psalmist is the Jamaican American poet and seminal Harlem Renaissance figure Claude McKay, who composed a melancholic and intensely personal meditation in 1922, writing in his simply titled "A Prayer," "'Mid the discordant noises of the day I hear thee calling; / I stumble as I fare along Earth's way; keep me from falling," a declaration that perhaps most sharply differentiates prayer as a subset of poetry—for unlike the latter, the former is always obligated to be honest (for its reader would know if it wasn't). In a theme that has motivated religious narrative from Paul to Augustine to Hank Williams Sr., McKay tells God that the "wild and fiery passion of my youth consumes my soul; / In agony I turn to thee for truth and self-control." The rhyming couplets, as critically out of fashion as they were and continue to be, give the prayer the singsong quality of hymn; their formal innocence adds to the sense of helplessness that motivates the most intense of prayers.

That great wit and raconteur Dorothy Parker, more famous for her cutting gin-and-vermouth-fueled quips at the Algonquin Round Table than piety, penned a beautiful and sad prayer in 1930 that James P. Moore Jr. described in *One Nation under God: A History of Prayer in America* as "conveying a rare tenderness in the midst of personal loss." Written in light of infidelity, miscarriage, and the omnipresent companion of alcoholism, Parker pleaded, "Dearest one, when I am dead / Never seek to follow me. / Never mount the quiet hill / Where the copper leaves are still, / As my heart is, on the tree / Standing at my narrow bed." Parker's sadness is a rejoinder to those who see in prayer only the myopia of personal contentment, the asking of a cosmic favor. Rather, her prayer is an artifact of the broken ego that defines the tragedy of any prayer uttered truthfully—that prayer, if it's to be heard, must be a ritual of ego extinction, of Hesychasm. "Only of your tenderness, / Pray a little prayer at night," wrote Parker, "Say: 'I have forgiven now— / I, so weak and sad; O Thou, / Wreathed in thunder, robed in light, / Surely Thou wilt do no less.'"

If prayer was "effective," then people wouldn't die young, alone, sick, spurned, and forgotten; if prayer was "pragmatic," then loved ones wouldn't suffer and pass, people wouldn't be in debt, and homes wouldn't be foreclosed; if prayer was "useful," then we'd never be despairing and broken. That prayer's purpose isn't to be effective, pragmatic, or useful speaks to a far deeper thirst that the practice quenches. Prayer isn't about avoiding bad things; it's about how one approaches their inevitability in a fallen world. Because I am a broken person who once drank too much and discovered that it was impossible for me to drink less without drinking everything, I decided that it would be easier to not drink at all. As such, there's a perhaps predictable and clichéd prayer that I've long been partial toward but that has as much significance to me as the Jesus Prayer had to John Cassian. In *Prayer: A History*, Philip and Carol Zaleski write of the Serenity Prayer, "Nothing in it smacks of ideology or sectarianism, and yet its demands, if followed faithfully and to the letter, require Solomonic insight and saintly fortitude."

Commonly attributed to the liberal Protestant minister and theologian Reinhold Niebuhr, who claimed that he first preached it in a sermon at an Evangelical church in western Massachusetts during World War II, the prayer was attributed by the founder of Alcoholics Anonymous, Bill W., to everyone from an "ancient Greek, an English poet, [or] an American naval officer," as the Zaleskis write. As seen on coffee mugs, wall hangings, key chains, and cross-stitches, the Serenity Prayer implores, "God grant us the serenity to accept the things we cannot change, / Courage to change the things we can, / And wisdom to know the difference." This Stoic injunction is often misinterpreted as maudlin pablum by those who stop at the first sentence, misinterpreting the call to surrender as unthinking capitulation, whereas in reality, it is often good sense. It's the second sentence that has the pathos, however, and in the third, there is the ingredient for all true narrative. When people are unable to know the difference, we call it tragedy; when they can, we call it something else—even if tragedy remains forever a possibility.

The prayerful greatest hits have much to recommend in themselves as well, of course. Each of the great Abrahamic faiths is poetically bound by defining prayers, whether the Jewish Shema Yisrael, the Christian Pater Noster, or the Islamic Shahadah. The Shema's blessing is both principle and poem, the short declaration "Hear, O Israel: The Lord is our God, the Lord is One" a statement of divine synthesis, unity, consilience. The imploration that the collected people must listen raises our profane realm into the transcendent. As with the Hesychasts or Whitman, humanity itself is transposed into the very flesh of the prayer. Melvin Konner describes the phylacteries used by observant Jews in the recitation of the prayer, writing in *Unsettled: An Anthropology of the Jews* about "tefillin, the black leather boxes that hold the words of the Shema, fulfilling the commandment to place them as 'a sign upon the hand' and 'frontlets between the eyes.'" The Shahada does something similar, presenting an axiom as a prayer, the drama implicit within it a statement about reality itself. "There is no god but God," prays the observant Muslim, and part of the beauty of the statement lies in its tautological simplicity, self-referentiality only broken in English transliteration by orthographic convention regarding the capitalization of certain words. The Pater Noster has a similar sense of the ways in which heaven (and perhaps hell) dwells not in a beyond but in the here and now, as clear as a poem placed in a box and affixed to the forehead. What could be more tangible than the forgiveness of debts and of our "daily bread"?

America's greatest psalmist, Emily Dickinson, in poem 437, defined the genre as being "the little implement / Through which Men reach / Where Presence—is denied them," the gap of that characteristic dash saying everything we've ever felt, thought, or wondered about the spaces at the center of that absent Writer we call G-d. Perhaps that old language of adoration, thanksgiving, contrition, and so on is limited. Better to think of prayer as being the poetry that you internalize and take with you, a consumptive implement that burns away the detritus of personality to leave behind (w)holy ash. Prayer is the poetry that possesses the body, the kernel of a soul left over when everything else has been immolated. Poems are written for audiences, readers, the poets themselves, but only prayers are written for God.

Prayer is no doubt the literary genre for which there is the greatest number of compositions but for which the vast majority of them will never be heard or read by any living person. The only literary genre in which there need not even be words for it to be a poem. All true prayers have as their subject the drama of salvation, redemption, reconciliation, peace. Such was the request of the great Iranian poet Jalāl al-Dīn Rūmī, who in the thirteenth century ecstatically implored us to "come, come, whoever you are. Wanderer, worshiper, lover of learning—it doesn't matter, / Ours is not a caravan of despair. / Come, even if you have broken your vow a hundred times, / Come, come again, come." So prayer is, even when it seems to despair, a fundamentally optimistic genre. What it presupposes is that every second is a portal through which some kind of grace may enter. What it hopes is that there is somebody on the receiving end, listening.

3

Recall, Orpheus

Recall, Jacob. The Hebrew patriarch's nocturnal wrestling with that unnamed angel, presumed to be God himself. The story is sublimely strange, in the manner of the Scriptures at their most powerful. As a book, or rather a collection of books, the poetry of the Bible is the most true when it is the most inexplicable. To wit, Jacob fought with the supernatural being and prevailed, earning him his blessed new name, *Israel* (he who fights with God), but when desiring to learn the name of his assailant, God demurs. Genesis 32:29: "And Jacob asked him, and said, Tell me, I pray thee, thy name. And he said, Wherefore is it that thou dost ask after my name?" The patriarch is victorious in all but finding the true name for this being he has wrestled with. The story remains supremely disquieting in what it doesn't say.

There is one possible interpretation, rooted in the Axial Age beliefs of the men who repeated such stories and the scribes who wrote them down, and in many ways, it is an interpretation that remains true in a primal and visceral way. In this interpretation, the story conveys the singular, powerful, and literally magical possibilities within language—the supreme, spooky, transcendent capabilities inherent within the word. There is significance in a name, and in a manner, all words are names of a sort. Men and women of Jacob's day understood how powerful the word could be; to know someone's name was to have the possibility to supernaturally control them. This being, this God who Jacob struggled with could lose the night battle but must never lose the war. Jacob can never know his true name. This fear motivates the commandment against taking the Lord's name in vain. Restricting the use of God's name is not a simple issue of the perceived disrespect inherent in blasphemy but rather a need to prevent the use of magical language so as to ensnare or somehow control the being who created the universe. In this way, creatures will never have dominion over their creator, and the Word must remain ineffable. In the beginning, there may have been the Word, but as Jacques Derrida would remind us, it must endlessly defer to itself.

The word is simultaneously profane—that which we use to communicate every day—and the Word is sacred—that which exists and justifies the ground of being. This is worth remembering, for it is just as true today as it was in Jacob's era. When the Word itself is considered, there's a special category of language that's all the more intense, all the more rarefied, all the more explosive. I'm speaking of poetry, which, for all of the traditional attributes we apply to it—rhythm, meter, rhyme, and so on—is only ever really distinguished from other forms of language by what it does, not necessarily how it does it. And what poetry does is use all of its tricks, tropes, and conceits to draw attention to the artifice of language, to make language strange and thus all the more miraculous.

There is magic in poetry, not just as a metaphor, but in a literal sense as well. Narrative, fiction, language, prosody—all of these, despite the calipers of criticism, maintain a sort of charged and enchanted power. There is something sacred in poetry that is greater than and before that of even religion: the power of language. This ability of language—to conjure completely different worlds that exist only in the grammatical relationships of abstract words to one another, to maintain the ability to affect the objective world of material existence, and to function as a totem of meaning that can travel from mind to mind—was as visceral for Jacob wrestling with his angel as it is for any of us wrestling with meaning today.

In the ancient world of the Mediterranean, Greek and Jew alike were united in this alphabetic predisposition and shared a belief that letters, words, and language were uniquely capable of a special kind of power. This is not an entropic jeremiad. I do not believe that the power of language has lost any of its magic; it still permeates and pulses through conversation, paper, and unseen electrons. Language is so all-encompassing a medium that like a fish in water, we don't even need to recognize it for its magic to work. Where ancient papyri were perhaps inscribed with special combinations of letters used to protect, condemn, conjure, and divinate, the great literary lines of our own culture spread meme-like throughout the system of interconnected humans who constitute our species. Not all combinations of letters are equal, of course—just as a misplaced diacritical in ancient Hebrew could indicate the wrong vowel and thus nullify any power a given line may have had, a misplaced word that makes a line unmemorable can negate the effectiveness of a poetic line. If the first part of my argument is that poetry remains in some sense enchanted, the second is that no poem can be fully enchanting if there is not a line that can function as a fragment shored against your ruin. Not all lines can be memorable; indeed, a hypothetical cento of only excellent turns of phrase negates the power of the memorable line, which defines itself contextually in opposition to the ones that function as supporting actors. But when a line aphoristically rises to the level of magic, then being able to call it forth is like the power of knowing God's real name.

In lyric, or in the now sadly undercelebrated genre of epic, the memorable line is the fundamental currency. If any poem does not have a line that sticks inside your skull, it is not a good poem. For the mind is its own place and in itself can make a heaven of hell, a hell of heaven. As the ancient Hebrews and Greeks understood, the abecedarian that was human language constitutes a communal tongue shared by all of us, and our best thoughts are often crafted by others, for as William Burroughs said, the word is a virus, but viruses are the very substance of inoculation. Poems are remembered by phrases: "In Xanadu did Kublah Khan" or "Shall I compare thee to a summer's day?" and "Do not go gentle into that good night." These fragments are like pottery shards we excavate from a site and imperfectly glue together to constitute our own selfhoods. We do this because a thing of beauty is a joy forever. And though no poem is supposedly as lovely as a tree, the tree only has existence because we are able to name it.

National Poetry Month recently ended in that cruelest of months. Critics often take aim at the kitschification of poetry, which once supposedly existed at the heights of Parnassian influence, as if now the Academy of American Poets and the Poetry Foundation have conspired to force Orpheus to write copy for those magnets and greeting cards with inspirational sayings on them available for purchase near the checkout line at Whole Foods. That is the critique of those who think the month commercializes poetry; it is not necessarily (or at least, not always) my critique. As the only things that have ever been done at large scale have only ever been facilitated through the power of language, it is very much true that poets unironically are, always have been, and always will be the unacknowledged legislators of the world. This is true for both good and evil; kitschification is irrelevant to that. No amount of denigration or celebration can either exult or diminish the simple fact that language is all-consumingly powerful, and poetry is the most distilled, crystalline, and perfect example of language.

All language is magical, and all poetry is language, but not all language is poetry. The unique capabilities of verse are that it simultaneously refers to something beyond itself as all language does (whether something real or not) while also drawing attention to its own artifice. In this way, poetry is both the means of expression and the object itself. Poetry, through the use of certain incantatory effects we call rhythm, meter, rhyme, consonance, assonance, metaphor, simile, and so on, makes its own artifice obvious and thus is honest about and admits its magic. Poetry can be about all sorts of things; it can be political, religious, personal, propagandistic, doggerel, what have you. But one of the most important subjects of every poem, without exception, is the idea of poetry itself. If all language, in its infinite, endlessly recursive ability to create new worlds and to alter the one in which we live, is a form of magic, then poetry is when that system becomes self-conscious. Poetry is when language thinks about itself. It is not about consciousness; it is consciousness.

Perhaps the fears about a decline in poetry (which is a priori impossible, since wherever language exists, poetry must also exist by definition) are because we simply do not recognize the fact that our very lives are poems themselves and that the stuff of verse is in the protean everyday. We always have been, and still are, composed of poetry. Lines of verse always rattle about in our heads, whether promoted by the academy or not. Those Svengalis of Madison Avenue are sometimes great poets; often those fragments shorn against our ruin were penned there. Witness one example: the Foote, Cone & Belding slogan for insecticide, "Raid Kills Bugs Dead," which was written by the Beat poet Lew Welch when he worked in advertising and is a perfect example of spondaic bimeter. Or if not advertising, then surely popular music should be seen as a reservoir of contemporary poetry without controversy, harkening back to when the psalms were sung. As the novelist Michael Chabon once said, Warren Zevon's line "Little old lady got mutilated late last night" from "Werewolves of London" taught him everything he needed to know about consonance, assonance, and alliteration.

W. H. Auden wrote in his lyric "In Memory of W. B. Yeats" that "poetry makes nothing happen," and in a way, he is right, especially if we understand the broader implications of what he meant (especially considering the rarely quoted line later in the stanza where he confesses that poetry is "a way of happening"). Like the great God of the medieval mystics, a poem exists unto itself, and only for itself, meaning radiating out from it. A poem sells nothing but itself, not even insecticide. But of course, poems make things happen whether we see them as poems or not, for language makes things happen, because to know the name of God gives you dominion over him even if you are his creation. As we are the creation of language, the ability to manipulate that language generates its own power. This is true whether there is a month to acknowledge that power or not, because it exists whether we see it or not. As for God, one assumes our prayers are appreciated but hardly necessary for his existence. The same is true for poetry.

4

Poetry before the Fall; or, The Pathetic Fallacy in Paradise

Spare a thought of pity for the person who has felt the warmth of the sun and not smiled, espied the mysteriousness of the moon without acknowledging her meditative melancholy, or been upon a raging ocean and not empathized with its mad fury. Such personifications, the imbuing of the inanimate with the energy of emotion, have a deep literary history. Shakespeare's *Julius Caesar* prefigures the treachery of the Ides of March with "scolding winds," an "ambitious ocean," and "threatening clouds," and in *Macbeth*, the playwright informs his audience that the "night has been unruly." John Keats with his weeping clouds and William Wordsworth with his lonely mists went in for this sort of thing, and Emily Brontë's heights were wuthering. Charles Dickens bucked against furious winds, and even Bob Dylan stepped in the "middle of seven sad forests." A faint shimmer of that old pagan perspective, of enchanted meaning glowing like embers in a chill, contemplative autumn bonfire.

Killjoys will observe that winds do not scold and cannot be furious, oceans have no ambition, clouds do not threaten or weep, and forests cannot be sad—even if the people within them are. Such a perspective—that projecting our consciousness onto nature is fundamentally flawed—is a position against what is called the "pathetic fallacy." The adjective is from the Greek *pathos* for emotion, but the more common pejorative meaning of the word might as well be noted, for the positivist who disparages representations of the environment exhibiting human subjectivity argues that there is something pathetic about such language. A tendency to inflect the literal storms of the outside world with the metaphorical storms of the inner goes back deep into antiquity, with poet Edward Hirsch in *A Poet's Glossary* explaining that the practice "has been a central poetic device of archaic and tribal poetries everywhere, which view the natural world as alive in all its parts," even if mostly associated with Romantic poets writing about sad sea foam and chipper birds—though the critic who explicated the fallacy would argue that "the greatest poets do not often admit this kind of falseness." The literary definition of the "fallacy" has its origin in the Victorian critic John Ruskin, who saw such blurring of human consciousness with the inert world as sentimental, illogical, inartful, and in a word, *wrong*. When poet Charles Kingsley wrote in his poem "The Sands of Dee" about the "cruel, crawling foam," Ruskin bitchily responded that "foam is not cruel, neither does it crawl."

Ruskin's 1856 treatise *Modern Painters*, from which his previous quote derives, contains his outline of the supposed pitfalls and perils of the pathetic fallacy, and though the critic's esteem has risen and fallen since the nineteenth century, his contention that depicting nature with human emotions is flawed endures as an assumption of creative writing seminars and book reviewers alike.

Not always unfairly, these critics of the pathetic fallacy see such personification as rank and simplistic symbolism, of anthropomorphizing nature rather than mimetically conveying the reality of an individual character's experience. In their view, such pathos is lazy writing, and it's used in expression by lazy narrators, for whom it's easier to say that the foam is cruel than that what's actually cruel is the disposition of the said individual who is observing the foam. To his credit, Ruskin doesn't universally condemn the trope, though he takes great pains to describe why such instances in poets he respects like Dante or Homer aren't examples of the pathetic fallacy and why instances in poets like Wordsworth, Blake, Keats, and Burns are. It's helpful to center Hirsch's reminder in *The Demon and the Angel* that "this projection of feeling has also flourished as a strain in epic poetry from Homer onward, as a feature of prophetic poetry from the major and minor prophets of the Hebrew Bile to Smart and Blake, Coleridge and Shelley, Whitman and Crane." Despite such venerable practitioners (though Ruskin wrote before Crane), it was in a pique of positivism that the former would have us concur that the "state of mind which attributes to [nature] these characters of a living creature is one in which the reason is unhinged by" emotion, a style that results from a tepid "temperament which admits the pathetic fallacy," born from "mind and body . . . too weak to deal fully with what is before them or upon them; born away, or over-clouded, or over-dazzled by emotion." Heady criticism from a man so terrified by his wife's pubic hair that on his wedding night, he ran away from her and ultimately filed for divorce, and telling that such a man would abjure instances of the pathetic fallacy for their "emotional falseness."

As with any literary criticism that is prescriptivist rather than descriptivist—that is, which seeks to tell writers how they should write rather than to explain how they do write—there are certain errors of historicizing implicit in Ruskin's argument, and there is also the cultural context of the time period that lent itself to the germination of the concept in the first place. Ruskin was, after all, writing in Victorian London, in a massive, stuffed, filthy, stinking, dirty, gray, ash-besotted metropolis held captive to smoky and smoggy factories, where the mechanical had replaced the natural and the environment was as apt to be brown as green. His criticism was of an industrial age and was no less inadvertently indebted to the fallacies of techno-utopianism than our own besotted era. How can one see the sun smile through smog, hear the wind roar over turbines, or observe the ocean's mood when it's caked with obscuring pollution? Ironically, and with fairness to Ruskin, it should be noted that he was an early acolyte for environmentalism, presumably in spite of the vagaries of the pathetic fallacy. Scholar Bernard Dick in his 1968 paper "Ancient Pastoral and the Pathetic Fallacy" writes that the "origins of the pathetic fallacy probably lie in a primitive homeopathy . . . wherein man regarded himself as part of his natural surroundings." A salient point that calls for humility concerning any who approach Ruskin's injunction as absolute dicta rather than as suggestion; it is necessary to recall how in archaic days, both writer and reader, orator and audience, muse and poet would approach the personification of nature with due reverence. More than that, it's imperative to fully question the claim that the ancient poet simply "regarded" herself as indivisible from the natural world, for the prophetic, poetic, scientific, and spiritual truth is that we *are* part of the natural world.

That, then, is Ruskin's great error, his embrace of what could be called the "logolatry fallacy." I define this as when a critic unfairly attacks the personification of nature or the anthropomorphizing of creatures, as that attack is based not on objective considerations of reality but rather on the embrace of a pernicious dualism separating humans from the circumstances of our natural environment. This separation is an exceedingly modern malady, certainly when

Ruskin was writing and all the more so in the world of smartphones and Facebook. For the Victorian critic, it certainly seemed as if nature was inert, inanimate, dead, and without emotion, as it does for all of us in the digital cocoon. But what nature seems like and what it actually is are two very different things, and there is a reason why bards heard birds belt, makers approached minds in mountains, and poets understood pines as people. Assuming that the pathetic is a fallacy in the first place is to take it as a given that there is no mind in nature, no consciousness in our environment, no subjectivity in the world outside of our own narrow, circumscribed skulls. Such an ascientific perspective is contrary to some very ancient wisdom, and if you are quiet enough and humble enough, you can surely still understand how a dull, aching consciousness thrums through all of creation.

Who is responsible for the severing of that connection is the subject of a debate for which there is no convenient answer. A pagan might say that it was Paul, a Catholic could finger Luther, and a spiritualist might blame Descartes. Perhaps the most accurate explanation of who is responsible folds each one of those figures into the previous one, seeing that fall as occurring when early Christians first turned from the prophetically sensual "amen" of Jerusalem to the cerebral philosophical "ergo" of Athens, preferring rather to see bodies as lumpen piles of foul deformity unimbued with spirit and, in the process, doing violence to both the original biblical text and the pantheistic truths of the Greeks, who'd rather turned over to the divisions of Plato. That disenchantment has been our lot in the long modernity is a historical matter of course, but if we must simplistically blame someone, we could do worse than to pin it on that French Renaissance philosopher.

After all, it's Descartes whose name graces that reductionist dualism that haunts contemporary philosophy like a ghost in the machine, a metaphysical bugaboo that can't adequately explain how it is that mind and matter interact, venturing half hypotheses about the pineal gland and holding to Homer Simpson's dictum, "What is mind? No matter. What is matter? Never mind." Western ontology has always been bedeviled by dualisms, from Plato's distinction between Forms and the mundane world to Derrida's prescriptions about binary oppositions. Certainly the most damaging example of that last category could be Cartesian dualism, with its bloody cleaving between body and brain, corpse and spirit. Descartes argued that there was an irreducible difference between the "thinking thing" and "the thing that exists," and so we have the philosophical underpinnings of Ruskin's aesthetics, where to conflate the former with the latter is to commit an egregious fallacy, except that the error was always in assuming that any such distinction exists.

It was in his 1641 *Meditations on First Philosophy* that Descartes carefully illuminated his metaphysics based on a priori principles, and there has always been reason to see that writing as the initiation of a certain type of modern thought. In many ways, Descartes was simply giving logical justification for that initial severance between heaven and earth, for Cartesian dualism is completely compatible with orthodox pronouncements about indivisible, individual, living souls animating inert bodies. In his sixth meditation, the philosopher wrote, as translated by John Veitch, "[I] clearly and distinctly understand my existence as a thinking thing (which does not require the existence of a body)," and in principle six, he wrote, "God can create a body independently of a mind," which leads to the conclusion, "My mind is a reality distinct from my body. . . . So I (a thinking thing) can exist without a body." The logolatry fallacy is old, albeit not as old as the more accurate perspective, which gives proper reverence to psalms sung by brooks and prayers supplicated by the wind, but certainly it predates Descartes. Yet in Descartes,

we can see the irrevocably cold and cruel conclusions of such dualism, for he held it undeniable that "animals are without feeling or
awareness of any kind," seeing them as being "automata," as if an
exuberant dog were simply a furry robot or a slinking cat a programmed android. The implications of such a self-evidently incorrect presupposition are endemic in modernity and contrary to the
wisdom of our foremothers and forefathers who, even if they were
carnivores, had an innate respect for the sovereignty, individuality,
and agency of our fellow creatures. These, after all, were people who
saw no disjunction between eating animals and putting them on
trial, but that's no less absurd than Descartes's scaly, furry robots. If
modernity refuses to see the consciousness in our animal familiars,
then how much less likely are they to see faces in stones and hear
voices in the rustling of leaves?

Descartes's may be remembered as the primogeniture of modern skepticism, but true to being the devout Catholic who made a
pilgrimage to the shrine of the Virgin at Loreto so as to offer thanks
for her intercession in producing the very text that supposedly incubated a pernicious doubt in the Western psyche, Descartes's perspective is heavily saturated with the old distinctions between flesh
and spirit that go back to Paul, who said in Galatians 5:17, "For the
flesh lusteth against the Spirit, and the Spirit against the flesh: and
these are contrary the one to the other." Cartesian dualism, which
refuses to empathize with the emotions in supposedly inanimate
things, has a history that goes back two millennia even if its logocen-
tric formulation waited until the seventeenth century. Ruskin was
inculcated in the positivist enthusiasms of such a perspective, and
these enthusiasms define his particular manifestation of the logolatry fallacy. Perhaps it's correct to think of disenchanted modernity
not as something that was birthed wholesale when Descartes sat by
a fire contemplating melting wax, or when Luther nailed his theses

to the Wittenberg Castle Church door, but rather as something that has been slowly crawling like Ruskin's despised sea foam. Descartes marks one figure in this process, Luther another, and Paul still an earlier one, but heaven has never been completely mute, even as the narrative of human history records her becoming ever quieter. Prelapsarian Eden, in which God spoke to all of us with the visceral granularity of sand and the striking chords of snow, is an abstraction, and yet it's undeniable that our myths speak to us as relics from a time when the consciousness of nature was more immediate. Sometimes foam crawls. Sometimes foam is cruel.

Psychologist Julian Jaynes, in his brilliant and underread *The Origin of Consciousness in the Breakdown of the Bicameral Mind*, argued that it is possible to read "the story of the Fall" as a "myth of the breakdown" of that primeval order, when once we heard chanting in the trees and saw intentional benevolence in sunlight's smile. Rather than any definitive break from this archaic reality, Jaynes identifies a "long retreat from the sacred" in which poetry that describes "external events objectively" is "subjectified into a poetry of personal conscious expression." That is to say that examples of the pathetic fallacy are faint whispers from the before, the cosmic background radiation of the fall, echoes of our expulsion from Eden that remind us of when consciousness permeated everything and our language was also the thing-in-itself. Animism is simply pantheism without a dictionary. That way of hearing and seeing and sensing and understanding was the natural state of our ancestors and for those who still live the "old ways," as anthropologist Elizabeth Marshall Thomas explains when writing about the !Kung of the Kalahari Desert in *The Old Way: A Story of the First People*. She describes their hunter-gatherer lifestyle as "governed by sun and rain, heat and cold, wind and wildfires." For the !Kung, an intuition of the pathetic fallacy's truth is instrumental in staying alive. There have been varying degrees of separation between the sacred and the profane, heaven and earth since we first stumbled out of Olduvai Gorge, but for the !Kung, their very clicks are the language of paradise, and this language defines a startlingly ancient permanence, which led Thomas to describe the !Kung as having the "most successful culture that our kind has ever known," one predicated upon the complete rejection of those divisions promoted by the logolatry fallacy.

Fully copping to my own lack of desire to live as a subsistence gatherer in the Namibian wilderness, and fully admitting to the dangers of romanticizing some sort of "noble savage" archetype (perhaps not convincingly), I do ask us to consider the benefits of rejecting Ruskin's denigration of the pathetic fallacy, turning instead against the error of logolatry, which permanently renders asunder humans from nature and thus both does grave violence to the environment and makes humanity a permanent diasporic from the very place we were born into, our insulated, unnatural lives in exile from the environment itself. In that spirit, I consider philosopher George Santayana's declaration in his marginalia that "the pathetic fallacy is a return to that early habit of thought by which our ancestors people the world with benevolent and malevolent spirits; what they felt in the presence of objects they took to be part of the objects themselves." Two reasons why this is advisable: first, because the so-called pathetic fallacy more accurately reflects how we are actually constituted as beings in space and time, born into a reality not of our own creation, and second, because when facing the perils of the Anthropocene generated entirely out of the mistake of dualism, a rejection of logolatry may be that which is required to save us from complete ecological collapse, since as Hirsch argues the pathetic fallacy is indicative of "empathetic feeling for the overlooked world."

Regarding the first contention, consider Portuguese neurobiologist Antonio Damasio, who took direct aim at the fallacious dualisms defining modernity, writing in 1994's *Descartes's Error: Emotion, Reason, and the Human Brain* that our disciplinary attitudes have been defined by a "remarkable neglect of the mind as a function of the organism." In his work, Damasio emphasized the role that emotion plays in the development of reason and, even more importantly, how as embodied creatures, the human mind is not separate from physicality but indeed an integral part of the body, so any division between the two is nonsensical. Mind is not just in our skulls but radiates out through our nerves, our appendances, and our very flesh. Mind is more than a wet and squishy organ inside our heads. Scottish philosopher Andy Clark sees the mind as not just encompassing our bodies but indeed extending outward into the very physical universe that Ruskin so carefully delineated from our own emotional subjectivities. Clark sees a process called "extended cognition" as explaining how it is that humans live metaphorically as "cyborgs," using supposedly inanimate things to store and jog memories. In a *New Yorker* interview with Larissa MacFarquhar, Clark claims that it is a prejudice to assume "that whatever matters about my mind must depend solely on what goes on inside my own biological skin-bag, inside the ancient fortress of skin and skull," a prejudice that can be defined by the logolatry fallacy.

Neurobiologists Giulio Tononi and Christof Koch have argued an even more radical form of scientific panpsychism, claiming that a type of rudimentary consciousness permeates most objects with any form of even slightly complex organization. Tononi, in an *Atlantic* article by Joshua Lang, tells the author that "within this empty, dusty universe, there would be true stars. And guess what? These stars would be every living consciousness." Let's not forget the Gaia hypothesis of biologists Lynn Margulis and James Lovelock, which configures the entire ecosystem of the planet earth as an integrated, synthesized, comprehensive organism, whereby it's not just metaphor but reality to think of the environment as a single living being of which we're simply a cellular part. A hypothesis that encouragingly sees pantheism as science. Margulis writes with her son Dorion Sagan that the "question 'What is Life?'" which is also the title of the book they wrote, "is . . . a linguistic trap. To answer according to the rules of grammar, we must supply a noun, a thing. But life on Earth is more like a verb," as indeed is consciousness. Thought is a thing that happens, and mind is a verb, an activity engaged for writers writing or for sea foam cruelly crawling. There are many mansions in Mother Earth's house and in her skull as well. With such expansive definitions of mind, Ruskin's initial pronouncement seems not only snobbish but erroneous as well.

Such integrative models of consciousness may do much to exonerate the pathetic fallacy, but what of my second contention, that rejection of logolatry is necessary to our very environmental survival? Sidney Burris, in defining the pathetic fallacy for the *New Princeton Encyclopedia of Poetry and Poetics*, observes, "Modern usage of the pathetic fallacy ironically emphasizes the individual and the natural world; and in its implied envy of an older world where such communion once existed, it resurrects yet another remnant of its ancient origin, pastoral nostalgia." But the rejection of logolatry isn't only a form of pastoral nostalgia, it's a reaffirmation of that fundamental truth that we're inseparable from the natural world and that when we look out at the wilderness with uncertain eyes, we're sometimes gazed back at by knowing ones. Environmental collapse's precipice has been justified by the exact sort of dualistic thinking that Ruskin's condemnation of the pathetic fallacy serves to affirm, a perspective that refuses to see agency in what it classifies as inert, which can't see mind in what it has misclassified as moribund.

No wonder we now see ourselves on a planet threatened by cataclysmic climate change, for we've believed the lie that we were granted dominion over the creeping things upon the earth, and we've been very bad stewards indeed (since we were never intended to be such in the first place, anyhow). In his 2015 encyclical *Laudato si'*, Pope Francis writes that "the post-industrial period may well be remembered as one of the most irresponsible in history," an understated truth. Now more than ever there is a need for the wisdom of what's been denigrated as the pathetic fallacy, the verbal reminder that consciousness extends out beyond our own lonely cells. We need a view related to the Norwegian philosopher Arne Naess's concept of "deep ecology," a mystically inflected understanding that consciousness exists beyond the simple reductionisms of Cartesian dualism and that our civilizational embrace of that ossified philosophy has brought us to the possible brink of calamity. Australian environmentalist, philosopher, and theorist of sustainability Freya Mathews has argued that an embrace of a certain ecological panpsychism can liberate us from the very system that has brought us to this brink. She writes in *For Love of Matter* that if we "assume a panpsychist worldview," we can perhaps "extricate oneself, to a significant degree, from the ideological grid of capitalism."

In her *For Love of Matter: A Contemporary Panpsychism*, Mathews points out how her "own sense of the sacred . . . had been mainly stirred by my experiences in the natural world. It was there that I had experienced the feelings usually associated with the sacred—wonder, exultation, a sense of plenitude and expansiveness, beauty and awe." Ruskin, I would imagine, would reject any wonder, exultation, plenitude, or expansiveness in nature itself, preferring rather to only locate such emotions in the lucky individual who projects such feelings onto empty nature. He, it should be said, had no use for the hypotheses of Romantics or Transcendentalists either. In Ruskin's estimation, verse that locates meaning in the subject of nature is naive, but the poem that locates meaning in the poet is sophisticated. And yet the orthodox strictures of this sort of Western dualism have proven remarkably malignant, for as Mathews writes, it was by "draining matter of any animating principle" that we ideologically "ensured that the world itself could no longer be regarded either as morally significant in its own right or as the lodestar for human meanings and purposes: henceforth, we would have to find out own ends and meanings in ourselves, by means of our innate power of reason." That "reason," for all of its benefits, has also brought upon the specter of collective suicide in the form of nuclear war and radical climate change.

Though such logolatry is the norm, Western culture isn't completely inundated by dualism. Mathews explains that in her youth, "the Christianity of my teachers was strangely mute on the meaning of the sunrise, the wind, the creek, the herons, and cranes, the light before the storm—the things that spoke so palpably, if inscrutably, to me," but there have been any number of mystics and seekers who rejected the Pauline division of nature from humanity, who saw all things numinous, all things luminous, the very substance of all things shining. Sing that canticle of the sun, that *Laudes creaturarum* of Saint Francis first whispered in ecstatic Umbrian in the thirteenth century. Received while convalescing at San Damiano among the Order of Poor Ladies in 1224, Saint Francis simply listened to the breathing lungs of creation—that organic, ever-shifting being of whom we're all composite persons. Francis sings of "Brother Sun, / who brings the day" and of "Sister Moon / and the stars . . . clear and precious and beautiful," as translated by Bill Barrett.

Having never heard of Ruskin, Francis had no anxiety about anthropomorphism, no disquiet concerning personification. Rather, he unabashedly could praise "Brother Wind," who was both "cloudy and serene," and "Sister Water," who in a paroxysm of supplicating polysyndeton was "very useful and humble and precious and chaste." In the monk's understanding, "Brother Fire" was "beautiful and playful and robust and strong," while "Sister Bodily Death" was an impartial judge from whom nobody can escape—and thus must be all the more respected. The ultimate conclusion of such personification—which is neither metaphor nor affectation, symbol, trope, or conceit but rather living gospel—is that we must shout a prayer reading, "Praised be You . . . through Sister Mother Earth, / who sustains us and governs us and who produces / varied fruits with colored flowers and herbs."

Francis's panpsychism would no doubt be distasteful to Ruskin, would exhibit "emotional falseness," as the critic would put it, save for the fact that it is the monk's vision rather than that of the Victorian that is fundamentally true, and it is Assisi's beautiful creed that is necessary if we're to hope that any collective salvation awaits us, if we're to apologize for what we've done to Sister Earth. Our lives and our existence upon this earth are a very poem, for words can be angry, and objects too. If there is any consciousness, it is between the relationship of language to itself and in the self-communion of matter. Our dying age cries out for a poetics of immanence, for a sacramental poetics, for the pathetic fallacy long denigrated. For who has not seen gnarled faces in the stumps of trees? Who has not been kissed by the sun or slapped by the rain? Who has not felt the drizzly damp November of the soul when the earth's very seasons conspire against us and the winter hangs heavy gray drapes within our minds? Lest spring forever be quiet, we must begin straining to hear her this instant, or our supplications will be passed over in her own eternal silence, when neither foam nor people crawl any longer, for there shall be no consciousness left to observe either.

5

Poetry without Poets; or, Spirit Is a Human Earth

"When I use a word," Humpty Dumpty said
in rather a scornful tone, "it means just what I
choose it to mean—neither more nor less."

"The question is," said Alice, "whether you can
make words mean so many different things."

"The question is," said Humpty Dumpty,
"which is to be master—that's all."

—Lewis Carroll, *Through the Looking-Glass,
and What Alice Found There* (1872)

In 1806, the good Christians of Leeds, England, prepared for the millennium after a certain Mary Bateman presented them with a prophetic hen that had been laying eggs with a simple, urgent, and simultaneously hopeful and terrifying message: "Christ is Coming." The chiliastic chickens of Leeds, pushing out signs of Judgment

Day, proving that you have to crack a few eggs to make an apocalypse. "Christ is Coming" would seem to be as unambiguous a message as one could imagine; it leaves little room for interpretation. If confronted with Bateman's eggs, and if one were confident they were not a hoax, it would seem as good a bit of evidence as any that Christ was indeed soon coming.

Of course Christ did not come in 1806 (or 1666, or 1844, or 2000, or any of the other predicted dates for his second coming—and every year has been a predicted year), and of course Bateman's Sibylline poultry was a hoax. She'd been etching the messages to the shells in acid and then gingerly shoving them back up into the hen. Perhaps not entirely unrelated, she's also arguably one of the last women to hang for witchcraft in England, strung up on a scaffold among those Yorkshire hills some three years after the trick with the chickens—though part of her conviction was related to her murdering an associate with poisoned pudding. That's incidental, though, since what I'd like you to consider is that even if Bateman's hen were not a hoax, what confidence could there be in such a message? Even genuine, what assurances could such a miraculous fowl actually give? Because we expect that the voice of God is an assured one and that trumpets and broken seals herald not just the arrival of the millennium but *confidence* in that arrival. We envision, even the atheists among us, the possibility of some sort of eschaton that could forever dispel such doubts. In other words, we can hypothesize a state of epistemic absolute zero, an imaginary utopian kingdom where *meaning* reigns as queen. A clear, and defined, and immutable, and most of all, obvious meaning.

Why would a hen laying eggs that say "Christ is Coming" mean that Christ is coming? For that matter, should the stars rearrange themselves in the sky to say "I'm up here," why would that mean that anyone was? Maybe this astronomical anomaly is a shockingly coincidental new natural phenomenon, or perhaps the engineers who programmed our reality are playing a joke at our expense, or maybe the psilocybin is bad. If God is a hypothesis, then by necessity, she will only be one of those myriad possibilities (which is why the true worshipper never reduces God to mere hypothesis). No, we are humans, and as humans, our mortal lives must be shot through with ambiguity. We also, by necessity, evolved as meaning-making creatures, and the world of symbol (even if pareidolia) is our savannah. That's the genius of Tom Perrotta's novel *The Leftovers*— were the rapture to happen, why would we even be sure that it was really the rapture and not something else?

That meaning exists can't be doubted, but the contours of that monarch's face must remain uncertain. An infinity of space exists between word and thing, and in that space is the ever-chaotic, ever-shifting, ever-mercurial kingdom of meaning—and that can be a terrifying place. God may be dead, and the author too (maybe especially him), but rumors of meaning's demise have always been overrated. Deconstructionists can defer to the end of days, but undefined meaning keeps ticking along, like a clock simultaneously wound up and next to her partner timepiece of reality, somehow making us get at least part of the message even though the mechanism remains ever a mystery. From Pythagoras to John Searle, how meaning is constituted has been the central question of the human disciplines.

Really, meaning is the central question of any discipline, of any life. "What does it *mean*?" the stock penitent implores to the stock unanswering cosmos. At this point in time, and in our culture broadly defined, we assume certain things about meaning: that some things mean something and others things don't, that meaning is a message, and that a message requires a messenger. In the past, different models of meaning reigned supreme. For a seventeenth-century

Puritan scanning the pages of his almanac and the gathering stormy darkness on the western horizon of Massachusetts, everything meant something, and all of it was a message from God. If anything, this typological persona has been more the norm throughout human history—wind and rain and clouds and all manner of simple things under the dome of heaven read for providential assurances or warnings. In the past, meaning pulsated like unseen currents of electricity through the very network of life, all things glowing with an enchanted thrum like some bioluminescent neon squish in a deep-ocean vent. Humans read the signs like a schizophrenic scanning newspaper print for messages from the CIA, for if God was supposedly killed by Nietzsche in the nineteenth century, then our ancestors before that deicide lived in a world in which the Lord couldn't keep quiet. If we fear that meaning now lays silent, then generations past had to grapple with an overabundance of her.

Medieval exegetes read Scripture, literature, and literature performed (which we deign to call life) in four different ways: literally, morally, allegorically, and mystically. Since Luther first nailed his *Ninety-Five Theses* to one of Christ's wrists, we've slowly seen the last three of those listed hermeneutics collapse into the first one. Good Augustinian that he was, such a result couldn't have been his intent, and there is, of course, no dearth of the allegorical Reformed (like our friend the Puritan). But *sola scriptura* couldn't help but enthrone a pope of paper, and where text is made immutable, pretty soon literalism will reign. As a result, literally literal literalism has become the faith of our modern world over the past half millennia. Unintentional perhaps, but the infinite shade of connotation that had defined the hermeneutics of everyday life was drained from both Scripture and life until only the poets could see the old chain of ever-varying, shifting, living meanings.

Positivism and fundamentalism, twin specters of that correspondence theory of truth that posits a simple relationship between word and thing, a vanilla version of meaning shorn of all of that anagogical kinkiness where the truth sometimes actually resides. All the more ironic, because literalism can beget that nihilism where if one believes in nothing, they're willing to fall for anything. The reduction of metaphorical and mystical truth introduced a strangely crude kind of relativism where meaning was reduced but the messenger became king. Do what thou wilt with the disenchantment hypothesis (I for one think that the great god Pan never truly died), but Luther's diatribe was a potent early version of false news.

So whereof does meaning now reside? Where is her home, her origin, her birthplace? What is the omphalos that tethers meaning to some grander thing, whether God or truth? This, it should be said, is not a question of minor significance, for what meaning means is arguably that which has structured all ideologies, philosophies, and religions. *Meaning* as a word has many connotations, from the New Age pablum I come dangerously close to skirting, to the rhizomic definitional trees of the lexicographer compiling her dictionary, to the arid postulates of the analytical philosopher still chaffing at the indignation of being a failed mathematician. Whether one's model of meaning is of limitless deferring in an ultimately endless (and thus meaningless?) chain of connections or of a transcendent signified through from which all meaning ultimately radiates, that meaning means something (even nothing) ultimately means something. Maybe. With apologies to Noam Chomsky, perhaps "colorless green ideas sleep furiously" does say it all.

Meaning, like all things, has a history, and our understanding of her has an evolution. That once the world brimmed with glowing significance but now meaning is reduced to whether a few testable postulates are confirmed by the data is of no significance. Whether her kingdom is bound in a walnut shell or is the universe itself matters not, for as long as meaning exists somewhere, meaning still exists everywhere—even if we're blind to it today. That's the nature of meaning; no country is too small for her. This enduring haunting is why Blake feared not the Nobodaddy and wrote that jingle about universes and eternity and seconds and sand. But though meaning still exists (because otherwise, you couldn't comprehend what I'm saying—then again, perhaps I presume too much about both of us), culture and philosophy are defined by our relationship to her. How we define her, whether meaning requires the intercession of some messenger, whether divine or human. The medieval exegete and the Puritan typologist looked for signs in their respective perfumed pleasure garden and upon their rocky shoal, but the messenger was God. After her wake, meanings were human affairs and the messenger a man. But though one generation saw meaning everywhere and delivered from on high and ours sees it as limited and passed from person to person like some communicable disease, the messenger is still the medium and thus the message. But what if we could forget the messenger and listen to only the message? What if meaning need not have any face at all?

Imagine that one day, you're lucky enough to find yourself with some much-needed rest and recreation, and you're strolling along a pristine white-sand beach while on vacation. The tide washes in, and as it pulls back, you see that the ocean has etched into the sand the appearance of Latin letters organized into English words and sentences; furthermore, these sentences are broken into what are identifiably poetic stanzas, reading, "A slumber did my spirit seal; / I had no human fears: / She seemed a thing that could not feel / The touch of earthly years."

If you were paying attention in your British literature survey, you'd recognize the verse as being Wordsworth's, but whether you know it's the Romantic poet or not, you clearly understand that it is—or at least, appears to be—a fairly ornate and complicated manifestation of the English language. But assuming that you are a sober, sane, rational person who believes neither that the former poet laureate of Great Britain has somehow possessed this aforementioned pristine white-sand beach nor that God or some other supernatural being enjoys posting English literature GRE identification questions through intricate miracles, you are forced to admit that this is a particularly stunning, totally natural coincidence. You'd conclude that this is a remarkable example of pareidolia, an illusion that meaning-making creatures such as ourselves misinterpret as significant but is no more legitimate than someone who thinks that a tortilla conveys the face of Christ. In short, the surf-carved "poem" might seem to make sense, but in reality, it is random and totally meaningless.

However, the philosophical problem endures: when we flip through a copy of *Lyrical Ballads* and come across this poem, we know that it has meaning that can be interpreted. In 1798, Wordsworth—a real person with emotions and a biography—composed this poem with some intention and design that can be interpreted by us, its readers. While readers and scholars can argue about the proper interpretation of the poem, there can be little doubt that it means something, since it was an expression of a person trying to communicate an idea or a feeling. There were conscious decisions in the composition of this poem. Yet this short lyric, designed with intentionality and conveying meaning, appears physically identical to our anomalous beach phenomenon, which we all agree was meaningless. So the thought experiment presents us with our favored conundrum: What exactly is meaning, and where does it reside?

This scenario first appeared in the literary scholars Steven Knapp and Walter Benn Michaels's 1982 paper in *Critical Inquiry* entitled "Against Theory." Knapp and Michael were attempting to illustrate a divide that has bedeviled literary theory since the

New Critics of the 1920s first put typewriter ribbon to paper. That is to say that all approaches to interpretation must side either with the text itself or with the author. Through materialisms, and historicisms, and Marxisms, and feminisms, and poststructuralism, and all the rest, the biggest distinction has always been who listens to the song versus who listens to the singer. Knapp and Michael's essay illustrates through its starkness the difference between literary formalists and historicists.

For the latter, this miraculous Wordsworth poem upon the sand must be meaningless, the contours of its letters and its semantic organization only so much coincidence. If there is no author, no creator, then there can be no meaning. (Our straw Puritan would of course know that the message was obviously that of God, or else Mary Bateman was out there at low tide scratching her contemporary Wordsworth's verse into the beach.)

The formalist, on the other hand—with the New Critical "intentional fallacy" as their solemn rallying cry—understands that the text is primary, and since the Barthian death of the author, the formalist (whether they're a T. S. Eliot or a Jacques Derrida) understands that the play is the thing. For the formalist, meaning exists in the form of the text itself regardless of the intentions of its creators, or if it even has creators. Of course, literary critics of even the most strictly formalist bent understand that texts are produced by humans with intentions, but Knapp and Michael's gedanken-experiment expresses the ultimate desire of any true formalist criticism: the existence of poetry without poets, where meaning requires not a messenger.

Late capitalism has given us the opportunity to resurrect the voiceless god, the pantheistic pulse of meaning in every syllable and every word, to give us verse without versifier and poetry in search of a poet. I sing a song of the digital golem, of course: artificial intelligence (AI), the computer. We can wait an eternity of eternities, and

Wordsworth is never going to be carved out of the chalk cliffs of Dover Beach, and a thousand monkeys at typewriters still haven't given us Lear, but a plug-and-play online computer doodad can randomly generate poetry as surely as a drunk falling onto their refrigerator and scrambling their magnetic poetry playset can. So I picked my favorite Wordsworthian nouns, and using an online poetry generator, I was able to let an AI program fashion its own poem, sans any human intention. But does it have *meaning*? The attempt is below:

> *Spirit, course, and spirit.*
> *Fears, force, and course.*
> *My, course!*
> *Where is the no stones?*
> *Things touch!*
>
> *All things motion neither, diurnal earths.*
> *Spirit is a human earth.*
>
> *My, spirit!*
> *Fears, fears, and fears.*
> *Why does the stones touch?*
> *Trees seal!*
>
> *My, force!*
> *Fears is a human earth.*
> *My, spirit!*
> *Never rolled a thing.*
> *Fears, force, and spirit.*

The literary historicist, obsessed as he is with intention and circumstance, would have nothing to say about interpreting such a poem. The computer has no gender, no race, no class; it is born of no culture, and no psychology affects it. The humanities are, after all, the realm of the human, and the interpretation of meaning can only be vested toward subjects capable of expressing meaning, while the electronic tarot, the digital tea leaves only scramble bits of code as preprogrammed by somebody else. Where there is no intentionality, there is no meaning, so saith the historicist.

However, the formalist, or at least the null-zero hypothetical Platonic formalist critic, would see no reason why meaning can't be interpreted from such a text, for meaning is not a message from a messenger but intrinsic to the form itself. It's not the return address on the letter but the words inside the envelope. So what was my computer trying to say?

Appropriately enough, the subject appears to be about this essay's very subject—the distance between reality and expression wherein meaning lies, or as the last sentence of the first verse puts it emphatically, where "Things touch!" AI-Wordsworth begins the poem with a monosyllabic tricolon, the first line starting with a trochaic substitution and ending with the same word. It's an interesting rhythm, if not completely amenable to regular scansion: "Spirit, course, and spirit." What distinguishes "course" from "spirit"? Are we to interpret the use of the word *spirit* twice as meaning that we're speaking of two different varieties of spirit, or is there only one type, altered by some process (the "course" AI-Wordsworth speaks of)? The first line would lose some of its frustrating ambiguity were the second comma deleted, then "course and spirit" could be bundled conveniently together, but as it is, each word is stubbornly separated out.

The second line is aurally pleasing by utilizing that most Anglo-Saxon of rhetorical conceits, alliteration, while it also contains a simple but affective internal rhyme. Is "course" here read as "of course"? Or is it the same "course" mentioned in the previous line? Or even more provocatively, the "My, course!" in the third? The odd punctuation in the third line further confuses the ultimate meaning of the poem (its deletion would make the sentence more straightforward in its interpretation), even if the short lines call to mind Dickinson and the enthused exclamation mark alludes to Whitman. AI-Wordsworth is fond of emphatic declarations in this manner: we have "My, force!" and "My, spirit!" twice, always with that troubling comma. Is the punctuation mark to be read merely to indicate a pause? And if so, why is the speaker pausing, especially in the middle of a line that the exclamation point would seem to indicate is forcefully uttered?

"Where is the no stones?" is a fascinating paradox. Are "no stones" the class of all things that are not stones (which would include the majority of things in existence), or are they some sort of negations of stoniness? And if they are nothing, a "no stone," then how can the question of where they are make any semantic sense? Even more provocatively, this leads into the crux of the poem, AI-Wordsworth's contention that "Things touch!" emphatically and enthusiastically declared. If things touch, there seems to be hope in closing that gap between reality and expression and charting a navigable course of meaning. Yet in the third stanza, AI-Wordsworth pensively asks, "Why does the stones touch?" Grammatical inaccuracy aside, there is an anxiety about that which was celebrated only a few lines before. Of course, it should be noted that "things" and "stones" are not reducible to one another, even if the latter is by necessity a subset of the former, and the claim in stanza one must imply the question in stanza three. The anxiety of AI-Wordsworth's interrogative declaration is compounded by the sentence before, the second line of the third stanza, where it (or he or she?) writes, "Fears, fears, and fears." As an example of dialogic intertextuality, it almost calls to mind Hamlet's withering expression of ennui: "Words, words, words." Indeed, the addition of the conjunction in some sense furthers AI-Wordsworth's sense of fear by prolonging the expression of it.

Some lines are particularly interesting by skirting the border of comprehensibility while deferring easy interpretation (in the manner of some Dadaist verse)—for example, "All things motion neither, diurnal earths." AI-Wordsworth revels in contradiction and has a fondness for paradoxical aphorism, for the Heraclitean declaration that "All things motion" is immediately negated by the Parmenidean injunction of "neither." Or consider the line "Spirit is a human earth." There seems to be a contrast between the transcendent qualities of "spirit" placed in comparison to the material one of "earth," balanced on the fulcrum of the "human." An expression of a certain incarnational poetics, perhaps? AI-Wordsworth could be stating a postulate of theological orthodoxy, humankind strung as it is between soul and flesh, the sacred and profane, spirit and earth. But of course, that's based on the placement of words; it requires us to read the poem as a sort of word sculpture. As a literal statement, "Spirit is a human earth" is gnomic and cryptic. Are there earths that are not human, which require the specificity of a particular "human earth"? And why would spirit—often defined precisely by not being of this earth—be by AI-Wordsworth's definition a specifically "human earth"? I would argue that the reconciliation of these irreconcilable contradictions is precisely the point, only underscored by the ominous declaration that "Fears is a human earth." AI-Wordsworth seems to identify "Fears" (importantly plural) as being that which defines the very nature of what it means to be a person, a Hobbesian domain of "Fears, force, and spirit" (ending the poem, as it began, on a forceful tricolon). Yet AI-Wordsworth finds a poignancy in the observation that "Spirit is a human earth," a humble declaration that despite the "Fears," we may through "force" finally arrive at "spirit." A type of metempsychotic *Pilgrim's Progress* ascending to the higher palaces of the human soul.

Or something, I don't know. A fucking computer wrote the thing.

But here's its significance: despite its aesthetic proficiencies or deficiencies, AI-Wordsworth's "Spirit Is a Human Earth" (as I've elected to title it) is not necessarily without meaning, even if it's a message without a messenger. There is semantic comprehension to the thing, and one can spin interpretations (even if they're kind of bullshit) from such a text. There is no reason why a more advanced computer can't (and they already do) produce more adept examples of verse and, undoubtedly someday soon, narrative. The internet as of late has been delighted by the inadvertently hilarious and sometimes strangely (if nihilistically) wise faux-inspirational posters of AI. From the *I Ching* to AI-Wordsworth, the random clinamen of aleatory literature has sometimes provided strange moments of comprehension, a consciousness that seems to emerge from the void like a natural pattern mistaken for a face. Poetry without poets is not just possible but already a reality.

And here's the second point: maybe all poetry is as if a poem without a poet. Maybe there is no messenger, transcendent or otherwise; maybe the message is identical with that of the messenger who has uttered it. Atman is Brahman and all the rest of that stuff. And in this model, intentionality is not an either/or but rather a particularly thick bundle of meaning, for when it comes to meaning itself, she is democratically spread throughout the whole country of being from east to west. Can we reenchant reality again in that way? Why not? For even if the deity is no longer responding to our questions, can we not say that meaning permeates everything and trickles down as if a stream of cool water over all of us? And do not mistake me, I speak not of signs and portents or of any anthropic principle, for they can be a meaning that points to nothing beyond her own existence. No need to read those darkening western skies as a sign of the apocalypse or even see doomsday in an egg declaring that "Christ is coming."

Scholastics looked for a soul in the head, Cartesians for the ghost in the machine, neuroscientists for transmitters in the brain. Consciousness has always been a vexing thing. There is a class of mystical-minded materialist and pantheist alike who've conjectured that perhaps the whole damn thing is conscious—no mind-body dualism and no pesky question of the soul interacting with matter at the pineal gland. There are only thicker glops of consciousness (that's us) and thinner ones (trees, and rocks, and shit). Why should meaning be any different? There are big dollops of it (Shakespeare and whatnot) and more modest ones (trees, and rocks, and shit), but meaning permeates the whole thing through and through, and that's the overall meaning. Whether the brazenness of an egg declaring the end of days or the seven types of ambiguity threaded throughout a poem, meaning is forever mercurial in most models, but if meaning permeates everything—if we can envision a secular reenchantment, if you will—then both anxiety and confidence become moot points. For if you seek her, if you look for meaning, simply look around you. For when it comes to her, when it comes to meaning, you see, it's turtles all the way down.

6

Another Person's Words
Poetry Is Always the Speaker

Blessedly, we are speakers of languages not of our own invention, and as such, none of us are cursed with only a private tongue. Words are our common property; it would take a brave iconoclast to write entirely in some Adamic dialect of her own invention, her dictionary locked away (though from the Voynich manuscript to Luigi Serafini's *Codex Seraphinianus*, some have tried). Almost every word you or I speak was first uttered by somebody else— the key is entirely in the rearrangement. Sublime to remember that every possible poem, every potential play, every single novel that could ever be written is hidden within the *Oxford English Dictionary*. The answer to every single question, too, for that matter. The French philosophers Antoine Arnauld and Claude Lancelot enthuse in their 1660 *Port-Royal Grammar* that language is a "marvelous invention of composing out of twenty-five or thirty sounds that infinite variety of expressions which, whilst having in themselves no likeness to what is in our mind, allow us to . . . [make known] all the various stirrings of our soul." Dictionaries are oracles. It's simply an issue of putting those words in the correct order. Language is often spoken of in terms of *inheritance*, where regardless of our own origins, speakers of English are the descendants of the languid ecstasies of Walt Whitman, the psalmic utterances of Emily Dickinson, the stately plain style of the King James Bible, the witty innovations of William Shakespeare, and the earthy vulgarities of Geoffrey Chaucer—not to forget the creative infusions of foreign tongues, from Norman French to Latin, Ibo, Algonquin, Yiddish, Spanish, and Punjabi, among others. Linguist John McWhorter puts it succinctly in *Our Magnificent Bastard Tongue: The Untold History of English*, writing, "We speak a miscegenated grammar."

There is a glory to this, our words indicating people and places different from ourselves, our diction an echo of a potter in a Bronze Age East Anglian village, a canting rogue in London during the golden era of Jacobean theater, or a Five Points Bowery Boy in antebellum New York. Nicholas Oster, with an eye toward its diversity of influence, its spread, and its seeming omnipresence, writes in *Empires of the Word: A Language History of the World* that "English deserves a special position among world languages," as it is a "language with a remarkably varied history." Such history perhaps gives the tongue a universal quality, making it a common inheritance of humanity. True with any language, but when you speak, it would be a fallacy to assume that your phrases, your idioms, your sentences, especially your words are your own. They've been passed down to you. Metaphors of inheritance can be either financial or genetic; the former has it that our lexicon is some treasure collectively willed to us, the latter posits that in the DNA of language, our nouns are adenine, verbs are cytosine, adjectives like guanine, and adverbs are thymine. Either sense of inheritance has its uses as a metaphor, and yet they're both lacking to me in some fundamental way—too crassly materialist, too eugenic. The proper metaphor isn't inheritance but *consciousness*. I hold that a language is as if a living thing, or to be more specific, as if a *thinking thing*. Maybe our linguistic inheritance isn't a metaphor at all; perhaps we're simply conduits for the thoughts of something bigger than ourselves, the contemplations of the language we speak.

Philosopher George Steiner, forever underrated, writes in his immaculate *After Babel: Aspects of Language and Translation*, "Language is the highest and everywhere the foremost of those assents which we human beings can never articulate solely out of our own means." We're neurons in the mind of language, and our communications are individual synapses in that massive brain that's spread across the earth's eight billion inhabitants and back generations innumerable. When that mind becomes self-aware, when language knows that it is language, we call those particular thoughts poetry. Argentinean critic (and confidant of Jorge Luis Borges) Alberto Manguel writes in *A Reader on Reading* that poetry is "proof of our innate confidence in the meaningfulness of wordplay"; it is that which demonstrates the eerie significance of language itself. Poetry is when language consciously thinks.

More than rhyme and meter or any other formal aspect, what defines poetry is its self-awareness. Poetry is the language that knows it is language and that there is something strange about being such. Certainly, part of the purpose of all the rhetorical accoutrement we associate with verse, from rhythm to rhyme scheme, exists to make the artifice of language explicit. Guy Deutscher writes in *The Unfolding of Language: An Evolutionary Tour of Mankind's Greatest Invention* that the "wheels of language run so smoothly" that we rarely bother to "stop and think about all the resourcefulness that must have gone into making it tick." Language is pragmatic; most communication doesn't need to self-reflect on, well, how *weird* the very idea of language is. How strange it is that we can construct entire realities from variations in the breath that comes out of our mouths or the manipulation of ink stains on dead trees (or of liquid crystals on a screen). "Language conceals its art," Deutscher writes, and he's correct. When language decides to stop concealing, we have poetry.

Verse accomplishes that unveiling in several different ways, chief among them the use of the rhetorical and prosodic tricks, from alliteration to terza rima, which we associate with poetry. Some of the most elemental and beautiful aspects of language that poetry draws attention toward are the axioms implied earlier in this essay—that the phrases and words we speak are never our own—and that truth is found not in the invention but in the rearrangement. In *Problems of Dostoevsky's Poetics*, the Russian literary theorist Mikhail Bakhtin wrote that we receive "the word from another's voice and filled with that other voice." Our language is not our own, nor is our literature. We communicate in a tongue not of our own creation. We don't have conversations; we are the conversation. Bakhtin reasons that our "own thought finds the world already inhabited." Just as the organization of words into enjambed lines and those lines into stanzas demonstrates the beautiful unnaturalness of language, so to do allusion, bricolage, and what theorists call *intertextuality* make clear to us not that we're not individual speakers of words but that words are speakers of us. Steiner writes in *Grammars of Creation* that "the poet says: 'I never invent.'" This is true: the poet never invents, none of us do. We only rearrange—and that is beautiful.

True of all language, but few poetic forms are as honest about rearrangement as a forgotten Latin genre from late antiquity known as the cento. Rather than inheritance and consciousness, the originators of the cento preferred the metaphor of textiles. For them, all of poetry is a massive patchwork garment, squares of fabric borrowed from disparate places and sewn together to create a new whole. Such a metaphor is an apt explanation of what exactly a cento is—a novel poem that is assembled entirely from rearranged lines written by other poets. Centos were written perhaps as early as the first century, but the fourth-century Roman poet Decimus Magnus Ausonius was the first to theorize about their significance and to give rules for their composition. In the prologue to *Cento nuptialias*, where he composed a poem about marital consummation from fragments of Virgil derived from the *Aeneid*, *Georgics*, and *Eclogues*, Ausonius explained that he has, "but out of a variety of passages and different meanings," created something new that is "like a puzzle."

The editors of *The Penguin Dictionary of Literary Terms and Literary Theory* explain that while forgotten today, the cento was "common in later antiquity." Anthologizer and poet David Lehman writes in the *American Scholar* that "historically, the intent was often homage, but it could and can be lampoon," with critic Edward Hirsch writing in *A Poet's Glossary* that centos "may have begun as school exercises." Though it's true that these poems were written for educational reasons, to honor or mock other poets, or as showy performances of lyrical erudition (the author exhibiting their intimacy with Homer and Virgil), none of these explanations does service to the cento's significance. To return to my admittedly inchoate axioms of earlier, one function of poetry is to plunge "us into a network of textual relations," as the theorist Graham Allen writes in *Intertextuality*. Language is not the provenance of any of us but rather a common treasury, with its other purpose being what Steiner describes as the "rec-compositions of reality, of articulate dreams, which are known to us as myths, as poetry, as metaphysical conjecture." That's to say that the cento remixes poetry, it recombines reality, so as to illuminate some fundamental truth hitherto hidden. Steiner claims that a "language contains within itself the boundless potential of discovery," and the cento is a reminder that fertile are the recombinations of poetry that have existed before, that literature is a rich, many-varied compost from which beautiful new specimens can grow toward the sun.

A demonstration of the literary potential of the cento is particularly apparent in the verse of the fourth-century Roman poet Faltonia Betitia Proba. Hirsch explains that one of the purposes of the cento, beyond the pedagogical or the parodic, was to "create Christian narratives out of pagan text," as was the case with Proba's *Cento virgilianus*, the first major Christian epic by a woman poet. Allen explains that "works of literature, after all, are built from systems, codes and traditions established by previous works of literature"; what Proba's cento did was a more literal expression of that fundamental fact. The classical past posed a difficulty for proud Roman Christians, for how were the faithful to grapple with the paganism of Plato, the Sibyllines, and Virgil? One solution was *typological*—that is, the assumption that if Christianity was true, and yet pagan poets like Virgil still spoke the truth, then Christianity must be encoded within his verse itself, part of the process of *Interpretatio Christiana*, whereby pagan culture was reinterpreted along Christian lines.

Daughter of Rome that she was, Proba would not abandon Virgil, but Christian convert that she also was, it became her task to internalize that which she loved about her forerunner and repurpose him, to place old wine into new skins. Steiner writes that one aspect of authorship is how the "poet's consciousness strives to achieve perfect union with that of the predecessor," and though those lyrics are "historically autonomous," as reimagined by the younger poet, they are "reborn from within." This is perhaps true of how all influence works, but the cento literalizes that process in the clearest manner. And so Proba's solution was to rearrange, remix, and recombine the poetry of Virgil so that Christianity could emerge, like a sculptor chipping away all of the excess marble in a slab to reveal the statue hidden within.

Inverting the traditional pagan invocation of the muse, Proba begins her epic (the proem being the only original portion) with both conversion narrative and poetic exhortation, writing that she is "baptized, like the blest, in the Castalian font— / I, who in my thirst have drunk libations of the Light— / now being my song: be at my side, Lord, set my thoughts / straight, as I tell how Virgil sang the offices of Christ." Thus she imagines the prophetic Augustan poet of Roman republicanism who died two decades before the Nazarene was born. Drawing from a tradition that claimed Virgil's *Eclogue* predicted Christ's birth, Proba rearranged 694 lines of the poet to retell stories from Genesis, Exodus, and the Gospels, the lack of Hebrew names in the Roman original forcing her to use general terms that appear in Virgil, like "son" and "mother," when writing of Jesus and Mary. Proba's paradoxically unoriginal originality (or is its original unoriginality?) made her popular in the fourth and fifth centuries, the *Cento virgilianus* taught to catechists alongside Augustine and often surpassing *Confessions* and *City of God* in popularity. Yet criticism of Proba's aesthetic quality from figures like Jerome and Pope Gelasius I ensured a millennium-long eclipse of her poem, forgotten until its rediscovery with the Renaissance.

Rearranging the pastoral *Eclogues*, Proba envisions Genesis in another poet's Latin words, writing that there is a "tree in full view with fruitful branches; / divine law forbids you to level with fire or iron, / by holy religious scruple it is never allowed to be disturbed. /

And whoever steals the holy fruit from this tree, / will pay the penalty of death deservedly; / no argument has changed my mind." There is something uncanny about the way that such a familiar myth is reimagined in the arrangement of a different myth—the way in which Proba is a redactor of Virgil's words, shaping them into (or pulling out from) this other, different, unintended narrative. Scholars have derided her poem as juvenilia since Jerome (jealously) castigated her talent by calling her "old chatterbox," but to be able to organize, shift, and shape another poet's corpus into orthodox Scripture is an unassailable accomplishment. Writers of the Renaissance certainly thought so, for a millennium after Proba's disparagement, a new generation of humanists resuscitated her.

Cento virgilianus was possibly the first work by a woman to be printed, in 1474; a century before that, the father of Renaissance poetry, Petrarch, extolled her virtues in a letter to the wife of the Holy Roman emperor, and she was one of the subjects of Giovanni Boccaccio's 1374 *On Famous Women*, his 106-entry consideration of female genius from Eve to Joanna, the crusader queen of Jerusalem and Sicily. Boccaccio explains that Proba collected lines of Virgil with such "great skill, aptly placing the entire lines, joining the fragments, observing the metrical rules, and preserving the dignity of the verses, that no one except an expert could detect the connections," in Pier Giorgio Ricci's translation. As a result of her genius, a reader might think that "Virgil had been a prophet as well as an apostle," the cento suturing together the classic and the Hebraic, Athens and Jerusalem.

Ever the product of his time, Boccaccio could still only appreciate Proba's accomplishment through the lens of his own misogyny, writing that the "distaff, the needle, and weaving would have been sufficient for her had she wanted to lead a sluggish life like the majority of women." Boccaccio's myopia prevented him from seeing that that was the precise nature of Proba's genius—*she was a weaver*. The miniatures that illustrate a fifteenth-century edition of Boccaccio give truth to this, for despite the chauvinism of the text, Proba is depicted in gold-threaded red with white habit upon her head, a wand holding aloft a beautiful, blue expanding sphere studded with stars, a strangely scientifically accurate account of the universe as the poet sings the song of Genesis in the tongue of Virgil. Whatever anonymous artist saw fit to depict Proba as a mage understood her well; for that matter, they understood creation well, for perhaps God can generate ex nihilo, but artists must always gather their material from fragments shored against their ruin.

In our own era of allusion, reference, quotation, pastiche, parody, and sampling, you'd think that the cento would have new practitioners and new readers. Something of the disk jockeys Danger Mouse, Fatboy Slim, and Girl Talk in the idea of remixing a tremendous amount of independent lines into some synthesized newness; something oddly of the Beastie Boys' *Paul's Boutique* in the very form of the thing. But centos proper are actually fairly rare in contemporary verse, despite T. S. Eliot's admission in *The Sacred Wood* that "mature poets steal." Perhaps with more charity, Allen argues that reading is a "process of moving between texts. Meaning because something which exists between a text and all the other texts to which it refers and relates." But while theorists have an awareness of the ways in which allusion dominates the modernist and postmodernist sensibility—what theorists who use the word *text* too often call "intertextuality"—the cento remains as obscure as other abandoned poetic forms from the Anacreontic to the Zajal (look them up). Lehman argues that modern instances of the form are "based on the idea that in some sense all poems are collages made up of other people's words; that the collage is a valid method of composition, and an eloquent one."

Contemporary poets who've tried their hand include John Ashbery, who wove together Gerard Manley Hopkins, Lord Byron, and Eliot, as well as Peter Gizzi, who in "Ode: Salute to the New York School" made a cento from poets like Frank O'Hara, James Schuyler, and Ashbery. Lehman has tried his own hand at the form, to great success. In commemoration of his *Oxford Book of American Poetry*, he wrote a cento for the *New York Times* that's a fabulous chimera whose anatomy is drawn from a diversity that is indicative of the sweep and complexity of four centuries of verse, including, among others, Robert Frost, Hart Crane, W. H. Auden, Gertrude Stein, Elizabeth Bishop, Edward Taylor, Jean Toomer, Anne Bradstreet, Henry Wadsworth Longfellow, Edna St. Vincent Millay, Wallace Stevens, Robert Pinsky, Marianne Moore, and this being a stolidly American poem, our grandparents Walt Whitman and Emily Dickinson.

Lehman contributed an ingenious cento sonnet in the *New Yorker* assembled from various Romantic and modernist poets, his final stanza reading, "And whom I love, I love indeed, / And all I loved, I loved alone, / Ignorant and wanton as the dawn," the lines so beautifully and seamlessly flowing into one another that you'd never notice that they're respectively from Samuel Taylor Coleridge, Edgar Allan Poe, and William Butler Yeats. Equally moving was a cento written by editors at the Academy of American Poets, which contains lines from Charles Wright, Marie Ponsot, Dickinson, Sylvia Plath, and Samuel Beckett.

Take this rather remarkable little poem, which begins with Wright's line "In the Kingdom of the Past, the Brown-Eyed Man is King," on its own accord. Its ambiguity is remarkable, and the lyric all the more powerful for it. In the second line, where it repeats a line from Ponsot which reads "Brute. Spy. I trust you. Now you reel & brawl," to whom is the narrator speaking, and who has been trusted and apparently violated that loyalty? Note how the implied narrative of the poem breaks after the dash that end-stops the third line with a fragment from Dickinson that reads "After great pain, a formal feeling comes —." In the first part of the poem, we have declarations of betrayal; somebody is impugned as "Brute. Spy." But from that betrayal, that "great pain," there is some sort of transformation of feeling; neither acceptance nor forgiveness but almost a tacit defeat, the "vulturous boredom" described in the fourth line, which is borrowed from Plath. The narrator psychologically, possibly physically, withers. They become less present to themselves, "of less use to myself," as the Wright fragment used in the penultimate line reads. And yet there is something to be said for the complexity of emotions we often have toward people, for though it seems that this poem expresses the heartbreak of betrayal, the absence of its subject is still that which affects the narrators so that the "hours . . . are so leaden," as words originally written by Beckett are used in the final line. Does the meaning of the poem change when I tell you that it was stitched together by those editors, drawn from a diversity of different poets in different countries living at different times? That the "true" authors are Wright, Ponsot, Dickinson, Plath, and Beckett?

Steiner claims, "There is, *stricto sensu*, no finished poem. The poem made available to us contains preliminary versions of itself. Drafts [and] cancelled versions." I'd go further than Steiner, even, and state that there is no individual poet. Just as all drafts are ultimately abandoned rather than completed, so is the task of completion ever deferred to subsequent generations. All poems, all writings (and all language, for that matter) are related to something else written or said by someone else at some point in time, a great chain of being going back to the beginnings immemorial. We are, in the most profound sense, always finishing one another's sentences. Far from something to despair at, this truth is something that binds us together in an untearable patchwork garment, where our lines and words have been loaned from somewhere else, given with the solemn promise that we must pay it forward. We're all just lines in a conversation that began long ago and, thankfully, shall never end. If you listen carefully, even if it requires a bit of decipherment or decoding, you'll discover the answer to any query you may have. Since all literature is a conversation, all poems are centos. And all poems are prophecies whose meanings have yet to be interpreted.

7

Marks of Significance

On Punctuation's Occult Power

Prosody, and orthography, are not parts of grammar, but
diffused like the blood and spirits throughout the whole.
—Ben Jonson, *English Grammar* (1617)

Erasmus was enraptured by the experience, by the memory, by
the very idea of Venice. For ten months from 1507 to 1508, Erasmus would be housed in a room of the Aldine Press, not far from
the piazzas of St. Mark's Square, with their red tiles burnt copper
by the Adriatic sun, the glory and the stench of the Grand Canal
wafting into the cell where the scholar would expand his collection
of 3,260 proverbs entitled *Thousands of Adages*, his first major work.
Venice was the home to a "library which has no other limits than
the world itself"—a watery metropolis and an empire of dreams
that was "building up a sacred and immortal thing."

Erasmus composed to the astringent smell of black ink rendered
from the resin of gall nuts, the rhythmic click-click-click of movable

type of alloyed lead-tin keys being set, and the whoosh of paper feeding through the press. From that workshop would come over a hundred titles of Greek and Latin, all published with the indomitable Aldus Manutius's watermark, an image filched from an ancient Roman coin depicting a strangely skinny and piscine Mediterranean dolphin inching down an anchor. Reflecting on that watermark (which has since been filched again by the modern publisher Doubleday), Erasmus wrote that it symbolized "all kinds of books in both languages, recognized, owned and praised by all to whom liberal studies are holy." Adept in humanistic philology, Erasmus's entire career was made by understanding the importance of a paragraph, a phrase, a word. Of a single mark. As did his publisher.

Erasmus's printer was visionary. The Aldine Press was the first in Europe to produce books made by folding the sheets of paper in a bound book not once (as in a folio) or four times (as in a quarto) but eight times to produce volumes that could be as small as four to six inches, the so-called octavo. Such volumes could be put in a pocket, what constituted the forerunner of the paperback, which Manutius advertised as "portable small books." Now volumes no longer had to be cumbersome tomes chained to the desk of a library; they could be squirreled away in a satchel, the classics made democratic. When laying the typeface for a 1501 edition of Virgil in the new octavo form, Manutius charged a Bolognese punchcutter named Francesco Griffo to design a font that appeared calligraphic. Borrowing the poet Petrarch's handwriting, Griffo invented a slanted typeface that printers quickly learned could denote emphasis, which came to be named after the place of its invention: *italic*.

However, it was an invention seven years before that restructured not just how language appears but, indeed, the very rhythm of sentences; for in 1496, Manutius introduced a novel bit of punctuation, a jaunty little man with leg splayed to the left as if he was pausing to hold open a door for the reader before they entered the next room, the odd mark at the caesura of this byzantine sentence that is known to posterity as the semicolon. Punctuation exists not in the wild; it is a function not of how we hear the word but rather of how we write the word. Punctuation is what the theorist Walter Ong described in his classic *Orality and Literacy* as marks that are "even farther from the oral world than letters of the alphabet are: though part of a text they are unpronounceable, nonphonemic." None of our notations are implied by mere speech, as they are creatures of the page: comma, and semicolon; (as well as parentheses and what Ben Jonson appropriately referred to as an "admiration" but we call an exclamation mark!)—the pregnant pause of a dash and the grim finality of a period. Has anything been left out? Oh, the ellipses . . .

No doubt the prescriptivist critic of my flights of grammatical fancy in the previous few sentences would note my unorthodox usage, but I do so only to emphasize how contingent and mercurial our system of marking written language was until around four or five centuries ago. Manutius may have been the greatest of European printers, but from Johannes Gutenberg to William Caxton, the era's publishers oversaw the transition from manuscript to print with an equivalent metamorphosis of language from oral to written, from the ear to the eye. Paleographer Malcolm Parkes writes in his invaluable *Pause and Effect: An Introduction to the History of Punctuation in the West* that such a system is a "phenomenon of written language, and its history is bound up with that of the written medium." Since the invention of script, there has been a war of attrition between the spoken and the written; battle lines drawn between rhetoricians and grammarians, between sound and meaning. Such is a distinction as explained by linguist David Crystal in *Making a Point: The Persnickety Story of English Punctuation*, whereby "writing and speech are seen as distinct mediums of expression, with different communicative aims and using different processes of composition."

Obviously, the process of making this distinction has been going on for quite a long time. The moment the first wedged stylus pressed into wet Mesopotamian clay was the beginning, through ancient Greek diacritical and Hebrew pointing systems, up through when Medieval scribes began to first separate words from endless *scriptio continua*, whichbroachednogapsbetweenwordsuntiltheendofthemiddleages. Reading, you see, was normally accomplished out loud, and the written word was less a thing-in-itself and more a representation of a particular event—that is, the event of speaking. When this is the guiding metaphysic of writing, punctuation serves a simple purpose—to indicate how something is to be read aloud. Like the *luftpause* of musical notation, the nascent end stops and commas of antiquity existed not to clarify syntactical meaning but to let you know when to take a breath. Providing an overview of punctuation's genealogy, Alberto Manguel writes in *A History of Reading* how by the seventh century, a "combination of points and dashes indicated a full stop, a raised or high point was equivalent to our comma," an innovation of Irish monks who "began isolating not only parts of speech but also the grammatical constituents within a sentence, and introduced many of the punctuation marks we use today."

No doubt many of you, uncertain of the technical rules of comma usage (as many of us are), were told in elementary school that a comma designates when a breath should be taken, only to discover by college that that axiom was incorrect. Certain difficulties, with, that, way of writing, a sentence—for what if the author is Christopher Walken or William Shatner? Enthusiast of the baroque that I am, I'm sympathetic to writers who use commas as Hungarians use paprika. I'll adhere to the claim of David Steel, who in his 1785 *Elements of Punctuation* wrote that "punctuation is not, in my opinion, attainable by rules . . . but it may be procured by a kind of internal conviction." Steven Roger Fischer correctly notes in his *A History of Reading* (distinct from the Manguel book of the same title) that "today, punctuation is linked mainly to meaning, not to sound," but as late as 1589, the rhetorician George Putten-ham could in his *Art of English Poesie*, as Crystal explains, define a comma as the "shortest pause," a colon as "twice as much time," and an end stop as a "full pause." Our grade school teachers weren't wrong in a historical sense, for that was the purpose of commas, colons, and semicolons, to indicate pauses of certain amounts of time when Scripture was being read aloud. All of the written word would have been quietly murmured under the breath of monks in the buzz of a monastic scriptorium.

For grammarians, punctuation has long been claimed as a cap-tured soldier in the war of attrition between sound and meaning, these weird little marks enlisted in the cause of language as a pri-marily written thing. Fischer explains that "universal, standardized punctuation, such as may be used throughout a text in consistent fashion, only became fashionable . . . after the introduction of printing." Examine medieval manuscripts and you'll find that the orthography—that is, the spelling and punctuation (insomuch as it exists)—is completely variable from author to author, in keeping with an understanding that writing exists mainly as a means to perform speaking. By the Renaissance, print necessitated a degree of standardization, though far from uniform. This can be attested to by the conspiratorially minded who are flummoxed by Shake-speare's name being spelled several different ways while he was alive or by the anarchistic rules of eighteenth-century punctuation, the veritable golden age of the comma and semicolon. When punctu-ation becomes not just an issue of telling a reader when to breathe but a syntactical unit that conveys particular meanings that could be altered by the choice or placement of these funny little dots, then a degree of rigor becomes crucial. As Fischer writes, punctuation came to convey "almost exclusively meaning, not sound," and so the system had to become fixed in some sense.

If I may offer an additional conjecture, it would seem to me that there was a fortuitous confluence of both the technology of printing and the emergence of certain intellectual movements within the Renaissance that may have contributed to the elevation of punctuation. Johanna Drucker writes in *The Alphabetic Labyrinth: The Letters in History and Imagination* how Renaissance thought was gestated by "strains of Hermetic, Neo-Pythagorean, Neo-Platonic and kabbalistic traditions blended in their own peculiar hybrids of thought." Figures like the fifteenth-century Florentine philosophers Marsilio Ficino and Giovanni Pico della Mirandola reintroduced Plato into an intellectual environment that had sustained itself on Aristotle for centuries. Aristotle rejected the otherworldliness of his teacher Plato, preferring rather to muck about in the material world of appearances, and when medieval Christendom embraced the former, they modeled his empirical perspective. Arguably, the transcendent nature of words is less important in such a context; what difference does the placement of a semicolon matter if it's not conveying something of the eternal realm of the Forms? But the Florentine Platonists like Ficino were concerned with such things, for as he writes in *Five Questions concerning the Mind* (printed in 1495—one year after the first semicolon), the "rational soul . . . possesses the excellence of infinity and eternity . . . [for we] characteristically incline toward the infinite." In Renaissance Platonism, the correct ordering of words (and their corralling with punctuation) is a reflection not of speech but of something larger, greater, higher. Something infinite and eternal, something transcendent. And so we have the emergence of a dogma of correct punctuation, of standardized spelling—of a certain "orthographic Platonism."

Drucker explains that Renaissance scholars long searched "for a set of visual signs which would serve to embody the system of human knowledge (conceived of as the apprehension of a divine order)." In its most exotic form, this involved the construction of divine languages, the parsing of kabbalistic symbols, and the embrace of alchemical reasoning. I'd argue in a more prosaic manner that such orthographic Platonism is the wellspring for all prescriptivist approaches to language, where the manipulation of the odd symbols we call letters and punctuation can lend themselves to the discovery of greater truths, an invention that allows us "to converse even with the absent," as Parkes writes. In the workshops of the Renaissance, at the Aldine Press, immortal things were made of letters, and eternity existed between them, with punctuation acting as the guideposts to a type of paradise. And so it can remain for us.

Linguistic prescriptivists will bemoan the loss of certain standards, how text speak signals an irreducible entropy of communication, or how the abandonment of arbitrary grammatical rules is as if a sign from Revelation. Yet such reactionaries are not the true guardians of orthographic Platonism, for we must take wisdom where we find it, in the appearance, texture, and flavor of punctuation. Rules may be arbitrary, but the choice of particular punctuation—be it the hushed pause of the dash or the rapturous shouting of the exclamation mark—matters. Literary agent Noah Lukeman writes in *A Dash of Style: The Art and Mastery of Punctuation* that punctuation is normally understood as simply "a convenience, a way of facilitating what you want to say." Such a limited view, which is implicit for those who advocate punctuation either as an issue of sound or as one of meaning, ignores the occult power of the question mark, the theurgy in a comma. The orthographic Platonists at the Aldine Press understood that so much depended on a semicolon; it signified more than a longer-than-average pause or the demarcation of an independent clause. Lukeman argues that punctuation is rarely "pondered as a medium for artistic expression, as a means of impacting content," yet in the most "profound way . . . it achieves symbiosis with the narration, style, viewpoint, and even the plot itself."

Keith Houston in *Shady Characters: The Secret Life of Punctuation, Symbols, and Other Typographical Marks* claims that "every character we type or write is a link to the past," every period takes us back to the dots that Irish monks used to signal the end of a line, every semicolon back to Manutius's Venetian workshop. Punctuation, as with the letters whom they serve, has a deep genealogy; their use places us in a chain of connotation and influence that goes back centuries. More than that, each individual punctuation has a unique terroir; they do things that give the sentence a waft, a wisdom, a rhythm that is particular to them. Considering the periods of Ernest Hemingway, the semicolons of Edgar Allan Poe and Herman Melville, and the sublime dash of Emily Dickinson, Lukeman writes, "Sentences crash and fall like the waves of the sea, and work unconsciously on the reader. Punctuation is the music of language."

To get overly hung up on punctuation as an issue of either putting marks in the right place or letting the reader know when they can gulp some air is to miss the point—a comma is a poem unto itself, and an exclamation point is an epic! Cecelia Watson writes in *Semicolon: The Past, Present, and Future of a Misunderstood Mark* that Manutius's invention "is a place where our anxieties and our aspirations about language, class, and education are concentrated," and she is of course correct, as evidenced by all of those partisans of minimalism from Kurt Vonnegut to Cormac McCarthy who've impugned the Aldine mark's honor. But what a semicolon can do that other marks can't! How it can connect two complete ideas into a whole; a semicolon is capable of unifications that a comma is too weak to do alone. As Adam O'Fallon Price writes in *The Millions*, "Semicolons . . . increase the range of tone and inflection at a writer's disposal." Or take the exclamation mark, a symbol I've used roughly four times in my published writing (until this essay, that is) but I deploy no less than fifteen times per average email. A maligned mark due to its emotive enthusiasms, Nick Ripatrazone observes in *The Millions* that "exclamation marks call attention toward themselves in poems: they stand straight up." Punctuation, in its own way, is conscious; it's an algorithm, as much thought itself as it is a schematic showing the process of thought.

To take two poetic examples, what would Walt Whitman be without his exclamation mark? What would Dickinson be without her dash? They didn't simply use punctuation for the pause of breath or to logically differentiate things with some grammatical-mathematical precision. Rather, they did do those things, but also so much more, for the union of exhalation and thought gestures to that higher realm the Renaissance originators of punctuation imagined. What would Whitman's "Pioneers! O pioneers!" from the 1865 *Leaves of Grass* be without the exclamation point? What argument could be made if that ecstatic mark were abandoned? What of the solemn mysteries in the portal that is Dickinson's dash when she writes, "'Hope' is the thing with feathers—"? Orthographic Platonism instills in us a wisdom behind the arguments of rhetoricians and grammarians; it reminds us that more than simple notation, each mark of punctuation is a personality, a character, a divinity in itself.

My favorite illustration of that principle is in dramatist Margaret Edson's sublime play *W;t*, the only theatrical work I can think of that has New Critical close reading as one of its plot points. In painful detail, *W;t* depicts the final months of Dr. Vivian Bearing—a professor of seventeenth-century poetry at an unnamed, elite, eastern university—after she has been diagnosed with stage four cancer. While undergoing chemotherapy, Bearing often reminisces on her life of scholarship, frequently returning to memories of her beloved dissertation adviser, E. M. Ashford. In one flashback, Bearing remembers being castigated by Ashford for sloppy work that she did, providing an interpretation of John Donne's "Holy Sonnet VI" that is based on an incorrectly punctuated edition of the cycle. Ashford asks her student, "Do you think the punctuation of the last line of this sonnet is merely an insignificant detail?" In the version used by Bearing, Donne's immortal line "Death be not proud" is end-stopped with a semicolon, but as Ashford explains, the proper means of punctuation as based on the earliest manuscripts of Donne is simply a comma. "And death shall be no more, *comma*, Death thou shalt die."

Ashford imparts to Bearing that so much can depend on a comma. The professor tells her student, "Nothing but a breath—a comma—separates life from everlasting. . . . With the original punctuation restored, death is no longer something to act out on a stage, with exclamation points. . . . Not insuperable barriers, not semicolons, just a comma." Ashford declares, "This way, the *uncompromising* way, one learns something from this poem, wouldn't you say?" Sometimes I imagine great works of literature with all the letters deleted and only those strange little marks left behind. There would be a torrent of commas, semicolons, dashes across pages and pages in the works of Dickens, only an occasional comma here or there with Hemingway, and a succession of periods for McCarthy. Each resultant litany of punctuation is as unique and personal as somebody's genetic code. Such is the mark of significance, an understanding that punctuation is as intimate as breath, as exulted as thought, and as powerful as the union between them—infinite, eternal, divine.

8

Lost in Lexicography

And they shall say to me, What is [God's]
name? what shall I say unto them?
—Exodus 3:13

Language is only the instrument of science,
and words are but the signs of ideas.
—Samuel Johnson, *A Dictionary of the English Language* (1755)

Attar of Nishapur, the twelfth-century Persian Sufi, wrote of a pilgrimage of birds. His masterpiece *The Conference of Birds* recounts how thirty fowls were led by a tufted, orange hoopoe (wisest of his kind) to find the Simurgh, a type of bird god or king. So holy is the hoopoe that the Arabic blessing of *bismillah* is etched onto his beak as an encouragement to his fellow feathered penitents. From Persia the birds travel to China, in search of the Simurgh, a gigantic eagle-like creature with the face of a man (or sometimes a dog) who has lived for millennia, possesses all knowledge, and like the Phoenix, has been immolated only to rise again.

In the birds' desire to see the Simurgh, we understand how we should yearn for Allah: "Do all you can to become a bird of the Way to God; / Do all you can to develop your wings and your feathers," Attar writes. An esoteric truth is revealed to the loyal hawk, the romantic nightingale, the resplendent peacock, and the stalwart stork: there is no Simurgh awaiting them in some hidden paradise, for the creature's name is itself a Farsi pun on the phrase "thirty birds." Attar writes that "all things are but masks at God's beck and call, / They are symbols that instruct us that God is all." There is no God but us, and we are our own prophets.

As a dream vision, *The Conference of Birds* appears to be borderline atheistic, but only if you're oblivious that such mysticism is actually God-intoxicated. And as with all mystical literature, there is (purposefully) something hard to comprehend, though the text includes a clue to its interpretation when Attar writes, "The shadow and its maker are one and the same, / so get over surfaces and delve into mysteries." Equivalence of shadow and maker—it's a moving understanding of what writing is as well, where the very products of our creation are intimations of our souls. My approach to these mysteries, plumbing past the surfaces of appearance, is an illustration of the epic's themes done in the characteristic Islamic medium of calligraphy. Alongside the intricate miniatures that defined Persian art, there developed a tradition whereby ingenious calligraphers would present Arabic or Persian sentences in artful arrangements so that whole sentences would compose the illusion of a representational picture.

One such image is nothing but the word *Simurgh* itself, yet the way in which the artist has configured letters like the ascending *alif*, horizontal *jim*, rounded *dhal*, and complex *hamzah* presents the appearance of a bird rearing with regal countenance—all feather, claw, and beak. A beautiful evocation of Attar's very lesson itself, for as the avian penitents learn, that there is no Simurgh save for their collective body, so too do we see that the illusion of the picture we're presented with is simply an arrangement of letters.

This illustration is a pithy demonstration of the paradox of literature as well. If the Simurgh of *The Conference of the Birds* is simply composed by the fowl themselves, and if the image of the calligrapher's art is constituted by letters, might there be a lesson that divinity itself is constructed in the latter way? Just as each bird is part of the Simurgh, may each letter be part of God? For as images have been historically understood as violating the prohibition on idolatry, pictures still can't help but arise out of these abstracted letters, these symbols imbued with a fiery life. Little wonder that incantations are conveyed through words and that we're warned not to take the Lord's name in vain, for letters both define and give life. A certain conclusion is unassailable: God is an alphabet—*God is the alphabet.*

* * *

Bereshit is the word that inaugurates Genesis, and it's from that word that the name of the book derives in its original language. No text more explicitly deals with the generative powers of speech than Genesis, and in seeing the Torah as both product of and vehicle for God's creation, we get closer to the sacredness of the alphabet. *Bereshit* begins with the second letter of the Hebrew alphabet, bet, which looks like this: ב. Something about the shape of the abstracted letter reminds me of a tree with a branch hanging out at an angle, appropriate when we consider the subject of the book.

There's something unusual in the first letter of the Torah being bet, for why would the word of God not begin with her first letter, aleph? Medieval kabbalists, adept in numerology, had an answer: it was to indicate that reality has two levels—the physical and the spiritual, or as Attar called them, the surfaces and the mysteries. But if the surface of the sheep vellum that constitutes a physical Torah is one thing, the actual reality of the letter is another. A deeper truth is conveyed by the mystery of letters themselves, the way in which abstract symbols can make us hallucinate voices in our heads, the way in which entire worlds of imagination can be constructed by dyeing the skin of dead animals black with ink.

We dissuade ourselves against magic too easily, especially since literacy itself is evidence of it. That language is sacred should be an obvious truth. Even as the old verities of holiness are discarded, the unassailable fact that language has magic is intuited at the level of an eye scanning a page and building universes from nothingness. Jewish sages believed that the alphabet preceded that initial *bereshit*; indeed, letters had to exist before creation, for how would God's accomplishment of the latter even be possible without her access to the former? As the kabbalistic book *Sefer Yetzirah* explains, "Twenty-two letters did [God] engrave and carve, he weighed them and moved them around into different combinations. Through them, he created the soul of every living being and the soul of every word."

* * *

Chiseled onto the sandy-red shoulder of a sphinx found at Serabit el-Khadim in the Sinai Peninsula is evidence of the alphabet's origins that is almost as evocative as the story told in the *Sefer Yetzirah*. As enigmatic as her cousins at Giza or Thebes, the Sinai sphinx is a votive in honor of the Egyptian goddess Hathor, guardian of the desert, and she who protected the turquoise mines that dotted the peninsula and operated for close to eight centuries producing wealth for distant Pharaohs. The Serabit el-Khadim sphinx is only a little under twenty-four centimeters, more than diminutive enough to find her new home in a British Museum cabinet. Excavated in 1904 by Flinders and Hilda Petrie, founders of Egyptology as a discipline, the little Hathor lioness lay in wait for perhaps 3,800 years, graffiti etched into her side attesting to alphabetic origins.

This graffiti was carved by laborers whose language was a Semitic tongue closely related to Hebrew (and indeed, some have connected the inscription to the Exodus narrative). John Man in *Alpha Beta: How 26 Letters Shaped the Western World* describes how these "twelve marks suggest links between Egyptian writing and later Semitic letters," for though what's recorded at Serabit el-Khadim are glyphs like "an ox-head, an eye, a house, a snake, and water," what is found on the haunches of Hathor's sphinx are the abstracted "roots of our own *a*, *b*, *v*, *u*, *m*, *p*, *w*, and *t*." By 1916, Alan Gardiner used the decipherable Egyptian hieroglyphic inscription between the sphinx's breasts, which read "Beloved of Hathor, Lady of the Turquoise," to translate the eleven marks on her side, making this one of the earliest examples of a script called "proto-Sinaitic," the most ancient instance of alphabetic writing to ever be found. Gardiner hypothesized that this was an alphabetic letter system, arguing that it was either a form of pidgin Egyptian used by the administrators or a simplified system invented by the workers. By streamlining the process of communication, the alphabet's purpose was pragmatic, but its implications rank it among the most important paradigm shifts of history.

In his book *In the Beginning: A Short History of the Hebrew Language*, Joel M. Hoffman explains that if it's "easier to learn the tens of hundreds of symbols required for syllabic system than it is to learn the thousands required for a purely logographic system," then it is easier still to learn consonantal systems (as both proto-Sinaitic and Hebrew are), as these systems "generally require fewer than 30 symbols." Vowels may be the souls of words, but consonants are their bodies. The former awaited both the Greek alphabet and the diacritical marks of Masoretic Hebrew, but the skeletons of our alphabet were already recorded in homage to the goddess Hathor.

Man writes that three features mark the alphabet as crucial in the history of communication: "its uniqueness, its simplicity and its adaptability." Perhaps even more importantly, where pictograms are complicated, they're also indelibly wed to the tongue that first uttered them, whereas alphabets can, "with some pushing and shoving, be adapted to all languages." The alphabet, a Semitic invention born from Egyptian materials for practical ends, "proved wildly successful," as Hoffman writes, with proto-Sinaitic developing into the Phoenician alphabet and then the Hebrew, which was "used as the basis for the Greek and Latin alphabets, which, in turn, along with Hebrew itself, were destined to form the basis for almost all the world's alphabets." Birthed from parsimony, proto-Sinaitic would become the vehicle through which abstraction could be spread. Still, the blurred edges of our letters proclaim their origin in pictures—the prostrate penitent worshipping prayerfully in an *E*; in an *S*, the slithering of the snake who caused the fall.

* * *

Every single major alphabetic system, save for Korean Hangul developed in the fifteenth century, can trace its origins back to this scratching on a sphinx. The Phoenicians, a people who spoke a Semitic language, developed one of the first proper alphabets in the Late Bronze Age, more than a millennium before the Common Era. Michael Rosen in *Alphabetical: How Every Letter Tells a Story* explains that the Phoenicians "used abstract versions of objects to indicate letters: a bifurcated (horned?) sign was an 'ox' (in their language 'aleph'), and on down through the words for 'house,' 'stick,' 'door' and 'shout' up to 'tooth' and 'mark.'" The alphabet is universal, applicable in any cultural setting, and yet the immediate context of its creation is of sailors and turquoise minors living in the Bronze Age.

An alphabetic epiphany when some turquoise miner abstracted the intricate pictures of Egyptian hieroglyphics but used them not for ideas but rather for units of sound. The seafaring Phoenicians, clad in their Tyrian purple cloth dyed from the mucus of clams, would disseminate the alphabet around Mediterranean ports. The Phoenician alphabet is the origin of elegant Hebrew, which God used when he struck letters of fire into the tablets at Sinai, the genesis of Arabic's fluid letters by which Allah dictated the Qur'an. The Greeks adapted the Phoenicians' invention (as they acknowledge) as a medium into which the oral poems of Homer could finally be recorded; the death-obsessed Etruscans whose tongue we still can't hear appropriated the symbols of Punic sailors, as did the Romans, who would stamp those letters on triumphant monuments throughout Europe and Africa in so enduring a way that you're still reading them now. Languid Ge'ez in Ethiopian gospels, blocky Aramaic written in the tongue of Christ, Brahmic scripts that preserved dharmic prayers, the mysterious ogham of Irish druids, the bird-scratch runes of the Norseman, the stolid Cyrillic of the czars—all derive from that initial alphabet. Even Sequoyah's nineteenth-century Cherokee, though a syllabary and not technically an alphabet, draws several of its symbols from a Latin that can be ultimately traced back to the mines of Serabit el-Khadim.

Matthew Battles in *Palimpsest: A History of the Written Word* writes how this "great chain of alphabetical evolution collapses in a welter of characters, glyphs, and symbols, mingling in friendly, familial and even erotic enthusiasms of conversant meaning." We sense familiarity across this family tree of alphabetical systems— how in an English *A* we see the Greek α, or how the Hebrew ח evokes the Greek η. But as the French rabbi Marc-Alain Ouaknin explains in *The Mysteries of the Alphabet*, all of our letters were ultimately adapted by the ancient Canaanites from Egyptian pictures, for before there was an *A* there was the head of an ox; before there was an *H* there was an enclosure. Ouaknin writes that the "history of meaning is the history of forgetting the image, the history of a suppression of the visible." In the beginning, there was not the word but rather the image.

* * *

During the seventeenth century, the German Jesuit polymath Athanasius Kircher was bedeviled by the question of how image and word negotiated over dominion in the kingdom of meaning. Kircher is an exemplar of the Renaissance; born not quite in time for the Enlightenment, he was fluent in conjecture rather than proof, esoterica rather than science, wonder rather than reason. His was the epistemology not of the laboratory but of the *Wunderkammer*— the wonder cabinet. Art historian Johanna Drucker in *The Alphabetic Labyrinth: The Letters in History and Imagination* writes that Kircher's studies included that of the "structure of the subterranean world of underground rivers, volcanic lava flow and caves, an exhaustive text on all extant devices for producing light," and most importantly, "compendia of information on China, [and] Egypt."

Kircher is both the first Egyptologist and first Sinologist, even as his conclusions about both subjects would be proven completely inaccurate in almost all of their details. His 1655 *Oedipus Aegyptiacus* was both an attempt to decipher the enigmatic symbols on papyri and monuments as well as a "restoration of the hieroglyphic doctrine," the secret hermetic knowledge the priest associated with the ancients. He concurred with the ancient Neoplatonist Plotinus, who in his *Enneads* claimed that the Egyptians did not use letters "which represent sounds and words; instead they use designs of images, each of which stands for a distinct thing. . . . Every incised sign is thus, at once, knowledge, wisdom, a real entity captured in one stroke," as translated by James Fentress. Kircher thus "translated" an inscription on a two-millennia-old obelisk that sat in the Villa Celimontana in Rome, explaining that the hieroglyphs should read as "His minister and faithful attendant, the polymorphous Spirit, shows the abundance and wealth of all necessary things." Not a single word is accurate.

For Kircher, what made both hieroglyphics and Chinese writings so evocative was that they got as close to unmediated reality as possible; they were not mere depiction but essence. Umberto Eco in *The Search for a Perfect Language* explains that Kircher's enthusiasms were mistaken, because his "assumption that every hieroglyph was an ideogram . . . was an assumption which doomed his enterprise at the outset," for contrary to his presupposition, neither Mandarin nor ancient Egyptian operated like some sort of baroque rebus.

Still, Kircher's was a contention that "hieroglyphs all *showed* something about the natural world," as Eco writes. Pictograms were as a window unto the world; fallen letters were simply scratches in the sand. Where Kircher and others faltered was in letting abstraction obscure the concreteness of the alphabet. If you flip an *A* upside down, do you not see the horns of the ox that letter originally signified? If you turn a *B* on its side, do you not see the rooms of a house? Or in the curvature of a *C* that of the camel's hump?

* * *

Iconoclasm explains much of our amnesia about the iconic origins of our letters, but it's also that which gives the alphabet much of its power. Imagery has been the nucleus of human expression since a Cro-Magnon woman blew red ochre from her engorged cheeks onto the cave wall at Lascaux so as to trace the outline of her hand. But the shift from pictographic writing to alphabetic inaugurated the reign of abstraction, whereby the imagistic forbearers of our letters had to be forgotten. Ouaknin explains that "behind each of the letters with which we are so familiar lies a history, changes, mutations based on one or more original forms."

Since Gardiner's translation of Serabit el-Khadim, there have been a few dozen similar abecedarians found at sites mostly in the Sinai. From those sparse examples, scholars trace the morphology of letters back to their origins, when they brewed from that primordial soup of imagery and held meanings that are now obscured. From our Latin letters, we move back to the indecipherable Etruscan, from those northern Italians, we trace to the Greeks, and then the purple-clad Phoenicians, finally arriving at the ancient Semites, who crafted the alphabet, finding that our letters are not *a*, *b*, and *c*; or alpha, beta, and gamma; or even aleph, bet, and gimel but rather their original pictures—an ox, a house, and a camel.

Philologists and classicists have identified all of the images from which the twenty-six letters derive. In proto-Sinaitic, *D* was originally a door. If you flip an *E* on its side, you see the arms outstretched above the head of a man in prayer. *I* was originally a hand; the wavy line of *M* still looks like the wave of water it originally was. *R* still has at its top the head above a body it originally signified; *U* still looks like that which an oar was placed upon in a boat. Kircher thought that hieroglyphics were perfect pictures of the real world, but hidden within our own alphabet, absconded from the courts of Egypt, are the ghostly afterimages of the originals.

*   *   *

The alphabet spread something more than mere convenience—it spread monotheism. Man argues that the "evolution of the belief in a single god was dependent on an ability to record that belief and make it accessible; and that both recording and accessibility were dependent on the invention of the alphabet." God made the alphabet possible, and it would seem that the alphabet returned the favor. What first had to be forgotten, however, was the meaning of the letters' original shapes, for in pictograms, there lay the risk of idolatry, of conjuring those old gods who birthed them.

At Mount Sinai, the Lord supposedly used fire to emblazon Moses's tablets with his commandments, the second of which demands that none shall make any "likeness of any thing that is in heaven above, or that is in the earth beneath, or that is in the water under the earth" (Exod 20:4). When writing those letters, God very well couldn't use ones that happened to look like a man, or an ox, or a camel's hump. Ouaknin conjectures, "Iconoclasm required the Jews to purge proto-Sinaitic of images," for the "birth of the modern alphabet created from abstract characters is linked to the revelation and the receiving of the law." The rabbi argues that it was "under the influence of monotheistic expression [that] hieroglyphics began to shed some of its images, resulting in the first attempt of an alphabet." Accessible abstractions of the alphabets were not a fortuitous coincidence but rather a demand of the Mosaic covenant, since the newly monotheistic Jews couldn't worship God if the letters of their writing system evoked falcon-headed Horus, the jackal Anubis, or baboon-faced Thoth with stylus in hand. Man writes that "both new god and new script worked together to forge a new nation and disseminate an idea that would change the world."

A skeptic may observe that the alphabet hardly caused an immediate rash of conversions to monotheism in Greece, Rome, or the north country, as Zeus, Jupiter, and Tyr still reigned among their respective peoples. Yet alphabetic writing's emergence occurred right before a period the Austrian philosopher Karl Jaspers called the "Axial Age." Jaspers observed that in the first millennium before the Common Era, there was surprising synchronicity between radically disparate cultures that nonetheless produced new ways of understanding reality that still had some unifying similarities between each other.

Monotheism in the Levant, Greek philosophy, Persian Zoroastrianism, and the Indian Upanishads can all be traced to the Axial Age. For Jaspers, a paradigm shift in consciousness resulted in abstraction. What all of these different methods, approaches, and faiths shared was enshrinement the universal over the particular, the reality that is unseen over the shadows on the cave wall. In *Origin and Goal of History,* Jaspers describes the Axial Age as "an interregnum . . . a pause for liberty, a deep breath bringing the most lucid consciousness."

Jaspers noted the simultaneous emergence of these faiths but proffered not a full hypothesis as to why. Ultimately, the abstractions of the alphabet were that which incubated the Axial Age. In *Moses and Monotheism,* Sigmund Freud claimed that this "compulsion to worship a God whom one cannot see . . . meant that as a sensory perception was given second place to what may be called an abstract idea—a triumph of intellectuality over sensuality." This triumph of abstraction included not just the prophets Isaiah and Elijah but the philosophers Parmenides and Heraclitus and the sages Siddhartha and Zarathustra, all of whose words were made eternal in the alphabet.

From the Aegean to the Indus River, the common thread of the Axial Age was alphabetic writing, with only China as an exception. Leonard Shlain in *The Alphabet versus the Goddess: The Conflict between Word and Image* observed that the rise of phonetic letters coincided with the disappearance of idol worship in the Levant, writing that the "abstract alphabet encouraged abstract thinking," a progeny born from the curve and line of the word. Yet old gods can always be born again, their voices barely heard, yet still present in a sacred phoneme, their faces peeking out from the spaces between our letters.

* * *

In the Babylonian desert, excavators frequently find small bowls ringed with Aramaic and designed to capture demons. Molded by magi, the demon bowls are a trap, a harnessing of the magical efficacy of the alphabet. These talismans combined word and image to tame the malignant lesser gods who still stalked the earth, even after God's supposed victory.

Appropriate that God's alphabet is that which is able to constrain in clay the machinations of erotic Lilith and bestial Asmodeus. One such bowl, which depicts the succubus Lilith at its center as an alluring woman with long hair barely obscuring breasts and genitalia, incants that "60 men . . . will capture you with copper ropes on your feet and copper shackles on your hands and caste collars of copper upon your temples." Israeli scholar Naama Vilozny, an expert on the images of demons painted on these bowls by otherwise iconoclastic Jews, says that you "draw the figure you want to get rid of and then you bind it in a depiction and bind it in words." There is control in the alphabet, not just in trapping demons, but in the ability to capture a concept's essence. Writing holds the theurgic power of writing, where curses against hell are as strong as baked clay.

Magic and monotheism are not strictly separated; a sense of paganism haunts our faith as well as our letters. The psychologist Julian Jaynes in his *The Origin of Consciousness in the Breakdown of the Bicameral Mind* posited a controversial hypothesis that human beings were only "conscious" relatively recently, since shortly before the Axial Age. The alphabet perhaps played a role in this development, theoretically eliminating the other gods in favor of the one voice of God, the only voice in your head. But Jaynes explains that the "mind is still haunted by its old unconscious ways; it broods on lost authorities." This explanation certainly holds true when a frightened Babylonian places a bowl in the earth to capture those chthonic spirits that threaten us even though their dominion has been abolished.

The alphabet facilitated a new magic. Consider that the fourth commandment in Exodus, which reads "Thou shalt not take the name of the Lord thy God in vain" (Exod 20:7), is not an injunction against blasphemy in the modern sense, for surely the omnipotent can abide obscenity, but in historical context, it specifically meant that you *shouldn't use God's name to perform magic*. To know the letters of someone's name is to have the ability to control them; there's a reason that the "angel" with whom Jacob wrestles refuses to be named. The four Hebrew letters that constitute the proper name of God—יהוה—are commonly referred to as the tetragrammaton, there being no clear sense of how exactly the word would have actually been pronounced.

These letters have a charged power, no mere ink stain on sheepskin, for the correct pronunciation was guarded as an occult secret. Hoffman writes that the letters were "chosen not because of the sounds they represent, but because of their symbolic powers in that they were the Hebrew's magic vowel letters that no other culture had." The yod, hay, vov, hay of the tetragrammaton demonstrated both the victory of monotheism and the electric power of the alphabet itself. God encoded into the very name, which in turn was the blueprint for our reality. A dangerous thing, these letters, for just as demons could be controlled with their names painted onto the rough surface of a bowl, so too could the most adept of mages compel the creator to do their bidding.

*   *   *

Incantation is sometimes called prayer, other times poetry, and occasionally, the alphabet can substitute for both. As acrostic, alphabetic possibilities have long attracted poets. In Edward Hirsch's *The Poet's Glossary*, he writes about "abecedarians"— that is, verse where each line begins with the respective letter of the alphabet. As all formal poetry does, the form exploits artificial constraint, in this circumstance so as to meditate upon the alphabet itself. The abecedarian, Hirsch explains, is an "ancient form often employed for sacred works," elaborating on how all of the "acrostics in the Hebrew Bible are alphabetical, such as Psalm 119, which consists of twenty-two eight-line stanzas, one for each letter of the Hebrew of the alphabet." The "completeness of the form," Hirsch writes, "enacts the idea of total devotion to the law of God."

Saint Augustine, the fourth-century Christian theologian, wrote an abecedarian against the Donatist heretics; nearly a millennium later, Chaucer tried his hand at the form as well. Centuries after that, the English journalist Alaric Watts wrote his account of the 1789 Habsburg Siege of Belgrade in alliterative abecedarian: "An Austrian army, awfully arrayed, / Boldly by battery besieged Belgrade. / Cossack commanders cannonading come, / Dealing destruction's devastating doom." There are, to the best of my knowledge, no major examples of abecedarian prose. Perhaps somebody will write something soon? Because as Hirsch notes, the form has "powerful associations with prayer," the rapturous repetition of the alphabet stripping meaning to its bare essence, emptying both penitence and supplication of ego in favor of the ecstasies of pure sound.

Such was the wisdom of the Baal Shem Tov, founder of Hasidism, who was inspired by the ecstasies of Pietists to return worship to its emotional core. He sought to strip ritual of empty logic and to reendow it with that lost sense of the glowing sacred. Sometimes prayer need not even be in words; the sacred letters themselves function well enough. The Baal Shem Tov's honorific means "Master of the Good Name," he who has brought within the very sinews of his flesh and the synapses of his mind the pulsating power of the tetragrammaton. So much can depend on four letters.

The Baal Shem Tov, or the Besht, as he was often called, lived in the Pale of Settlement, the cold, gray Galician countryside. Drucker writes that the Besht exhorted the "practicing Jew to make of daily life a continual practice of devotion," whereby "each of the letters which pass one's lips are ascendant and unite with each other, carrying with them the full glory." The Besht taught that letters were not incidental; the alphabet itself was necessary for "true unification with the Divinity."

According to Hasidic legend, one Yom Kippur, the Besht led his congregation in their prayers. Toward the back of the synagogue was a simple-minded but pious shepherd boy. The other worshippers, with fingers pressing prayer books open, repeated the words of the Kol Nidre, but the illiterate shepherd could only pretend to mouth along, to follow writing he could not read. Emotions became rapturous as black-coated men below and women in the balcony above began to sway and shout out the prayers. Finally, overcome with devotion but unable to repeat after the rest of his fellow Jews, the shepherd boy shouted out the only prayer he could: "Aleph. Bet. Gimel. Daleth . . ." and on through the rest of the eighteen Hebrew letters.

There was an awkward silence in the sanctuary. Embarrassed, the young man explained, "God, that is all I can do. You know what your prayers are. Please arrange them into the correct order."

From the rafters of the shul, decorated with Hebrew letters in blocky black ink, came the very voice of God, leading the entire congregation in the holiest of prayers, repeated from that of the simple shepherd: "Aleph. Bet. Gimel. Daleth . . ." And so, in the court of the Baal Shem Tov, in the early eighteenth century in a synagogue upon the Galician plain, God deigned to teach women and men how to worship once again in the holiest prayer that there is. The alphabet, repeated truthfully with faith in your soul, is the purest form of prayer.

* * *

Alphabets are undertheorized. Because our alphabet is seemingly omnipresent, there is a way in which it's easy to forget the spooky power of twenty-six symbols. Considering how fundamental to basic functioning the alphabet is, we frequently overlook the sheer, transcendent magnificence of the letters that structure our world. Disenchantment, however, need not be our lot, for there is a realization that letters don't convey reality; rather, *they are reality*. Ecstatic for us to comprehend, the manner in which stains on dead trees are the conduit through which all meaning traverses, much like the electrons illuminating our screens. Fundamentally, what I'm arguing for is not just that our alphabet is a means of approaching the divine—no, not just that. God is the alphabet, and the alphabet is God. Heaven is traversed through the alpha and the omega. The alphabet betrays its origins, for word and image are joined together in symbiosis, no matter how occluded.

Just as Kircher believed hieroglyphics contained reality, so too is the alphabet haunted by pictures obscure; as Ouaknin enthuses, it's in "unearthing the traces of the origin of letters and understanding how they evolved" that occult wisdom is provided. Knowing that letters shift back and forth so that they can return to the images that birthed them, as in the calligraphy that illustrates Attar's Simurgh, is a demonstration of their fluid nature. Literal though we may misapprehend Egyptian pictograms to be, their abstract progeny in the form of our twenty-six letters are still haunted by their origins, and we can resurrect that sense of their birthright now and again.

Moreover, the mysteries of the alphabet subconsciously affect us. As Battles claims concerning letters, since "whether alphabetic or ideographic, they start out as pictures of things," it makes all the more sense "why writing works for us, and why it has conserved these signs so well over these three millennia." Nevertheless, the haunting of previous incarnations of letters' past shapes can't alone explain their strange power. Only something divine can fully explicate how some marks on Hathor's hide chart a direct line to the letters you're reading right now. Perhaps *divine* is a loaded term, what with all of those unfortunate religious connotations; *transcendent* would be just as apt. Questions can certainly be raised about my contentions; I do not wish to be read as airy, but with every letter of my sentences, I can't help but believe that the kabbalists and Gnostics were right—the alphabet constitutes our being.

Reality, I believe, can be completely constituted from all twenty-six letters (give or take). Sift through all of them and realize that the answer to any question lies between aleph and tav, not just as metaphor, but those answers are simply uncovered by finding the proper organization of those letters. The answer to any inquiry, the solution to any problem, the very wisdom that frees can be discovered simply by finding the correct arrangement of those letters. Underneath the surface of these shapes are indications of their birth but also that fuller reality just beyond our gaze. Vexation need not follow such an observation; rather, embrace the endless transition between image and word that is the alphabet. We need not pick between letter and picture; there is room enough for both. Xenoglossic is what we should be—fluent in a language unknown to our tongues but spoken in our souls. You need only repeat the alphabet as if you're an illiterate shepherd in the assembly of the Baal Shem Tov. Zealots of the alphabet, with those very letters carved by fire into our hearts.

9

Possess the Origin
of All Poems

SATOR
AREPO
TENET
OPERA
ROTAS

—Anonymous (ca. 79)

Underneath the volcanic ash and debris of Herculaneum, the elegant smaller sister of Pompeii, there is the earliest example of a chiseled wall writing that has come to be called the Sator Square. Nine years after the Romans flattened most of Herod's Temple in Jerusalem, and the Lord apparently decided to return the favor in those twin cities on the Bay of Naples, for the Sator Square can be dated no later than 79 CE after Vesuvius blanketed Herculaneum with her asphyxiant gases, victims trapped in lava and preserved after what was physical of them had decomposed away. These bubbles, since filled with plaster, preserving an absence that used to be a dog, a lacuna that used to be a man. Near those nonexistent bodily remains, and those stony alleyways with their eerily preserved villas punctuated by singed erotic tiles, some anonymous mason carved onto the western wall of a wrestling academy a five-word Latin sentence organized into the perfect square of a latticework grid.

The sentence organized into this perfect five-by-five grid reads "Sator Arepo tenet opera rotas," with each five-numbered word constituting one line of the grid, each word situated one on top of the other. The result is that the lattice, in imitation of the math puzzles that are commonly known as "magic squares," organizes a short sentence that is a palindrome, which by the grammatical word order of Latin is possible to read the same way left to right and right to left, as well as top to bottom and bottom to top, and even in the archaic meandering of boustrophedon, which alternates directions between lines and draws its name from the Greek term for how an ox plows a plot of field from one direction in a row and then back toward its origin as it starts in on the next row, and so on. Maybe the boustrophedon provides a clue to what this odd little imagist poem means, for though classicists debate the exact translation, as context is lacking on deciding the particular meaning of words that have a multiplicity of potential definitions, a consensus has emerged that the nearest English for the Sator Square is "The farmer Arepo works a plow."

Cryptic in its simplicity, all the more mysterious for how prosaic it is. The word *Arepo* provides part of the difficulty in proper translation; it's an example of what linguists call a hapax legomenon—that is, the only example of that word's use in the entire corpus of Latin literature. From the sentence itself, it appears to be a proper noun, though the name isn't Italian, and some have argued that it sounds

Coptic, though others have claimed Aramaic or even Celtic origins. "The farmer Arepo works a plow," often parsed for a solution to the puzzle of the square, is, I would argue, a beautiful poetic evocation in its own right. A variety of Latin Zen classicism, a Roman imagist poem that reminds me of William Carlos Williams. In everything it doesn't say—who is Arepo?—there is something arresting about the visual itself, the farmer forever simply doing what it is that farmers must do. For how enigmatic the Sator Square is, the example at Herculaneum is only the oldest, for the five-word sentence in its characteristic grid appears throughout Europe. From perhaps the same period, an example is found in nearby Pompeii, hammered onto the wall of a man named Publius Paquius Proculus, though the Sator Square can also be found in the mosaics of the Duomo in Siena, in the Benedictine Abbey of Saint Peter ad Oratorium in Abruzzo, and in the Cistercian Valvisciolo Abbey near the Italian town of Sermoneta. Incidences of the Sator Square are limited not only to Italy or to the classical era, for Arepo is plowing his field in carving, engraving, and mosaic from Portugal to France and as far as chilly Sweden and England, with examples in Lancashire and Manchester from the era of Roman Britain through the Middle Ages.

Why the popularity of a palindrome that, if clever, is also obscure? In the Roman world, obscurity was no vice, for the ancient empire was a mélange of heterodox mysticisms and religious visions, when pilgrims of Mithras worshipped the bull from Smyrna to Londinium and Gnostics made supplication to archons with names like Yaldabaoth and Sabaoth. A Latin sentence organized into a palindromic five-by-five grid is never just a Latin sentence organized into a palindromic five-by-five grid. Something about Arepo ever driving his plow around the five rows of the palindrome, possibly a biblical reference as in Matthew 13:3–9, where Christ tells the parable about "a sower [who] went forth to sow," with his apparently bad scattering arm and all those rocks, thorns, and finally, good soil. Something about Euripides in the Sator Square as well, with Dionysius's injunction to Pentheus in *The Bacchae* that it is "hard for thee to kick against the pricks," in Gilbert Murray's rendering, a reference to a plow that won't scow, which was quoted by the well-read Lord to Saul on his road to Damascus.

The puzzler of the Sator Square left something encoded into its letters that indicates possible meaning more than the vague allusions that plowing implies—namely, that in addition to being read as a palindrome, the twenty-five letters of the grid also contain an anagram whereby they can be rearranged around the center axis mundi of the letter *n* into the shape of a cross that spells out both vertically and horizontally the words "Pater Noster," Latin for the Lord's prayer. Two *A*s and two *O*s are left over, possibly to punctuate each of the quadrants of the cross with Christ's declaration in Revelation 1:8 that "I am Alpha and Omega, the beginning and the ending." If the Sator Square is a bit of Christian esoterica, not dissimilar to the aquatic ichthys painted on catacomb walls, then its presence near Pompeii marks it as a shockingly early example, less than a generation after the crucifixion and older than most of the New Testament's composition. *Something* seems Christian about the Sator Square, but whatever it was has been subsumed into the more superstitious realms of practical magic by the Middle Ages, when repetition of the sentence or the writing of the grid itself was used by the English folk magicians known as cunning-women and cunning-men who deployed it in everything from care for a pregnancy to the warding off of fires, though some amount of the square's original meaning seems to have survived in Ethiopia, where a group of the Orthodox told the German Jesuit Athanasius Kircher that each one of the nails that affixed Christ to the cross had names that were clearly derived from every word in that sentence carved upon the wall of a gymnasium at Herculaneum.

Whatever the Sator Square was a spell for, however we interpret the incantatory magic of the thing, what's undeniably true is that to have whatever efficacy it's supposed to have, not a single letter can be off. Every single *A*, *R*, *E*, *P*, and *O* must be in the right place for the palindromic mechanism to work. The Sator Square is thus just like every other scrap of poetic language, because the positioning of letters can't be incidental to the nature of the text. So much depends on a letter; so much depends on a comma, and nobody understood better than the Christians of the era when the Sator Square was painted on church doors and inlaid in monastery floors that the deletion of a single iota between the Greek terms *homoousios* and *homoiousios* determined whether the Son is equal to the Father. With the most exacting of standards that even a New Critical extremist might be humbled by, all of proper Christology must hinge on either the inclusion or exclusion of a letter that is but a short vertical line with a happy little dot on top. For that matter, consult the 1631 "Wicked Bible," where a typographical error deleted a single word from Exodus 20:14—*not*—and consider the particular difference implied by that mistake.

Theology, that system of effective verbal idolatry that gestures to things beyond the field of vision, is nothing if not an incantatory genre. Don't think of my argument as being separate from any rational basis, because logic is another incantatory genre. Everything written is incantatory; it's that reality Walt Whitman sings of when he writes in *Leaves of Grass* that he shall help us "possess the origin of all poems." A model of poetics that doesn't acknowledge that poems must be understood, written, and experienced as incantations is a model of poetics that is operating blind and deaf. For that matter, so is any general theory of language that doesn't acknowledge the fusion of transcendence and immanence that defines the incantatory. No easy division can be made between poetry and the rest of language; if modernism has taught us anything, it's that the tropes of formalism can be discarded by poets at will. Rather, poetry is simply language that *knows* it's incantatory, but just because the rest of language might seem more prosaic doesn't mean it's not also miraculous. Incantation covers much more than the stereotypical wizard mumbling breathlessly a few nonsense words; incantation is language that announces itself as such. From my perspective, two of my favorite compendiums of incantations are *The Oxford Book of American Poetry* and *The Oxford Book of English Verse*, but I fully recognize how eccentric my classification may sound. So it is helpful to first parse that more conventional understanding of incantation and to meditate on how it relates more generally to language. If what I'm saying is true, then incantatory poetics is that which defines all of the words whispered, spoken, sung, chanted, and shouted by woman and man.

Incantation seems like simple abracadabra, that bastardized nonsense word that everyone knows and that comes from the unlikely source of the Gnostic Basilides's archon *Abraxas* and was first written in the second century by a Roman physician with the delicious name of Serenus Sammonicus. It conjures hocus-pocus and magical words, amulets shored against reality. For those who bracket magic away from profane reality, incantation is not Homer but rather the blackened Greek Magical Papyri and nonsense injunctions such as "ασκι κατασκι αασιαν ενδασιαν," found on a fourth-century BCE lead tablet in Crete whose semantic meaning remains obscure. Though both travel through a dark "wood of Woden," the sixth-century Germanic epic *Nibelungenlied* is considered poetry, while the compilation of spells known as the Merseburg charms, with their practical considerations of "bone-sprain, so blood-sprain / so joint-sprain: / Bone to bone, blood to blood, / joints to joints, so may they be mended," is simply archaic superstition, even while the nineteenth-century Scottish philologist Alexander Macbain notes that the Gaelic replaced *Woden* with *Christ* while preserving the admirable rhetorical parallelism: "Sinew to sinew, / Flesh to flesh. / And skin to skin; / And as he healed that, / May I hear this." There's something charged in the line "May I hear this" because that's precisely what's affected in any of you who read those words. We can be as skeptical as we want to be about the efficacy of incantation, but any prosaic form of communication in and of itself is de facto a type of charm. The Sri Lankan anthropologist Stanley Tambiah writes in the *Journal of the Royal Anthropological Institute* that "words exist and are in a sense agent in themselves which establish connexions and relations between both man and man, and man and the world, and are capable of 'acting' upon them, they are one of the most realistic representations we have of the concept of force which is either not directly observable or is a metaphysical notion." If you're skeptical of a model of language that posits that all words are incantation, then consider how I've already used words to make you hallucinate that which is not immediately in front of you.

No compunctions in seeing *Beowulf* as poetry, but I'd contend it's just as much incantation as the Anglo-Saxon metrical charm found in the contemporary tenth-century collection of the Lacnunga book. The anonymous cunning man (or woman) of that compendium who edited in an England on the verge of the Norman Conquest noted, "A snake came crawling, it bit a man. / Then Woden took nine glory-twigs" (that Woden again!) and "smote the serpent so that it flew into nine parts. / There apple brought the pass against poison, / That she nevermore would enter the house." And so some scribe figured out practical magic to invalidate the very fall, an incantation whose glorious syncretism puts Jewish Eden and pagan Woden into synthesis. As a figurative conceit, it's just as moving as *Beowulf*'s cast of pagan Grendel and biblical Cain, an equivalent poetic achievement that should not be dismissed because it appears in a book of practical magic. Especially since all poetry—indeed, all language—is *practical magic*.

The Polish linguist Bronisław Malinowski wrote in *Coral Gardens and Their Magic* that "the belief that to know the name of a thing is to get a hold on it is . . . empirically true," with Tambiah, with shades of Wordsworth, explaining that "magical language was an emotive use of language, that magic was born of the emotional tension of particular situations and that the spells, ritual acts and gestures expressed a spontaneous flow of emotions." Malinowski's contention is radical in just how prosaic it is. We doubt the efficacy of incantation, and yet we're presented with examples of its utility every time we open our mouths, every time we type some abstract symbols and they *do something in the world*—even if, *maybe especially if,* that something is "nothing" more than making someone experience the illusion of an ingeniously constructed fictional universe. Most importantly, as the linguist Geoffrey Leach has observed in *Philosophical Transactions of the Royal Society of London*, when it comes to sacred language, the "uttering of the words itself is a ritual."

When it comes to that occluded, slightly musty form of the "incantation," most of us probably limit it to what Tambiah has enumerated as the "verbal forms which we loosely refer to as prayers, songs, spells, addresses, [and] blessings." Of course, that is the connotation we commonly have of incantation, a system whereby words are used to affect reality, and it's not an inappropriate connotation. In incantation, the words themselves are the same thing as that which they represent. But if all human expression, all language, is fundamentally defined by incantatory poetics, then a conclusion is drawn: there is no distinction between words and things, and so the proper order of words becomes crucially important. Call it the "Sator principle." Had a single letter been off in that square, reality itself would have been different—and so it ever is for all language. Modernity, with its attendant idols of positivism and puritanism, extols a particular theory of expression—namely, that the straight-forward, the literal, the nonfictional exists only as a vehicle to move meaning from some abstract realm to the world of human compre-hension. By contrast, figurative and poetic language are allowed to revel in their own medium, the language that is conscious of itself, that can draw attention to itself and the nature of artifice that defines abstract words. In place of this distinction, I argue that all language is about itself, that the disjunct between figurative and literal is erroneous, as is the opposition between poetry and prose, fiction and nonfiction. If the point of language was simply and only ever to convey meaning, then individual variations of it would mat-ter less than they do, but so much depends on where the line is enjambed. If even just a letter of the Sator Square was off, the pal-indrome would be broken, and that incantatory effect is true for all language, even literal language. *A spell can never be disrupted into not being a spell; it just becomes a different one.*

My formulation is close to Percy Shelley's old chestnut that poets are the unacknowledged legislators of the world. Strip away the Romantic affectations, and the contention to me seems unas-sailable. Nothing has happened of any consequence in human cul-ture, after the era of *Homo habilis* hitting one another with sticks, except through the intercession of language. When I speak of "incantatory poetics," that is what I sing of—that all of our words are charms and spells. What the Sator principle speaks to is the need for rigorously close reading and equivalent composition, for every slogan, aphorism, motto, meme, poem, story, play, novel, and essay is fundamentally an incantation, all doing different things and to different affect but all trading in the charged theurgy of that mysterious element known as language. I'm primarily a nonfiction writer myself, plying in that hoary chimera of a genre invented by Montaigne, which is neither quite here nor there. But as an essayist, the content of the piece has always been secondary to me (perhaps the critics among you might find that obvious). I do not see the words as mere vehicles for meaning; I see them, as a fiction writer might, as the *things-in-themselves*. Philosopher Roman Jakobson spoke of the various purposes of language in his essay "Linguistics and Poetics," including the "magic, incantatory function," but this, I believe, should be understood of all language, and we need a criticism commensurate with the universal incantatory poetics of our very words. To proffer an axiom for that criticism, I affirm an inviolate theoretical principle: "Rhetoric is content; aesthetics is epistemology."

10

Poetry Is Prayer

The English colony of Jamestown was only eighteen years old in 1625, during the midst of what the poet John Donne, preaching safely from London, had called the "barbarous years," when disease, starvation, and violence nearly destroyed the Virginian settlement. Its unfortunate colonists had been reduced in their most dire straits to exhuming the corpses of the recently dead so that the living would have something to eat. If anytime would necessitate prayer, it would seem to be when people resort to cannibalism, and no doubt there was rending of garments in Jamestown. Across the Atlantic too, for the collapse of the Virginia Company humbled an investor named Nicholas Ferrar. A courtier, and eventually an ordained Anglican deacon, Ferrar reacted to the financial implosion of his American investments by taking what money remained and purchasing an abandoned medieval church named St. John's in the Salisbury village of Little Gidding.

Orthodox in his Calvinism, Ferrar was still High Church and mourned for what had been lost from that Catholic past of multicolored stained glass and incense burning in thuribles. His little chapel had been stripped bare during the Reformation of a century before, and he hoped to restore some ornamentation to that ruined choir. At Little Gidding, Ferrar and his siblings dedicated themselves to founding a secular oratory, what later Puritan critics maligned as a "Protestant nunnery." The Ferrars were to live simply, by a rigorous schedule of prayer, study, service, and contemplation. Upon the whitewashed walls of their home, Ferrar and his brother John and sister Susan (and their respective families) painted psalms so as to "excite the reader to a thought of piety," as he wrote in a letter. As prayers are outward expressions of inner devotions, sent on vibrations of sound to whatever ear is listening, the community at Little Gidding displayed their psalms as a type of signpost to the divine, hoping that they'd be noticed. Appropriate for a family that had turned their walls into printed pages, their home into an anthology, because the Ferrars supported Little Gidding with the trade of bookbinding.

Critic Don Paterson writes in *The Poem: Lyric, Sign, Metre* that poetry has "invested itself with those magical properties, and also took the form of spell, riddle, curse, blessing, incantation and prayer. For those atavistic reasons, poetry remains an invocatory form." Like spells written on hidden parchments, there was enchantment to the textuality of the Ferrars' house, with its divinely graffitied walls. The house a book based on the book that produced books. None more famous or influential than a slender volume of poetry titled *The Temple*, written by a friend of Ferrar's named George Herbert, a priest. Ministering a village over, Herbert was a product of courtier culture as well and of similar social status to the Ferrars, his mother of the wealthy Newport family and a patron to

Donne. Like the pious Ferrars, Herbert had rejected the trappings of nobility that were his guaranteed birthright, preferring rather to work as a humble reverend on the Salisbury plain. When Herbert sent his friend a copy of his devotional poems in 1633, he said that he wished them to be printed, should they have "advantage of any dejected poor soul," and if Ferrar saw no such quality, the verse should be burned.

Herbert's *The Temple* pairs with Donne's "Holy Sonnets" as among not just the greatest of seventeenth-century metaphysical poetry but the greatest religious lyrics ever written in English. Poems like "The Collar," "Love (III)," and his "shape poems" (with typography working as image) such as "The Altar" and "Easter Wings" were as a type of worship. A century later, the Puritan schoolman Richard Baxter would enthuse, "Herbert speaks to God like one that really believes in God"; obvious faith beats like a metronome in the meter of his verse. "Heart-work and heaven-work make up his books," said Baxter, so that it's impossible to disentangle theology from his poetry, as it might be for modern readers of sexier metaphysical poets like Donne. Biographer John Drury writes in *Music at Midnight: The Life and Poetry of George Herbert* that "divinity saturated and enclosed his world: the whole of it, from the slightest movements of his own inmost being to his external circumstances in time and the natural world. . . . Divinity was the cause and the sum of how things are, without remainder." That being the case, Herbert's poetry itself couldn't help but be devotional, couldn't help but fundamentally be as if a prayer. What I'd venture is that *all poetry is fundamentally a prayer.*

My ideas may be muddled or inchoate, and for that, I beg your patience, but I think that some of my half-formed thinking (multitudinous as it will be) can be illustrated by a Herbert poem appropriately entitled "Prayer (I)." Of the poem's subject, Herbert describes it as "the church's banquet . . . God's breath in man returning to his birth, / The soul in paraphrase, heart in pilgrimage." There are two things happening in those lines: The obvious is the connection of God's spirit to the individual spirit of man, how the animus of our breath finds its origin in the divine. All fine and good, but what's more fascinating is the description of prayer as being a "soul in paraphrase," for that explicitly aligns prayer not with completism—axioms, treatises, arguments, syllogisms, or any other method of total explication—but with an intimation of what a soul is. "Prayer (I)" is replete with this language of incompleteness; it's in some ways a statement against method. Herbert writes of "The six-days world transposing in an hour," a type of paraphrase of creation itself, and of "A kind of tune," or the "Heaven in ordinary." The imprecision of Herbert's language is precisely the point: prayers are exemplary because they don't exist to say everything that can be said; they exist for all of that which can't be. The result of prayer, Herbert famously concludes, is "something understood."

Everything depends on that indefinite pronoun, for in the ambiguity of *something*, Herbert gestures at what prayer is. It's not necessarily that prayer deals with only the ineffable (though that concept intersects with prayer) but rather that the product of prayer is this amorphous, free-floating, mercurial *something* of which Herbert speaks. Prayer imparts a type of knowledge—*something has been understood*. But good luck in being able to simply or literally say what that something is. So Herbert differentiates prayer from other forms of sacred language. Prayer has not the delineation of a creed or the rigor of an argument; it has neither the logic of theology nor the narrative of Scripture. Prayer has this understood *something*, but by its nature, what exactly it is must be felt rather than known, believed rather than stated.

The poem is about prayer, but it's also about poetry. If Herbert is making an argument about prayer's significance being incompleteness, then the precise same thing must be said about poetry as well. Like prayer, poetry is not the same as creed or argument, thesis or claim, philosophy or pedagogy. Both prayer and poetry are synonyms, albeit respectively associated with the sacred and the profane. They concern things that can only be espied from multiple perspectives, for the ecstasy of ambiguity and the spurning of literalism, for the quality of having "something understood" even if such a thing is contradictory or indefinable or impossible to summarize. The two forms are mechanisms for approaching the unapproachable; they are engines driving us to that which is an infinite distance away. What's imparted is the mysterious *something*—when done well, both prayer and poetry can change you, but it's difficult to put into words what that change was. A sublimity in that paradox, for prayer and poetry are defined by being words that gesture beyond words themselves.

All literary language is a special case; all literary language is an exception. Since Plato, philosophers have found it difficult to categorize what exactly literature is supposed to be. Fictional narrative, after all, is simply a lie artfully arranged. Or at least that's one way to look at it, albeit a reductionist one that doesn't perform due diligence toward just how weird literature is, this process by which we hallucinate entire worlds after staring at abstract symbols. Because it seems real, literature compels questions like that jocularly posed by the Shakespeare scholar L. C. Knight, when in 1933 he asked, "How many children did Lady Macbeth have?" Knight was raising a point about the way we talk about fiction, where a question can be posed that is logically and semantically coherent yet totally meaningless. Lady Macbeth had no children, of course, since she wasn't real (or at least, not in the form that the Bard presented to us). A similar metaphysical conundrum was posed by the philosopher Bertrand Russell when he asked what the "truth status" was of the question "Is the present king of France bald?" There no longer being a king of France, it would seem that either an affirmative or a negative answer is completely meaningless, yet that's affectively the nature of all fiction.

Poetry and fiction aren't reducible to each other; if anything, they're sometimes contrasted (in part because narrative poetry, such as the epic, is a largely moribund genre today). But poetry also has an innate weirdness that makes it difficult to classify. What exactly defines it? What makes poetry *poetry*? Formal characteristics—rhyme, meter, rhythm, and so on—make little sense as distinguishing elements after almost two centuries of free verse. Russian linguist and critic Roman Jakobson argued (in a paper first published in Thomas A. Sebeok's anthology *Style in Language*) that the "poetic function" of language was neither to express nor to communicate clear-cut truth; rather, it existed with "the message for its own sake." Jakobson's claim was that poetry is basically always about poetry, that verse announces the strangeness of language itself rather than communicating literal facts. What defines poetry is not how it's constructed but what it does. Poetry announces itself as language through a process of defamiliarization—iambic pentameter and anaphora are ways in which a reader understands that something odd is happening—but it need not be facilitated only through formal rhetorical means. Paterson rightly condemns the fact that "too often our interpretations are unconsciously predicated on the real-world existence of a truth, albeit a truth conveniently veiled or missing," but to be overly hung up on the "truth" of poetry is to precisely miss the point. The medium truly is the message.

In an odd way, such pronouncements were anticipated by the Renaissance critic and poet Philip Sidney, who in his 1580 *Defense of Poesy* argued that "the poet, he nothing affirms, and therefore never lieth." Facts can be lied about, but a poem can't be evaluated on whether it's "true" or not, at least in any literal or logical way. What's the "truth status," Russell might ask, of the statement "I have measured out my life in coffee spoons?" Certainly, it's not literally accurate or privy to scientific falsification, but that it says something significant should be obvious. Poetry is thus a cracked type of speech, language that is about language, expressing truths that move beyond mere words but can be indicated in their splendiferous ambiguities. Poetry is rhetorically distinct from other uses we have for words, Jakobson would argue; it's not the dry literalism of logic, or the pragmatic utility of instruction, or even the dense world building of fiction (though that last certainly can intersect with poetry). Rather, verse is when language thinks about itself. Popularizer of religion Karen Armstrong argues something similar in the introduction to Thomas J. Craughwell's *Every Eye Beholds You: A World Treasury of Prayer* when she writes, "Prayer helps us to liberate ourselves and to use language in an entirely different way."

Functionally, I see no difference between prayer and poetry. I should emphasize that this has to do not with God per se but rather with what prayer and poetry do. And as both are, in some sense, very present-based genres, existing for their own purposes rather than to convey some other primary piece of information, what they do is ultimately the same. W. H. Auden famously declared, "Poetry makes nothing happen," but there is a theological profundity to that, the idea of something existing without pragmatic justification to some bottom line, having being rather as a glorious singularity unto itself. Not dissimilar to the God of the medieval scholastics, whose views the literary critic Terry Eagleton described in *The Meaning of Life*, writing that God's purpose for his creation isn't a "question about what the world is *for*, since in . . . [theological] opinion the world has no purpose whatsoever. God is not a celestial engineer who created the world with some strategically calculated goal in mind. He is an artist who created it simply for his own self-delight, and for the self-delight of Creation itself." The word of God thus becomes something very close to the word of Auden. Something close to the ecstasy of prayer as well. Poetry fulfills what Jay Hopler described in the preface to *Before the Door of God: An Anthology of Devotional Poetry* when he noted that "poems confront two of humankind's most powerful actuations: the drive to create and the drive to know a creator."

Both poetry and prayer are written in a type of transcendent tense; they seem to bring a voice forward from a certain perspective of eternity. The visceral *presentness* of both makes them different from other forms of language, for poetry and prayer don't merely correspond to things that have happened in the world; they are realities themselves. Kimberly Johnson writes in the introduction to *Before the Door of God* that "though a lyric poem may have a narrative that unfolds over its course, the first drama it relates is the coming into being of that speaking voice," for poetry is an ever-regenerative form. It is not an ossified representation of some outside subject; it is the subject. Unlike painter René Magritte's visual pun *The Treachery of Images*, with its depiction of a pipe with the sentence "Ceci n'est pas une pipe," a similar gambit makes no sense with a poem. There is no delay in verse; it has an immediacy that oracularly announces itself as a presence. Poetry and prayer share in this incantational quality because they trade not only in representation but in a certain theurgy. This is the position the narrator presents to God in Charles Simic's poem "Prayer" included in his collection *A Wedding in Hell*: "You who know only the present moment, / O Lord, / You who remember nothing / Of what came before." An encapsulation of prayer and lyric alike, as well as the experience of being God in eternity, for unlike other modes, verse exists perennially in this moment we live in right now.

Because poetry and prayer, as an experience, belong not to the past or the future but rather to a continual present, they both have the incantational quality of being able to resurrect that which is gone, of bringing to bear an actual presence with the reading of a poem, the chanting of a prayer. Eagleton, with good reason, sees something fallacious in this claim, arguing in *How to Read a Poem* that "on this view, form and content in poetry are entirely at one because the poem's language somehow 'incarnates' its meaning" but dismissing such romanticism by saying that "words which 'become' what they signify cease to be words at all." But that might be precisely the point: that which distinguishes poetry from prose isn't form but the quality by which the former does actually, in some way, invoke or "call down" a different reality from the one in which the reader exists—while making allowances to poetic "prose" being capable of that same quality.

The Harlem Renaissance poet Jean Toomer performs such an incantation in his lyric "Georgia Dusk." Toomer writes that a "lengthened tournament for flashing gold, / Passively darkens for night's barbecue." Men gather, and "their voices rise . . . the pine trees are guitars, / Strumming, pine-needles fall like sheets of rain. . . . / Their voices rise . . . the chorus of the cane / Is caroling a vesper to the stars." Poetry is not editorial or syllogism, but it is a calling forth, a transubstantiation. With Toomer's invocation of this rural Black town observing the simple eucharist of a barbecue, how is it not possible to feel the warm breeze of Georgia dusk whistling through the pines as the yolk dusk descends into the hills, the drone of cicada punctuating the gathering coolness? That Toomer can put the reader there, it seems to me, is not an example of the "incarnational fallacy"; it is simply an incarnation.

Paterson differentiates prose from poetry by noting that with the former, the "well-chosen word describes the thing as if it were present," but the latter "persists in its attempt to invoke, to call down its subject from above, as if there were no 'as if' at all." That's because when we read a poem, whether out loud or in our heads, we embody the speaker. We're possessed by the narrator, this spooky character who isn't quite equivalent with the poet herself. Johnson argues that "poetic speech endures with a kind of immortality. Among other effects, it preserves the human voice far beyond the scale of human life. . . . The voice that is preserved over centuries comes to the reader's corporeal as well as intellectual awareness, resurrected anew, as it were, through each new reader's ears and eyes and breath and heartbeats."

When we read Marianne Moore's poem "By the Disposition of Angels," which takes as its subject this quality of possession itself, we resurrect both Moore and the immanent voice that speaks and exists beyond mere personality, querying, "Messengers much like ourselves? Explain it. / Steadfastness the darkness makes explicit? / Something heard most clearly when not near it?" Moore's poem gives voice, literally and figuratively, to this precise strangeness of poetry and prayer: its ability to make us hear that which seems to not be there. "Poet and reader enter a bizarre cultural contract where they *agree* to create the poem through the investment of an excess of imaginative energy," argues Paterson. "This convergence of minds adds a holographic dimension to the poem, one denied other modes of human speech. A poem's elements can sometimes *appear* to have been summoned into existence with enough potency to engage our physical senses."

Possession isn't the same thing as transformation, however. When we pray, we speak to God; as when we read and write poetry, we perhaps speak to our narrators. At their most ecstatic, those things blur into our selves, but when we stand up from the kneeler or close the book, we return to being ourselves—what poet Malachi Black describes in his poem "Vespers" when he writes, "Lord, you are the gulf / between the hoped-for / and the happening." Any recitation, any reading, has a gulf between it and the actual divine, for a poem must be a mechanism of approaching an eternity that we never quite reach. Ronald Thomas, Welsh poet and Anglican priest, describes in his poem "Kneeling" the "moments of great calm, / Kneeling before an altar / Of wood in a stone church / In summer, waiting for the God / To speak." The simple physicality of his description takes part in that incantational poetics whereby we can transpose ourselves into that private moment, but the illusory nature of that experience isn't obscured. We are, after all, "waiting" for God to speak, and that uncertainty, that agnostic quiet isn't incidental to the prayerful qualities of poetry—it's instrumental to it. Thomas writes, quipping on Saint Augustine, "Prompt me, God; / But not yet. When I speak, / Though it be you who speak / Through me, something is lost. / The meaning is in the waiting." When Thomas humbly admits that "something is lost," it's an acknowledgment that the possessions of poetry are incomplete, yet that gulf between God's understanding and our fumbling is the vacuum into which poetry must dissipate.

Because if there is anything that poetry and prayer share, that distinguishes them from other forms of language—be they plays or novels, policy briefs or automobile manuals—it's that both must engage with that abiding sense of mystery that exists in those silent places where the soul dwells. A novel or a play or an essay can have mystery at its core, and can be all the better for it, but such mystery is incidental to it being in whatever particular genre it happens to be in. Philosopher George Steiner noted in *Language and Silence: Essays 1958–1967* that "when the word of the poet ceases, a great light begins," explaining that "language can only deal [with] . . . a special, restricted segment of reality. The rest, and it is presumably the much larger part, is silence." What differentiates poetry is not form or content. Poetry is the language that is written not in words but rather in the gaps between them. Poetry and prayer are implicated in that mystery, that sacrament. "Mysteries expound mysteries," writes Moore, and it's a good shared explanation of prayer and its identical twin poetry.

That sense of divine mystery is invoked by our most immaculate of modern devotional poets, Denise Levertov, in her "Mass for the Day of St. Thomas Didymus" from the collection *Candles in Babylon*. Writing at the mystical confluence of her duel Jewish and Christian background, between America and Europe, the political and the sacred, Levertov voiced the "deep unknown, guttering candle, / beloved nugget lodged in the obscure heart's / last recess" more fully than any poet after the Second World War. Levertov is an incarnational poet, able to describe "woodgrain, windripple, crystal, / in crystals of snow, in petal, leaf . . . fossil and feather, / blood, bone, song, silence." A poet of immanence, but one for whom all of this world is built not of exhalation but of inhalation, of "our hope . . . in the unknown, / in the unknowing." This is the subject of all poetry and prayer, the injunction "O deep, remote unknown, / O deep unknown, / Have mercy upon us." The beating heart of all poetry and prayer must be this blessed silence, this sacred unknown. Such a faith is what animates both vocations. For when we approach the sepulcher of that which Herbert called "something understood."

Part Two

The Conjurations of Prose

11

Missives from Another World

Literature of Parallel Universes

> He believed in an infinite series of times, in a growing,
> dizzying net of divergent, convergent and parallel times.
>
> —Jorge Luis Borges, *The Garden of Forking Paths* (1942)

> And you may tell yourself, "This is not my beautiful house"
> And you may tell yourself, "This is not my beautiful wife."
>
> —Talking Heads, "Once in a Lifetime" (1980)

By the release of their seventeenth album, *Everyday Chemistry*, in 1984, the Beatles had been wandering for years in a musical wilderness. Their last cohesive venture had been 1972's *Ultraviolet Catastrophe*, but the '70s were mostly unkind to the Beatles—an output composed of two cover albums of musicians like Ben E. King and Elvis Presley, rightly derided by critics as filler. Meanwhile, the Rolling Stones released their brilliant final album before

Keith Richards's death; the disco-inflected 1978 *Some Girls*, which marked them as the last greats of the British Invasion. By contrast, the Beatles' *Master Class* and *Master Class II* were recorded separately and spliced together by engineers at Apple Studios, a two-star *Rolling Stone* review from 1977 arguing that "Lennon and McCartney don't even appear in the same room with each other. Their new music is a cynical ploy by a band for whom it would have perhaps been better to have divorced sometime around *Abbey Road* or *Let It Be*."

Maybe it was the attempt on John Lennon's life in 1980 or the newfound optimism following the election of Walter Mondale, but by the time the Fab Five properly reunited to record *Everyday Chemistry*, there was a rediscovered vitality. All of that engineering work from the last two albums actually served them well as they reentered the studio; true to its title, with its connotations of combination and separation, catalyst and reaction, *Everyday Chemistry* borrowed from the digital manipulations of Krautrock bands like Kraftwerk and the synthesizer-heavy experimentation of Talking Heads. The Beatles may have missed punk, but they weren't going to miss New Wave.

With a nod to the Beatlemania of two decades before, Lennon and Paul McCartney sampled their own past songs, now overlaid with flourishes of electronic music, the album sounding like a guitar-heavy version of David Byrne and Brian Eno's avant-garde classic *My Life in the Bush of Ghosts*. This formula defined this reconstituted version of the band, now committed to digital production, whose influences are seen from Jay-Z's Lennon-produced *The Grey Album* to the tracks George Harrison played with James Mercer in Broken Bells.

By asking Eno to produce their new album, the Beatles signaled that they were once again interested in producing pop that didn't just pander. Always pioneers in sound effects, the modulation on

Revolver, Sergeant Pepper's Lonely Hearts Club Band, and *Ultraviolet Catastrophe* were a decidedly lo-fi affair, but by the era of the Macintosh, the Beatles had discovered the computer. Speaking to Greil Marcus in 1998, Ringo Starr said, "You know, we were always more than anything a couple of kids, but John was always into gizmos, and something about that box got his attention, still does." Billy Preston, officially the band's pianist since *Ultraviolet Catastrophe,* was also a zealous convert to digital technology. In Marcus's *Won't Get Fooled Again: Constructing Classic Rock,* Preston told the critic, "They were a bar band, right? Long before I met them, but I was a boogie-woogie guy too, so it was always copacetic. You wouldn't think we'd necessarily dig all that space stuff, but I think the band got new life with that album." From the nostalgic haziness of the opening track, "Four Guys," to the idiosyncratic closing of "Mr. Gator's Swamp Jamboree," *Everyday Chemistry* was a strange, beautiful, and triumphant reemergence of the Beatles.

Such a history may seem unusual to you, because undoubtedly you are a citizen of the same dimension that I am. Unless you're a brave chrononaut who has somehow twisted the strictures of ontological reality, who has ruptured the space-time continuum and easily slides between parallel universes, your Beatles back catalog must look exactly the same as mine. And yet *Everyday Chemistry* exists as a ghostly artifact in our reality, a digital spirit uploaded to the internet in 2009 by some creative weirdo who cobbled together an imagined Beatles album from the fragments of their solo careers. A bit of Wings here, some of the Plastic Ono Band there, samplings from *All Things Must Pass* and *Sentimental Journey,* edited together into a masterful version of what could have been.

Most of my narrative above is my own riffing, but claims that the album is from a parallel universe are part of the mythmaking that makes listening to the record so eerie. "Now this is where the story becomes slightly more unbelievable," the pseudonymous "discoverer" James Richards writes. *Everyday Chemistry* is a seamlessly edited mash-up done in the manner of Girl Talk or Danger Mouse, but its ingenious creator made a parallel universe origin of *Everyday Chemistry* the central conceit. Richards claims that a tape of the album was swiped after he fell into a vortex in the California desert and was gifted *Everyday Chemistry* by an interdimensional Beatles fan.

At *Medium*, John Kerrison jokes that "inter-dimensional travel probably isn't the exact truth" behind *Everyday Chemistry*, even if the album is "actually pretty decent." Kerrison finds that whoever created the album is not going to reveal their identity anytime soon. Unless, of course, it actually is from a parallel universe. While I *mostly* think that's *probably* not the truth, I'll admit that anytime I listen to *Everyday Chemistry*, I get a little charged frisson, a spooky spark up my spine. It's true that *Everyday Chemistry* is kind of good, and it's also true that part of me wants to believe. Listening to the album is like finding a red rock from Mars framed by white snow in your yard—a disquieting interjection from an alien world into the mundanity of our lives.

Part of what strikes me as so evocative about this hoax that mixes science fiction, urban legend, and rock 'n' roll hagiography is that we're not just reading about a parallel universe, but the evidence of its existence is *listenable right now*. Tales of parallel universes—with their evocation of "What if our world was different from how it is right now?"—are the natural concerns of all fiction. All literature imagines alternate worlds. But the parallel universe story makes such a concern explicit, makes it obvious. Such narratives rely on the cognitive ability to not accept the current state of things, to conjecture and wonder at the possibility that our lives could be different from how we experience them in the present.

Such stories are surprisingly antique, as in Livy's *History of Rome*, written a century before the Common Era, in which he conjectured, "What would have been the results for Rome if she had been engaged in a war with Alexander?" as Canon Roberts translates. Even earlier than Livy, the Greek father of history, Herodotus, hypothesized about what the implications would have been had there been a Persian victory at Marathon. Such questions are built into how women and men experience their lives. Everyone asks themselves how things would be different had different choices been made—what if they'd moved to Milwaukee instead of Philly, majored in art history rather than finance, asked Rob out for a date instead of Phil?

Alternate history is that narrative writ large. Such stories have been told for a long time. In the eleventh century, there was Peter Damian's *De divina omnipotentia*, which imagined a reality where Romulus and Remus had never been suckled by a she-wolf and the Republic was never founded. In 1490, Joanot Martorell's romance *Tirant lo Blanch*, perhaps the greatest work ever written in the Iberian Romance language of Valencian, envisioned a conquering errant knight who recaptures Constantinople from the Ottomans. Medieval Europeans were traumatized as the cross was toppled from the dome of the Hagia Sophia, but in Martorell's imagination, a Brittany-born knight is gracious enough so that "a few days after he was made emperor he had the Moorish sultan and the Grand Turk released from prison." What followed was a "peace and a truce for one hundred one years," his former enemies "so content that they said they would come to his aid against the entire world." Written only thirty-seven years after Mehmed II's sacking of Orthodoxy's capital, *Tirant lo Blanch* presents a Christian poet playing out a desired reality different from the one in which he actually found himself.

In the nineteenth century, the American writer Nathaniel Hawthorne did something similar, albeit for different ideological aims. His overlooked "P.'s Correspondence" from his 1846 *Mosses from an Old Manse* is credibly the first alternate history story written in English. An epistolary narrative where the titular character, designated by only his first initial, writes about all the still-living Romantic luminaries he encounters in a parallel version of Victorian London. Lord Byron has become a corpulent, gouty, conservative killjoy; Percy Shelley has rejected radical atheism for a staunch commitment to the Church of England; Napoléon Bonaparte skulks the streets of London, embarrassed and vanquished while kept guard by two police officers; and John Keats has lived into a wise seniority where he alone seems to hold to the old Romantic faith that so animated and inspired Hawthorne. P. is a character for whom the "past and present are jumbled together in his mind in a manner often productive of curious results," a description of alternate history in general. Hawthorne's is a message about the risks of counterrevolution but also an encomium for the utopian light exemplified by Keats, for whom there remains so "deep and tender a spirit of humanity."

Alternate history's tone is often melancholic, if not dystopian. An exercise in *this world might not be great, but think of how much worse it could be.* Think of authors like Philip K. Dick in *The Man in the High Castle* or Robert Harris in *Fatherland*, both exploring the common trope of imagining a different outcome to the Second World War. Such novels present Adolf Hitler running roughshod over the entire globe, crossing the English Channel and ultimately the Atlantic. Such narratives highlight the ways in which the evils of fascism haven't been as vanquished as was hoped, but they also serve as cautionary parables about what was narrowly averted. In his own indomitable amphetamine-and-psychosis kind of way, Dick expresses something fundamental about the interrogative that defines alternative history, not the "What?" but the "What if?" He asks, "Can anyone alter fate? . . . our lives, our world, hanging on it."

Such novels often trade in the horror of an Axis victory or the catastrophe of Pickett's Charge breaking through that Confederate high-water line in that quiet, hilly field in Pennsylvania. Some of the most popular alternate histories depict a dark and dystopian reality in which polished Nazi jackboots stomp across muddy English puddles and Confederate generals hang their ugly flag from the dome of the Capitol building, where an American *Kristallnacht* rages across the Midwest, where emancipation never happens. Gavriel Rosenfeld in his study *The World Hitler Never Made: Alternate History and the Memory of Nazism* argues that such stories serve a solemn purpose, that the genre has a "unique ability to provide insights into the dynamics of remembrance." Rosenfeld claims that alternate history, far from offering an impious or prurient fascination with evil, memorializes those regimes' victims, generating imaginative empathy across the boundaries of history and between the forks of branching universes.

Philip Roth in *The Plot against America* and Michael Chabon in *The Yiddish Policeman's Union* imagine and explore detailed alternate versions of the twentieth century. With eerie prescience, Roth's 2004 novel reimagines the alternate history genre by focusing on the personal experience of the author himself, interpolating his own childhood biography into a larger narrative about the rise of a nativist, racist, sexist, anti-Semitic American fascism facilitated through the machinations of a foreign authoritarian government. Chabon's novel is in a parallel universe a few stops over but examines the traumas of our past century with a similar eye toward the power of the counterfactual, building an incredibly detailed alternate reality in which Sitka, Alaska, is a massive metropolis composed of Jewish refugees from Europe. Such is the confused potentiality that defines our lives, both collective and otherwise; an apt description of our shared predicament could be appropriated from Chabon's character Meyer Landsman: "He didn't want to be what he wasn't, he didn't know how to be what he was."

For Rosenfeld, the form "resists easy classification. It transcends traditional cultural categories, being simultaneously a sub-field of history, a sub-genre of science fiction, and a mode of expression that can easily assume literary, cinematic, dramatic or analytical forms." More than just that, I'd suggest that these narratives say something fundamental about how we tell stories, where contradiction and the counterfactual vie in our understanding, the fog from parallel universes just visible at the corners of our sight, fingerprints from lives never lived smudged across all of those precious things we hold on to.

While long the purview of science fiction authors, with their multiverses and retconning, alternate history has been embraced by academic historians for whom such conjecture has traditionally been antithetical to the sober plodding of their discipline. In history, no experiment can ever be replicated, for we live in said experiment—and it is forever ongoing. Temporality and causality remain tricky metaphysical affairs, and it's hard to say how history would have turned out if particular events had happened differently. Nonetheless, true to its ancient origins in the conjectures of Herodotus and Livy, some scholars engage in "counterfactual history," a variety of thought experiment that plays the tape backward.

Seriously considering counterfactual history as a means of historiographical analysis arguably goes back to John Squire's 1931 anthology *If It Had Happened Otherwise*. Squire arguably assembled his compilation less for the literary edification of readers than as a means for scholars to analyze history by imagining backward, as it were. His volume included contributions by Hilaire Belloc, who, true to his monarchist sympathies, imagines a very much nondecapitated Louis XVI returning to the Bourbon throne; his friend G. K. Chesterton enumerating the details of a marriage between

Don John of Austria and Mary Queen of Scots; and none other than future prime minister Winston Churchill writing a doubly recursive alternate history entitled "If Lee Had Not Won the Battle of Gettysburg," narrated from the perspective of a historian in a parallel universe in which the Confederacy was victorious.

Churchill concludes the account with his desired reunification of the English-speaking peoples, a massive British, Yankee, and Southern empire stopping the Teutonic menace during the Great War. As with so much of Lost Cause fantasy, especially in the realm of alternate history (including Newt Gingrich's atrocious *Gettysburg: A Novel of the Civil War*—yes, that Newt Gingrich), Churchill's was a pernicious revisionism, obstinate fantasizing that posits the Civil War as being about something other than slavery. Churchill's imaginary Robert E. Lee simply abolishes slavery upon the conclusion of the war, even while the historical general fought in defense of the continuation and expansion of that wicked institution. Yet ever the Victorian Tory, Churchill can't help but extol a generalized chivalry, with something of his ideal character being implicit in his description of Lee's march into Washington, DC, and Abraham Lincoln's rapid abandonment of the capital. The president had "preserved the poise and dignity of a nation. . . . He was never greater than in the hour of fatal defeat." In counterfactual history, Churchill had been cosplaying dramatic steadfastness. Regardless of the literary qualities of Churchill's piece, there's an important cautionary element to deploying alternate history as a historiographical method. Fiction may betray the opinions of the writer—in part that's its point. But in mistaking fiction for historiography, there is the risk of a category mistake, a risk of appropriating the aura of empiricism without the rigor.

In a more metaphysical sense, counterfactuals raise the question of where exactly these parallel universes are supposed to be, these uncannily familiar story lines that seem as if they inhabit the space at the edge of our vision for a duration as long as an eyeblink. Like a dream where unfamiliar rooms are discovered in one's own house, alternate history has a spooky quality to it, and the mere existence of such conjecture forces us to confront profound metaphysical questions about determinism and free will, agency and the arc of history. Did you really have a choice about whether you would move to Philly or Milwaukee? Was art history ever a possibility? Maybe Phil was always going to be your date.

The frustration of the counterfactual must always be that since history is unrepeatable, not only is it impossible to know how things would be altered, but we can't even tell if they could be. How can one know what the impact of any one event may be, what the implications are for something happening slightly different at Marathon, or at Lepanto, or at Culloden, or at Yorktown? All those butterflies fluttering their wings, and so on. Maybe Voltaire's Dr. Pangloss in *Candide* is right, maybe this really is the best of all possible worlds, though five minutes on Twitter should make one despair at such optimist bromides. Which is in part why alternate history is so evocative—it's the *alternate*. James Richards found that other world easily; apparently there is a wormhole in the California desert that takes you to some parallel universe where scores of Beatles albums are available. But for all of those who don't have access to the eternal jukebox, where exactly are these parallel realities supposed to be?

Quantum mechanics, the discipline that explains objects at the level of subatomic particles, has long produced surreal conclusions. Werner Heisenberg's uncertainty principle proves that it's impossible to have complete knowledge of both the location and the momentum of particles, Louis de Broglie's wave-particle duality explains subatomic motion with the simultaneous mechanics of both particle and wave, and Erwin Schrödinger's fabled cat, who is simultaneously dead and alive, was a means of demonstrating the paradoxical nature of quantum supposition, whereby an atom can be both decayed and not at the same time. The so-called Copenhagen interpretation of quantum mechanics is comfortable with such paradoxes, trading in probabilities and the faith that observation is often that which makes something so. At the center of the Copenhagen interpretation is how we are to interpret that which physicists call the "collapse of the wave function," the moment at which an observation is made and something is measured as either a wave or a particle, decayed or not. For advocates of the orthodox Copenhagen interpretation, the wave function exists in blissful indeterminacy until measured, being both one thing and the other until we collapse it.

For a Pentagon-employed physicist in 1957 named Hugh Everett, such uncertainty was unacceptable. That a particle could be both decayed and not at the same time was nonsensical, a violation of that fundamental logical axiom of noncontradiction. If Everett thought that the Copenhagen interpretation was bollocks, then he had no misgivings about parallel universes, for the physicist would argue that rather than something being both one thing and its opposite at the same time, it's actually correct to surmise that the universe has split into two branching forks. In Schrödinger's fabled thought experiment, a very much not subatomic cat is imprisoned in some sadist's box, where the release of a poisonous gas is connected to whether an individual radioactive atomic nucleus has decayed. According to the Copenhagen interpretation, that cat is somehow dead and alive, since the nucleus is under the purview of quantum law and can exist in indeterminacy as both decayed and not until it is observed and the wave function collapses. Everett had a more parsimonious conclusion—in one universe, the cat was purring and licking his paws, and in an unlucky dimension right next door, all four fury legs were rigid and straight up in the air. Everett's theory is no weirder than the Copenhagen interpretation, and maybe less so. Writing of Everett's solution, the physicist David Deutsch in his book *The Fabric of Reality* claims that "our best theories are not only truer than common sense, they make more sense than common sense."

Maybe mathematically that's the case, but I still want to know where those other universes are. Whether in wardrobe or wormhole, it feels like Narnia should be a locale more accessible than in just the equations of quantum theorists, though perhaps those formulas aren't so different from fiction. For myriad people who congregate in the more eccentric corners of the labyrinth that is the internet, the answer to where those gardens of forking paths can be found is elementary—*we're all from them originally.* Those who believe in something called the Mandela effect believe they're originally from another dimension and that you probably are as well. Named after people on internet message boards who claim to have memories of South African president Nelson Mandela's funeral in the early '80s (he died in 2013), whole online communities are dedicated to enumerating subtle differences between our current timeline and wherever they're originally from—things like recalling a comedy about a genie starring Sinbad called *Shazaam!* or the ursine family from the *Berenstain Bears* spelling their surname "Berenstein" (I think I'm actually from that dimension).

Everett's calculations concern minuscule differences; the many-worlds interpretation deals in issues of momentum and the location of subatomic particles. That doesn't mean that there isn't a universe where the Berenstain Bears have a different last name—in a multiverse of infinite possibility, all possibilities are by definition actual things—but it does mean that universe's off-ramp is a few more exits down the highway. This doesn't stop believers in the Mandela effect from comparing notes on their perambulations among the corners and byways of our infinite multiverse, recalling memories from places and times as close as your own life and as distant as another universe. Looking out my window, I can't see the Prudential Center anymore, and for a second I wonder if it ever really existed before realizing that it's only fog.

Have some sympathy for those of us who remember Kit Kat bars as being spelled with a hyphen, or *Casablanca* having the line "Play it again, Sam." Something is lost in this universe of ours, here where whatever demiurge has decided to delete that line. Belief in the Mandela effect illuminates our own alterity, our own discomfort in this universe or any other—a sense of alienness, of offness. The Mandela effect is when our shoes pinch and our socks are slightly mismatched, when we could swear that we didn't leave our keys in the freezer. And of course, the Mandela effect is the result of simply misremembering. A deeper truth is that existence can sometimes feel so off-putting that we might as well be from a parallel universe. Those other dimensions convey the promise of another world, of another reality. That just because things are done this way where we live now doesn't mean that they're done this way everywhere. Or that they must always be done this way here either.

What's moving about *Everyday Chemistry* is that those expertly mixed songs are missives from a different reality, recordings from a separate, better universe. The album is a tangible reminder that things are different in other places, like the fictional novel at the center of K. Chess's brilliant new novel *Famous Men Who Never Lived*, which imagines that thousands of refugees from a parallel universe find a home in our own. In that novel, the main character clutches onto a science fiction classic called *The Pyronauts*, a work of literature nonexistent in our reality. *The Pyronauts*, like *Everyday Chemistry*, betrays a fascinating truth about parallel universes. We may look for physical, tangible, touchable proof of the existence of such places, but literature is all the proof we need. Art is verification that another world isn't just possible but already exists. All literature is from a parallel universe, and all fiction is alternate history.

Whether or not the Beatles recorded *Everyday Chemistry*, the album itself exists; if *The Pyronauts* is written not in our universe, then one only needs to transcribe it so as to read it. In the introduction to my collection *The Anthology of Babel*, I refer to "imagined literature"; an approach toward "probing the metaphysics of this strange thing that we call fiction, this use of invented language which is comprehensible and yet where reality does not literally support the representation." Every fiction is an epistle from a different reality. Even Hugh Everett would tell you that somewhere, a real Jay Gatsby pined for Daisy Buchanan; that a few universes over, Elizabeth Bennet and Mr. Darcy were actually married; and that somewhere, Mrs. Dalloway is always buying the flowers herself. *The Great Gatsby*, *Pride and Prejudice*, and *Mrs. Dalloway* are all, in their own way, alternate histories as well.

Alternate history provides a wormhole to a different reality—but that's what all literature does. That fiction engenders a deep empathy for other people is true, and important, but it's not simply a vehicle to enter different minds; it enters but different worlds as well. Fiction allows us to be chrononauts, to feel empathy for parallel universes, for different realities. Such a thing as fiction is simply another artifact from another dimension; literature is but a fragment from a universe that is not our own. We are haunted by our other lives—ghosts of misfortune averted, spirits of opportunities rejected—so that fiction is not simply the experience of another but a deep human connection with those differing versions on the paths of our forked parallel lives.

12

When Books Read You
A Defense of Bibliomancy

Now, here's something you might do if you see fit. Bring me the works of Virgil, and, opening them with your fingernail three times running, we'll explore, by the verses whose numbers we agree on, the future lot of your marriage. For, as by Homeric lots a man has often come upon his destiny.

—Francois Rabelais, *Gargantua and Pantagruel* (1532)

It's the fault of those physicists and that synchronicity theory, every particle being connected with every other; you can't fart without changing the balance in the universe. It makes living a funny joke with nobody around to laugh. I open a book and get a report on future events that even God would like to file and forget. And who am I? The wrong person; I can tell you that.

—Philip K. Dick, *The Man in the High Castle* (1962)

Toward the end of 1642, or possibly the beginning of 1643, but either way in the midst of a miserable winter of civil war, King

Charles I found himself an oft-uncomfortable refugee in Oxford's Bodleian Library. At that archetypal university, the king and his confidant Lucius Cary, the Second Viscount Falkland, held a monotonous vigil. Unlike Cambridge, which lent its name to that other college town named in its honor by schismatic coreligionists across the ocean and would come to be known for its steadfast Puritanism and positivism, Oxford was all dreaming spires and medieval dragon chasing, a perfect shelter for a king making his last stand against Roundheads that were closing in. A map of England was brushed with Parliamentarian red, with Oxford a dab of royalist purple, and there King Charles consulted his leather-bound volumes, reading by candlelight in cold rooms, hoping to find some perspective on his predicament. But the king consulted not Herodotus, or Thucydides, or Cicero but rather Virgil. And while the founding of the Roman Republic may seem apt enough to read in a situation such as this, Charles and Falkland conferred with Virgil's ghost not as political strategists but rather as eager and credulous customers having their tarot read. For Charles, the wisdom of Virgil was not literary but magical.

Charles was many things, not least of which a flippant man, every bit as superficial as the dog breed that bears his name. And as a stupid ruler, perhaps the stupidest thing he believed in was the literal divine right of kings. Despite his flippancy, he was, however, a lover of books, and for that, he deserves some modicum of our esteem, even if Milton was disgusted by Charles's ignoring Scripture as part of his parting speech upon the scaffold, opting rather to choose Pamela's prayer from the Philip Sidney romance *The Countess of Pembroke's Arcadia*. Even if he was an often juvenile and impetuous man, dissolving Parliament over perceived slights or failing to account for the deep dissatisfaction among the growing middle class and the religious nonconformists of both London and wider England, he was still in some ways a brave man. Loyally standing by deeply unpopular figures like his archbishop of Canterbury William Laud, Charles was the man who, while quoting a bit of pop culture upon the executioner's stage, was also one who requested an extra-heavy wool shirt, lest his shivering in the cold English morning be interpreted by his enemies as trepidation.

But that was still in the future, and here, in this library toward the end of 1642 (or again, possibly at the beginning of 1643), the king, whom we have already established was prone to literary flights and the palliative of diversionary trifles, asked Falkland if he knew of any games adequate to pass the time in the gloomy, dark, cold Bodleian. A Dr. Welwood, in his account of the event, reports that Falkland "show'd among other Books, a Virgil nobly printed and exquisitely bound. The Lord Falkland, to divert the King, would have his Majesty make a trial of his fortunes." Both would use the Roman epic as an oracle; they would present their questions to Virgil and let the book function as a divination tool that would answer their inquiries, a trusted means of prophesizing that, according to Welwood, "everybody knows was a usual kind of augury some ages past." With the type of ardor only a bibliomaniac can muster, Charles turned to a book during what he assumed was the height of his political, military, and personal misfortunes, and with an affinity for superstition matched only by his belief that his very divine touch could cure sickness, Charles asked Virgil what his fortune would be. Letting the cracked leather spine hit the dark wooden surface of some Oxford desk, and with his eyes closed, the king pointed to some random line of Latin on some random page of Virgil. He did not like the fortune that had been cast. So he asked Lord Falkland to try casting his own lot, hoping for a better result. Falkland opened the volume at book 11, lines 150–57, which recounted the death of Evander's son Pallas. The viscount would be dead by September of the following year (or, of course, September of that year if it was 1643), felled by a Roundhead's bullet at the Battle of Newbury.

Fortuna's wheel seems to have crushed Charles with an extra heaviness. John Aubrey records that a year before the king's decapitation, Charles's son, then living in exile in Paris, asked the metaphysical poet Abraham Cowley to divert his own sorrows, writing that his friend offered "if his Highnesse pleased they would use 'Siortes Virgilianae,'" as the poet, of course, "alwaies had a Virgil in his pocket." This time, instead of letting the book fall open, Cowley rather took a pin and pushed it into the soft pages of the *Aeneid*, the prick arriving at the proper prediction for the royal estate. Both father and son, as it turned out, arrived at the exact same line regarding the Stuart family fortunes. What of Charles's lot, and that of the prince, which so distressed both of them? Book 4 of the *Aeneid*, line 615, which is Dido's prayer against her former lover, reading, "Nor let him then enjoy supreme command; / But fall, untimely, by some hostile hand," in John Dryden's version. In 1649, Charles would stand as upon the scaffold at Westminster, wearing his extra-heavy shirt and quoting his Sidney, awaiting the regicide's blade on his neck. Virgil may guide everyone to the truth, but that doesn't mean the truth will always set one free.

What Charles and the prince were so inadequately diverting their troubled minds with was a variety of divination known as bibliomancy, or the telling of the future with the aid of literature. Dr. Welwood was correct that the practice had an august history, across both East and West. One of many means of dubious divination, from the relatively well known such as tasseography (reading tea leaves) to the more obscure and thankfully extinct, like haruspicy (interpreting the organs, often livers, of sacrificed animals—popular in ancient Rome). All methodologies share a conception of *meaning* that is fundamentally different from the current dominant definition. While there is no shortage of people for whom astrologers, tarot, and palm readers offer some succor, it should be uncontroversial to note that the mainstream accepted definition of *meaning* departs from the magical in favor of the observable, the empirical, and the measurable. Science, it should be said, is not just a different form of magic where the terminology has been altered, palm reading replaced with MRI machines and tea leaves with spectroscopy. No, the very model of what constitutes meaning is fundamentally different as well, for Charles I and the prince, Falkland and Abraham Cowley understood meaning very differently from our current accepted norms. For them, the very world was pregnant with an enchanted, glowing significance. Weather indicated not just what storms might await in the future but what the course of one's life may be; anomalies and strange phenomena were to be read as harbingers of future events, as one might identify foreshadowing in a novel written with planning and intention. Nothing was divorced from a wider, if nebulous, meaning.

What the Stuart king was distracting himself with was a form of *rhapsodomancy*, which is the use of poetry to ascertain the future, and even more specifically, the previously mentioned *Sortes Virgilianae*, an example of what Virgil himself might have called "this dark technology of magic." Other popular varieties of rhapsodamancy included the *Sortes Homericae*, which utilized the two epic poems of Homer, and the *Sortes Sanctorum*, which, contrary to a prohibition against magic in Deuteronomy, used the Bible for fortune-telling. As bibliomancy and rhapsodamancy generally connote the use of literature for divination, the methodology of said readings could be accomplished in different ways. One could write an assortment of poetic lines on scraps of parchment or wood and draw them as lots, as was common with the use of those weird sisters and their

Sibylline prophecies in ancient Rome. Or, one could use some sort of "randomness generator," such as a die, coins, or yarrow sticks, as are used with the ancient Taoist *I Ching*.

Readers of Philip K. Dick's science fiction classic *The Man in the High Castle* (or viewers of its Amazon television adaptation) will be familiar with how the character Tagomi consults the almost three-thousand-year-old *I Ching* for advice. Dick himself used the ancient text to generate the narrative of the novel, harnessing randomness in his writing, a method referred to as "aleatory composition." This use of coins, and sticks, and dice can be contrasted to those methods in which the book is allowed to speak for itself (as it were), where a volume simply falls open so as to answer the questions posed to it, as with Charles at Oxford. This method relies on an innovation in information technology so ubiquitous that its radicalism may not be apparent: the codex. Simply the technical term for what we call a "book," the codex was first used as a means of Roman record keeping and, arguably, only began to supplant the scroll as the main method of literary transmission with the writing of the Gospels, and then shortly thereafter with the roughly simultaneous, if divergent, Jewish and Christian canonization of certain texts as officially scriptural. A codex, by its very architecture (circumscribed by cover and back), enshrines certain presuppositions about writing: it makes a text discrete and separate, and it turns the book into an individual. And an individual, of course, can have a question posed to it, with an expected answer. Yet the book's prehistory of being a scroll endures in the malleability and interconnectedness that bibliomancy presumes, where literature endures as a type of electromagnetic force field that an auger can master. Perhaps modern technology will generate further innovations in the field of bibliomancy studies (as with the Twitter handle @BiblioOracle).

But regardless of the procedure, what makes bibliomancy fascinating is that unlike other forms of divination, it trades in something that already has an interpretable meaning—words. Perhaps a butcher can figure out the narrative that a sheep's liver conveys, but that the *Aeneid*, as indeed all texts, has a meaning requires no suspension of disbelief, even if the meanings that are being derived seem far from authorial intention. What I find so interesting about bibliomancy is that it takes the written word, which we all assent to as composing the very atoms of meaning, and it interprets those lines and sentences *slant*. Furthermore, it wrenches the very interpretive center of a given text away from the authority of the author who created it toward the service of the reader who consults the text as a pilgrim at Delphi. Bibliomancy is thus a radical form of reading, one in which the reader becomes a figure in the text's narrative, for in presuming that the *Aeneid* (or Horace, or the Bible, or the *I Ching*) can predict our individual futures, even obliquely, is to assume that we're somehow encoded as characters in the text itself, like Moses reading of his own death in the Torah. A type of fantastic metafiction that breaks the cosmic fourth wall, finding our own fortunes hidden between the very letters in poems written millennia before we were born. Bibliomancy, in short, is one of the few opportunities in which the book is allowed to read *you*.

One could argue that such an approach cheapens literature, but I'd claim that far from a reduction, such an approach rather widens interpretive possibilities by making us partners in the creation of meaning. Note that in discussing an "approach" to bibliomancy, one need not embrace a literal belief that the *Aeneid* (or anything else) was actually predicting Charles's moment upon the scaffold. Rather, an openness to bibliomancy is simply to reaffirm literature as a vast, interconnected, endlessly mercurial field of potential where meaning is created by readers across centuries. While New Critics in the early part of the twentieth century may have preferred to view poems as dead butterflies mounted by pin and preserved on cardboard, the last three generations of literary theorists have been more amenable to the endlessly recursive play of literature. And yet for such a once profoundly popular practice, bibliomancy is underanalyzed and undertheorized. Underused as well. It's time we take bibliomancy seriously, not because it's literally an accurate means for ascertaining the future (though perhaps it's a diverting trifle as you wait for Parliamentary troops to arrive), but because it resurrects an archaic yet valuable manner of approaching language that has been in eclipse since the birth of modernity. I'm not really concerned with whether bibliomancy literally works in casting our futures (spoiler alert: I have my doubts); rather, I am interested in its potential as both totem in demonstrating the flexible interconnectedness of literature and as exercise in circumnavigating deficiencies in our own thought by leaving some aspects of interpretation up to *Fortuna*.

As book critic Jessa Crispin writes in defending the creative possibility of tarot, "The meaning of the cards comes from us." That is fundamentally the case with any type of literary theurgy, whether it's tarot, automatic writing, or bibliomancy—they present a method of circumnavigating the conscious mind, drawing connections that might not be apparent to either logic or literalism. A venerable way of understanding how meaning is connected by that unseen, golden web of connotation that literary theorists with their jargony talk of "intertextuality" and "heteroglossia" only dimly approach. There is an infinite richness in how those in centuries past approached words (and by proxy, the word).

The great scholar of Jewish mysticism Gershom Scholem described the process of connotative reading practiced by the thirteenth-century kabbalist Abraham Abulafia (who also, it should be noted, tried to convert the pope to Judaism—example under the dictionary entry for *chutzpah*) in his study *Major Trends in Jewish Mysticism*. Scholem explains that Abulafia read through "'jumping' or 'skipping.'" He elaborates that this is the "remarkable method of using associations as a way of meditation. . . . Every 'jump' opens a new sphere. . . . Within this sphere the mind may free associate. The 'jumping' unites, therefore, elements of free and guided association and is said to assure quite extraordinary results as far as the 'widening of the consciousness.'" Bibliomancy can be used to generate new ideas, or as Cicero explains in his work on divination, the truths that are generated "from mental excitement of some sort when the mind moves free and uncontrolled." The brain liberated by chance, fate, and fortune. Thus *fortuna* becomes a means of elucidating novel connections, while simple surface literalism remains largely mute. This is a type of reading where all interpretation is as bibliomancy, something the early twentieth-century avant-gardes from the surrealists to the Dadaists understood well. For in recasting all books as spell books, all literature as potential grimoire, we accomplish not just clarification but wonder as well.

Consider both that the Christian Gospel of John famously begins with a declaration that "In the beginning was the Word" (John 1:1) and that Jewish kabbalah presumes the preexistence of the Hebrew alphabet before all else emanated forward in creation. Take the example of the Catalan Franciscan Ramon Llull, a thirteenth-century contemporary of Abulafia. Llull, a beatified not-quite-saint, is primarily remembered for his *Ars magna*, or "The Great Art"—an intricate, baroque, labyrinthine method of calculation supposedly based on pure deductive axioms and in large part inspired by the work of Islamic logicians—which Llull believed was an engine capable of answering any philosophical question posed to it. A type of tony, engineered bibliomancy. Llull's *Ars magna* was manifested in an exceedingly odd book, whereby particular ideas had numeric assignations that could be combined in various permutations to arrive at novel conclusions (his work on combinatorics merits him as a potential "patron saint of computers"). Particularly unique in his manuscript were actual movable parts in the form of spinning paper wheels and gears, which could be manipulated in calculation. Central to Llull's understanding was an orientation similar to Abulafia's that the augury must "put the alphabet in this art in order to be able to make figures with it . . . for seeking the truth." This mystical Franciscan saw the alphabet as the very ground of being upon which reality was constructed, and thus approaching literature is a means of ascertaining reality.

That exact same view would be promulgated by an equivalently enigmatic figure some centuries later, when in the late sixteenth century, Elizabeth's court astrologer, John Dee, made a name for himself on the continent as an initiate in the occult and mystical arts. As with Abulafia and Llull, the alphabet (whether Hebrew, Latin, or the astral "Enochian" of his own discovery) was that with which divinity generated existence. Dee explains his views concerning the hieroglyphic arts in a letter to that most exulted of esoteric monarchs, Maximillian II of the Holy Roman Empire, whose Prague court featured all manner of wonders, from dancing dwarves to prophets, from the astronomer Johannes Kepler to the golem's father, Rabbi Judah ben Lowe. Dee explained to the king that "writings on the alphabet contain great mysteries . . . since He who is the only author of all mysteries has compared himself to the first letter and the last." For Abulafia, Llull, and Dee, the universe was born not from a primordial atom but from a primordial *A*, not from the breath of God but from his command, from the first Hebrew letter, aleph. Not as ridiculous as it first sounds—that the alphabet both underlines and constructs reality. Consider that the answer to any question you would ever have on any subject, that the composition of any narrative you could ever conceive from the most debased to the most beautifully exulted, that the correct description for any event that did or could have happened, that the accurate prophecy for anything that will or might happen actually already exists in print, albeit in disorganized form. All is answered in the very words of whatever dictionary is closest to you. The task of the writer, prophet, and bibliomancer is simply to put those words in the right order.

A premodern idea whose time may yet come again? Historian Stéphane Gerson observes that "like formulas and incantations, words had obtained therapeutic or magical powers. . . . They embodied hidden verities and divine ideas and the essence of things and people. By the Renaissance, they brimmed with meaning and could modify the natural world and sometimes transcend the symbolic realm to become analogies of the cosmos." Bibliomancy returns us to an almost mystical embrace of the transcendent ways in which interpretations permeate a reality pregnant with meaning. This view of how language operates—admittedly theological—is one that we must embrace if we're to resuscitate what is instrumental about literature. And it's a perspective that is the historical norm, across cultures and religions, only exorcised from our normal discourse upon the disenchantments of the world. Prosaic models of comprehending meaning understand it as a static kernel, but bibliomancic reading sees the text itself as sentient, as somehow conscious.

Books are thus beings unto themselves, capable of defining their own roles in the world—minds with agency capable of answering questions posed to them, of responding to queries beyond what's literally printed on their pages. Scholar Michael Wood says as much in his cultural study of oracles, *The Road to Delphi*, when he writes that "the point is to ask us to think of the world as haunted by the divine, and to see how the divinity can talk to us through the world," or as Walt Whitman put it in *Leaves of Grass*, "I find letters from God dropped in the street, and every one is signed by God's name." When we think of meaning as diffuse and capable of actually conversing with us, what results is an asynchronous theory of influence across time, evoking an observation I once heard a scholar of medieval literature make: "One of the best interpreters of T. S. Eliot was Dante." Bibliomancy abolishes the tyranny of time and the authoritarianism of age; books are liberated from being stationary and are transformed into full partners with whom we can converse. Whether or not we use novels and poetry to cast lots, bibliomancy is a reminder that literature itself is a breathing thing, and an ever mercurial one at that.

Both individual works of literature and all of collective literature compose the primordial alphabet, in which all answers to all questions lay dormant, occasionally becoming loud enough that we can hear them—and bibliomancy reminds us of that majesty. The French poet Max Jacob, reflecting on the writings of Nostradamus, once claimed that "the *Prophecies* contain the universe," but this is only partially correct—all language contains the universe, all dictionaries encapsulate reality, all literature holds the cosmos. Bibliomancy teaches that none of us are passive readers, for we are all characters within literature itself; that no book is an island, for all that has been written is like a giant continent crossed with highways; and that every book, every story, every poem, every line is not just permeated with meaning but conscious of it as well. Bibliomancy demonstrates that we've always been alive, hidden between the very words on the page. Even if it is superstition, it is also an exercise in literature's imaginative potential, where British kings can be hidden in Virgil, and where we all may live in Whitman, or Emily Dickinson, or whatever dog-eared volume we treasure, whose cracked spine points fate toward those particular passages that illuminate our own fortunes, where we reside before we've even breathed, where we live before we were even born. You can call it the alphabet of Abulafia and Llull, or what Leibnitz called the Monad, or what Jorge Luis Borges termed "the Aleph," that generative letter that shows us everything—"the coupling of love and the modification of death" where one can see "the earth and in the earth the Aleph and in the Aleph the earth" and where the Argentinean writer could see "your face; and I felt dizzy and wept, for my eyes had seen that secret and conjectured object whose name is common to all men but which no man has looked upon—the unimaginable universe."

Literature is the unimaginable and the imagined universe, books are the oracles that allow us to look upon that kingdom, and bibliomancy is the liturgy that reminds us of that sacred truth. Bibliomancy, as Scholem might say, "liberates us from the prison of the natural sphere and leads us to the boundaries of the divine sphere." And what, then, is life itself except a type of performative aleatory literature? A related observation: literary critics are the last theists. For those who spend any time amid the vagaries of plot, whether critic or novelist, often read the story of our lives as if it followed the dictates of narratology (or at least, I find myself doing that), as if some cosmic author penned that tale. That's not to imply that what the royals holed up in the Bodleian were doing was anything like literary criticism, and yet any reading of literature must defer to the strange glow of meaning that accrues on poetic language. We're meaning-making creatures, and more than that, we're storytelling animals, as the critic Jonathan Gottschall calls us, with brains evolved to find patterns, seeing faces in the pareidolia of mountains and clouds. We just as often interpret the texture of narrative in sequences of unrelated events. What is fascinating about bibliomancy, or any of the related methods of divination from literature, is that rather than looking at the green of a sheep's liver or the random distribution of some chamomile grounds in a saucer, the initiate is interpreting something that unequivocally already has intentional meaning—but it births it anew.

Bibliomancy returns us to the charged potential and innate weirdness of literature, of fiction and poetry, of the sacred origins of language itself. And so I ask myself, What is the critical potential of such a practice? And I pose that question to a dog-eared copy of Whitman's *Leaves of Grass*, and the book answers me, "They are but parts. . . . any thing is but a part," so as to confirm that all poetry is but a side on that infinite Monad, but a single letter in that eternal alphabet. And I ask myself, What hope can bibliomancy offer us in our own epoch of uncertainty, our anxious age? And I in turn deliver that query to *The Complete Poems of Emily Dickinson*, and she, cryptically as any at Delphi or among the Sibyllines, answers with another interrogative "Who has Paradise" with no question mark, only her eternally available em dash—signaling that all of literature is but a conversation that can never end, paradise always visible and yet never reached.

13

On Pandemic and Literature

Less than a century after the Black Death descended into Europe and killed seventy-five million people, as much as 60 percent of the population (90 percent in some places) all dead in the five years after 1347, an anonymous Alsatian engraver with the fantastic appellation "Master of the Playing Cards" saw fit to depict Saint Sebastian. Making his name, literally, from the series of playing cards he produced at the moment when the pastime first became popular in Germany, the engraver decorated his suits with bears and wolves, lions and birds, flowers and woodwoses. The Master of the Playing Cards's largest engraving, however, was the aforementioned depiction of the unfortunate third-century martyr who suffered execution by order of the emperor Diocletian. A violent image, but even several generations after the worst of the Black Death, Sebastian still resonated with the populace, who remembered that "to many Europeans, the pestilence seemed to be the punishment of a wrathful Creator," as John Kelly notes in *The Great Mortality: An Intimate History of the Black Death, the Most Devastating Plague of All Time.*

The cult of Sebastian had grown in the years between the Black Death and the engraving, and during that interim, the ancient martyr had become the patron saint of plague victims, particularly the promise that he could intercede in the horrors of the pandemic. His suffering reminded people of their own lot—that more hardship was inevitable, that the appearance of purpled buboes looked like arrows pulled from eviscerated flesh, and most of all, that which portion of bruised skin would be arrow pierced was seemingly as random as who should die from the plague. Produced roughly around 1440, when any direct memory of the greatest bubonic plague had long since passed (even while smaller reoccurrences occurred for centuries), the Master of the Playing Cards presents a serene Sebastian tied to a short tree while four archers pummel him with arrows. Unlike more popular depictions of the saint, such as Andrea Mantegna's painting made only four decades later—or El Greco's and Peter Paul Rubens's explicitly lithe and beautiful Sebastians made in, respectively, the sixteenth and seventeenth centuries—the engraver gives us a calm, almost bemused martyr. He has an accepting smile on his face. Two arrows protrude from his puckered flesh. More are clearly coming.

Sebastian became associated with the plague not just as a means of saintly intercession but also because in his narrative, there was the possibility of metaphor to make sense of the senseless. Medical historian Roy Porter writes in *Flesh in the Age of Reason: The Modern Foundations of Body and Soul* that the "Black Death of the mid-fourteenth century and subsequent outbreaks . . . had, of course, cast a long, dark shadow, and their aftermath was the culture of the Dance of Death, the worm-corrupted cadaver, the skull and crossbones and the charnel house." All of said accoutrement, which endures even today from the cackling skulls of Halloween to the pirates' flag, serves if not to make pandemic comprehensible then to at least tame it a bit. Faced with calamity, this is what the stories told and the images made were intended to do, and religion supplied the largest storehouse of ready-made narrative with which this was accomplished, even while the death toll increasingly made traditional belief untenable. As John Hatcher writes in *The Black Death: A Personal History*, many lost "faith in their religion and . . . [abandoned] themselves to fate," where fatality is as unpredictable as where an arrow will land.

A variation on this narrative was depicted forty years later. Made by the Swedish painter Albertus Pictor and applied to the white walls of the rustic Täby Church north of Stockholm, the mural presents what appears to be a wealthy merchant playing a (losing) game of chess against Death. Skeletal and grinning, Death appears with the same boney, twisted smile that is underneath the mask of every human face, the embodiment and reminder of everyone's ultimate destination. Famously the inspiration for director Ingmar Bergman's 1957 film *The Seventh Seal*, Pictor's picture is a haunting memento mori, a very human evocation of the desperate flailing against the inevitable. Both pictures tell stories about the plague, about the lengths we'll go to survive. They convey how in pandemic, predictability disappears; they are narratives about the failure of narratives themselves. What both of them court are Brother Fate and his twin, Sister Despair. The wages of fortune are the subject of which cards you're dealt and the tension of strategy and luck when you avoid having your bishop or rook taken. Life may be a game, but none of us are master players, and sometimes, we're dealt a very bad hand.

There has always been literature of pandemic because there have always been pandemics. What marks the literature of plague, pestilence, and pandemic is a commitment to try to forge if not some sense of explanation then at least a sense of meaning out of the raw experience of panic, horror, and despair. Narrative is an attempt to stave off meaninglessness, and in the void of a pandemic, literature serves the purpose of trying, however desperately, to stop the bleeding. It makes sense that the most famous literary work to come out of the plague is Giovanni Boccaccio's 1353 *The Decameron*, with its frame conceit of a hundred bawdy, hilarious, and erotic stories told by seven women and three men over ten days while they're quarantined in a Tuscan villa outside Florence. As pandemic rages through northern Italy, Boccaccio's characters distract themselves with funny, dirty stories, but the anxious intent from those young women and men self-exiled within cloistered walls is that, as G. H. McWilliam translates, "every person born into this world has a natural right to sustain, preserve and defend" their own life. Storytelling becomes its own palliative to drown out the howling of those dying on the other side of the ivy-covered stone walls.

The recounting of pandemic stories is a reminder that sense still exists somewhere, that if there is not meaning outside of the quarantine zone, there's at least meaning within our invented stories. Literature is a reclamation against that which illness represents—that the world is not our own. As the narrator of Albert Camus's *The Plague* says as disease ravages the town of Oran in French Algeria, there is an "element of abstraction and unreality in misfortune. But when an abstraction starts to kill you, you have to get to work on it." When confronted with the erraticism of etiology, the arbitrariness of infection, the randomness of illness, we must contend with the reality that we are not masters of this world. We have become such seeming lords of nature that we've altered the very climate and geologists have named our epoch after humanity itself, and yet a cold virus can have more power than an army. Disease is not metaphor, symbol, or allegory; it is simply something that kills you without consideration. Story is a way of trying to impart a bit of that consideration that nature ignores.

The necessity of literature in the aftermath of pandemic is movingly illustrated in Emily St. John Mandel's novel *Station Eleven*. Mostly taking place several years after the "Georgian Flu" has killed the vast majority of humans on the planet and civilization has collapsed, Mandel's novel follows a troupe of Shakespearean actors as they travel by caravan across a scarred Great Lakes region on either side of the US-Canadian border. "We bemoaned the impersonality of the modern world," Mandel writes, "but that was a lie." *Station Eleven* is, in some sense, a love letter to a lost world, which is to say, the world (currently) of the reader. Our existence "had never been impersonal at all," she writes, and the novel gives moving litanies of all that was lost in the narrative's apocalypse, from chlorinated swimming pools to the mindlessness of the internet. There is a tender love of every aspect of our stupid world so that how the crisis happened can only be explained because of the fact that we were so interconnected: "There had always been a massive delicate infrastructure of people, all of them working unnoticed around us, and when people stop going to work, the entire operation grinds to a halt." As survivors struggle to rebuild, it's the job of narrative to supply meaning to that which disease has taken away, or as the motto painted on the wagon of the traveling caravan has it, "Survival is insufficient."

The need to tell stories, to use narrative to prove some continuity with a past obliterated by pandemic, is the motivating impulse of English professor James Smith, the main character in Jack London's largely forgotten 1912 postapocalyptic novel *The Scarlet*

Plague. With shades of Edgar Allan Poe, London imagines a 2013 outbreak of hemorrhagic fever called the "Red Death." Infectious, fast moving, and fatal, the plague wipes out the vast majority of the world's population so that some six decades after the pestilence first appears, Smith can scarcely believe that his memories of a once sophisticated civilization aren't illusions. Still, the former teacher is compelled to tell his grandchildren about the world before the Red Death, even if he sometimes imagines that his memories are lies. "The fleeting systems lapse like foam," writes London. "That's it—foam, and fleeting. All man's toil upon the planet was just so much foam."

The Scarlet Plague ends in a distant 2073, the same year that Mary Shelley's 1826 forerunner of the pandemic novel, *The Last Man*, was set. Far less famous than Shelley's *Frankenstein*, her largely forgotten novel is arguably just as pathbreaking. As with *Station Eleven*, narrative and textuality are the central concerns of the novel. When the last man himself notes that "I have selected a few books; the principal are Homer and Shakespeare—But the libraries of the world are thrown open to me," there is the sense that even in the finality of his position, there is a way in which words can still define our reality, anemic though it may now be. Displaying the trademark uneasiness about the idea of fictionality that often marked nineteenth-century novels, Shelley's conceit is that what you're reading are transcriptions of parchment containing ancient oracular predictions that the author herself discovered while exploring caves outside of Naples that had once housed the temple of the Cumaean Sibyl.

Her main character is a masculinized roman à clef for Shelley herself, an aristocrat named Lionel Verney who lives through the emergence of a global pandemic in 2073 up through the beginning of the twenty-second century, when he earns the titular status of the novel's title. All of Shelley's characters are stand-ins for her friends, the luminaries of the rapidly waning Romantic age, from Lord Byron, who is transformed into Lord Randolph, a passionate if incompetent leader of England who bungles that nation's response to the pandemic; to her own husband, Percy, who becomes Adrian, the son of the previous king who has chosen rather to embrace republicanism. By the time Verney begins his solitary pilgrimage across a desolated world, with only the ghosts of Homer and Shakespeare and an Alpine sheepdog whom he adopts, he still speaks in a first person addressed to an audience of nobody: "Thus around the shores of deserted earth, while the sun is high, and the moon waxes or wanes, angels, the spirts of the dead, and the ever-open eye of the Supreme, will behold . . . the LAST MAN." Thus in a world devoid of people, Verney becomes the book, and the inert world becomes the reader.

The Last Man's first-person narration, ostensibly directed to a world absent of people who could actually read it, belies a deeper reason for the existence of language than mere communication—to construct a world upon the ruins, to bear a type of witness, even if it's solitary. Language need not be for others; that it's for ourselves is often good enough. Literature thus becomes affirmation—more than that, it becomes rebellion, a means of saying within pandemic that we once existed and that microbe and spirochete can't abolish our voices, even if bodies should wither. That's one of the most important formulations of Tony Kushner's magisterial play *Angels in America: A Gay Fantasia on National Themes*. Arguably the most canonical text to emerge from the horror of the AIDS crisis, Kushner's three-hour play appears in two parts, "Millennium Approaches" and "Perestroika," and it intermixes two narrative threads, the story of wealthy WASP scion Prior Walter's HIV diagnosis and his subsequent abandonment by his scared lover, Louis

Ironson, and the arrival to New York City of the closeted Mormon Republican Joe Pitt, who works as a law clerk and kindles an affair with Louis.

Angels in America combines subjects as varied as Jewish immigration in the early twentieth century, kabbalistic and Mormon cosmology (along with a baroque system of invented angels), the reprehensible record of the closeted red-baiting attorney and Joseph McCarthy acolyte Roy Cohn, the endurance of the gay community struggling against the AIDS epidemic and their activism opposing the quasi-genocidal nonpolicy of conservative politicians like Ronald Reagan. If all that sounds heady, Kushner's play came from the estimably pragmatic issue of how a community survives a plague. Born from the pathbreaking work of activist groups like the AIDS Coalition to Unleash Power (ACT UP), *Angels in America* has, not just in spite of but because of its mythological concerns, an understanding that pandemics and politics are inextricably connected. In answering who deserves treatment and how such treatment will be allocated, we've already departed from the realm of disinterested nature. "There are no gods here, no ghosts and spirits in America, no spiritual past," says Louis. "There's only the political, and the decoys and the ploys to maneuver around the inescapable battle of politics." Throughout *Angels in America*, there is an expression of the human tragedy of pandemic, the way that beautiful young people in the prime of life can be murdered by their own bodies. Even Cohn, that despicable quasi fascist, who evidences so little of the human himself, is entitled to some tenderness when, upon his death, kaddish is recited for him—by the spirit of Ethel Rosenberg, the supposed Soviet spy whom the lawyer was instrumental in the execution of.

At the end of the play, Prior stands at Bethesda Fountain in Central Park, with all of the attendant religious implications of that place's name, and he intones, "This disease will be the end of many of us, but not nearly all, and the dead will be commemorated and will struggle on with the living, and we are not going away. We won't die secret deaths anymore. . . . We will be citizens. The time has come." In telling stories, there is a means not just of constructing meaning, or of even endurance, but indeed of survival. Fiction is not the only means of expressing this, of course, or even necessarily the most appropriate. Journalist Randy Shilts accomplished something similar to Kushner in his classic account *And the Band Played On: Politics, People, and the AIDS Epidemic*, which soberly, clinically, and objectively chronicled the initial outbreaks of the disease among the San Francisco gay community.

In a manner not dissimilar to Daniel Defoe's classic *A Journal of the Plague Year, 1666* (even while that book is fictionalized), Shilts gives an epidemiological account of the numbers, letting the horror speak through science more effectively than had it been rendered in poetry. Such staidness is its own requirement and can speak powerfully to the reality of the event, whereby "the unalterable tragedy at the heart of the AIDS epidemic" was that "by the time America paid attention to the disease, it was too late to do anything about it," the shame of a nation whereby Reagan's press secretary Larry Speakes would actually publicly laugh at the idea of a "gay plague." Shilts waited till he finished *And the Band Played On* to be tested for HIV himself, worried that a positive diagnosis would alter his journalistic objectivity. He died of AIDS-related complications in 1994, having borne witness to the initial years of the epidemic, abjuring the cruel inaction of government policy with the disinfectant of pure facts.

Most people who read about pandemics, however, turn to pulpier books; paperback airport novels like Michael Crichton's clinical fictionalized report about an interstellar virus, *The Andromeda*

Strain; Robin Cook's nightmare fuel about a California Ebola pandemic in *Outbreak*; and Stephen King's magisterial postapocalyptic epic *The Stand*, which I read in the summer of 1994 and remains the longest sustained narrative I think I've ever engaged with. Because these books are printed on cheap paper and have the sorts of garish covers intended more for mass consumption than prestige, they're dismissed as prurient or exploitative. Ever the boring distinctions between genre and literary fiction, for though the pace of suspense may distinguish entertainment as integral as aesthetics, these novels too have just as much to say about the endurance of the written word in the face of disease, as well as about the fear and experience of illness, as do any number of explicitly more "serious" works.

The Stand is an exemplary example of just what genre fiction is capable of, especially when it comes to elemental fears surrounding plague that seem somehow encoded within our cultural DNA. Written as an American corollary to J. R. R. Tolkien's Lord of the Rings trilogy, King depicts a United States completely unraveled one summer after the containment loss of a government "Super-Flu" bioweapon nicknamed "Captain Trips." In that aftermath, King presents a genuinely apocalyptic struggle between good and evil that's worthy of Revelation, but intrinsic to this tale of pestilence is the initial worry that accompanies a scratchy throat, watery eyes, a sniffling nose, and a cough that seemingly won't go away. If anything, King's vision is resolutely in that medieval tradition of fortune as so expertly represented by the Master of the Playing Cards or Pictor, a wisdom that when it comes to disease, "life was such a wheel that no man could stand upon it for long. And it always, at the end, came round to the same place again."

Far from being exploitative, of only offering readers the exquisite pleasure of vicariously imagining all of society going to complete shit, there is a radical empathy at the core of much genre fiction.

Readers of Robert Kirkman and Tony Moore's graphic novels *The Walking Dead* (or the attendant television series) or viewers of George Romero's brilliant zombie classics may assume that they'll always be the ones to survive Armageddon, but these works can force us into a consideration of the profound contingency of our own lives. Cynics might say that the enjoyment derived from zombie narratives is that they provide a means of imagining that most potent of American fantasies—the ability to shoot your neighbor with no repercussions. More than expressing fantasies of unbridled violence, however, and I think that they state a bit of the feebleness of our civilization.

This is what critic Susan Sontag notes in *Illness as Metaphor* about how pandemic supplies "evidence of a world in which nothing important is regional, local, limited; in which everything that can circulate does, and every problem is, or is destined to become, worldwide" so that products and viruses alike can freely move in a globalized world. The latter can then disrupt the former, where plague proves the precariousness of the supply lines that keep food on grocery shelves and electricity in the socket—the shockingly narrow band separating hot breakfast and cold beer from the nastiness, brutishness, and shortness of life anarchic. Such is the grim knowledge of Max Brooks's *World War Z*, where "they teach you how to resist the enemy, how to protect your mind and spirit. They don't teach you how to resist your own people."

If medieval art and literature embraced the idea of fate, whereby it's impossible to know who shall be first and who shall be last once the plague rats have entered port, then contemporary genre fiction has a similar democratic vision, a knowledge that wealth, power, and prestige can mean little after you've been coughed on. When the Black Death came to Europe, no class was spared; it took the sculptor Andrea Pisano and the banker Giovanni Villani, the painter Ambrogio Lorenzetti and the poet Jeuan Gethin, the mystic Richard Rolle and the philosopher William of Ockham, and the father, mother, and friends of Boccaccio. Plague upended society more than any revolution could, and there was a strange egalitarianism to the paupers' body pit covered in lye. Sontag, again, writes that "illness is the night-side of life, a more onerous citizenship. Everyone who is born holds dual citizenship, in the kingdom of the well and in the kingdom of the sick. Although we all prefer to use only the good passport, sooner or later each of us is obliged, at least for a spell, to identify ourselves as citizens of that other place."

Such equality motivated the greatest of medieval artistic themes to emerge from the Black Death, that of the danse macabre, or "dance of death." In such imagery, painters and engravers would depict paupers and princes, popes and peasants all linking hands with grinning brown skeletons with hair clinging to mottled pates and cadaverous flesh hanging from bones, dancing in a circle across a bucolic countryside. In the anonymous *Totentanz* of 1460, the narrator writes, "Emperor, your sword won't help you out / Scepter and crown are worthless here / I've taken you by the hand / For you must come to my dance." During the Black Death, the fearful and the denialists alike explained the disease as due to a confluence of astrological phenomenon or noxious miasma, they claimed it was punishment for sin, or they blamed religious and ethnic minorities within their midst. To some, the plague was better understood as "hoax" than as reality. The smiling skulls of the danse macabre laugh at that sort of cowardly narcissism, for they know that pestilence is a feature of our reality, and reality has a way of collecting its debts.

Illness sees no social stratification—it comes for bishop and authoritarian theocrat, king and germophobic president alike. The final theme of the literature of pandemic, born from the awareness that this world is not ours alone, is that we can't avert our eyes from the truth, no matter how cankered and ugly it may be in the interim. Something can be both true and senseless. The presence of disease is evidence of that. When I was little, my grandma told me stories about when she was a girl during the 1918 Spanish influenza epidemic that took seventy-five million people. She described how wagons arrived carting coffins for those who perished in front of the courthouse of her small Pennsylvania town. Such memories are recounted to create meaning, to bear witness, to make sense, to warn, to exclaim that we were here, that we're still here. Narrative can preserve and remake the world as it falls apart. Such is the point of telling any story. Illness reminds us that the world isn't ours; literature lets us know that it is—sometimes.

14

Neo-Donatists in Eden

Edmund Spenser knew how to turn a phrase. His poetic vision, exemplified by his epic *The Faerie Queene*, remains in some ways unsurpassed. Though it is a dense, maximalist, incomplete poem of seven books and thousands upon thousands of lines, a complex religious allegory with a massive cast of characters, Spenser could deftly craft quivering lines of exquisite, whispered beauty, as he wrote in 1956's "Prothalamion": "Calm was the day, and through the trembling air / Sweet-breathing Zephyrus did softly play— / A gentle spirit, that lightly did delay / Hot Titan's beams, which then did glister fair." One might assume that Spenser's observation in *The Faerie Queene* that the "noblest mind the best contentment has" is true of its author, for as he celebrates his own genius in "Prothalamion," his is a verse that commands, "Sweete Themmes runne softly, till I end my Song."

Spenser's poetry is influential and important, and as is always more crucial, Spenser's poetry *is* sublime and sweet. He is able to march into an iambic rhythm like a poetic general, able to allude to the honey-scented winds of Zephyr or the clear waters of Parnassus, but for all of the immaculate lines he strung together, there is also his 1596 pamphlet, *A View of the Present State of Ireland*. In that piece, he argued that that colonized nation was a "diseased portion of the State, it must first be cured and reformed," which he recommended accomplishing through the scorched-earth eradication of Irish culture and people, the elimination of Gaelic, and the forced conversion of the natives. To argue that such a proposal is anything other than a form of ethnic cleansing would be revisionism, an attempt to ameliorate Spenser's guilt. Spenser's relationship to genocidal policy was more than just theoretical. He was present at Smerwick in 1580, where a surrendering garrison of Irish, Italian, and Spanish soldiers were massacred, and for his role, Spenser was gifted plantations at both Munster and Kilcolman by the British government. Spenser engaged authoritarian logic, the same type of logic since deployed from Wounded Knee to Wannsee in the language of Manifest Destiny and Lebensraum. He conceived of an Ireland where "in a shorte space there were none almost left, and a most populous and plentyfull countrye suddenly lefte voyde of man or beast." Despite his greatness as a poet, there must be a serious accounting of how we approach a man like Spenser and thus a poem like *The Faerie Queene*. As scholars, as teachers, as students, and most importantly, as readers, there must be a moral reckoning on how we reconcile the reality of the poet to the reality of the poem.

Spenser is not the only writer with a darkened biography, especially in his own era. Consider Spenser's fellow veteran in the Irish campaigns of the Nine Years' War, the ever-romanticized Sir

Walter Raleigh. The celebrated explorer, in addition to being a privateer, was also a poet of tremendous talent, whom the undersung modern critic Yvor Winters rightly championed as an exemplar of the anti-Petrarchan plain style, a versifier who wrote in his poem "The Nymphs Reply to the Shepherd,"

If all the world and love were young,
And truth in every shepherd's tongue,
These pretty pleasures might me move
To live with thee and be thy Love.

A poet of pastoral bounty no doubt, but also one who was at that very same siege in Smerwick that Spenser took part in and was in fact the officer who oversaw the beheading of those six hundred soldiers, turning that green Irish field a burgundy red. He was a man who could poignantly write in his own epitaph before his execution in the Tower of London in 1618, "Our youth, our joys, are all we have," and yet he was also responsible for the very beginnings of the English's genocidal policy toward the Indians, his advocacy was directly responsible for the institution of the transatlantic slave trade, and in importing tobacco to Europe, he was a potent trader in a deadly narcotic. Raleigh was a gorgeous poet, but today he'd be seen as a combination of Pablo Escobar and Lt. William Calley Jr.; in our time, his biography would certainly sully the picturesque scenes of his lovely poems.

For those who (often rightly) see something problematic in literature produced by those who range from disagreeable to outright monstrous, Renaissance literature presents a special problem. For who among that canon is remotely morally laudable? Even Shakespeare, that soul of his age, that master of what it means to be human, has a whole host of disreputable anecdotes about him that would unequivocally be understood as assault today, and as a rather wealthy shareholder in the King's Men, Shakespeare was also an investor in the colonial efforts of the Virginia Company. The author of the anticolonial *The Tempest* directly profited from the Calibans oppressed by men like Raleigh. What emerges is a network of complicity, whereby those visionary lights of an era—the creative poets and playwrights and scholars, men like Spenser and Raleigh and Shakespeare—were to varying degrees deeply involved with the authoritarianism of the state and were frequently reprehensible themselves even while producing works of exquisite beauty, meaning, and power. Which is to say that the Renaissance was a period absolutely like any other. If we remember only the virtues and forget the vices of those distant poets, it's only because their remove from our own age has blurred their edges and blunted injustice. For those who fret that perseverating on the cruelties of geniuses does them a disservice, there is a certain understandable logic.

But there is something common, and thus dangerously commonplace, in denying the crimes committed by those who have moved us. We must grapple with the beautiful fruit of art grown from malignant trees. The crux of the issue is a very human dilemma. We must not reduce a profound discussion into simple binaries, nor must we abdicate responsibility in a necessary conversation engaging complex, unsettling, and important questions at the nexus of ethics and aesthetics. Pundits have long critiqued humanities departments, in particular English departments, for an obsession with questions of "political correctness," with reducing literature to partisan issues of race, class, and gender. It barely warrants repeating the tired particulars, save to note that it's the sort of argument that sometimes bubbles up to the surface, and it seems we're at such a moment right now, albeit with popular culture. No doubt you're familiar with the terms of the debate: that English professors in their obsession with political correctness have enlisted the baroque jargon of theory to hammer into the heads of their impressionable students that Shakespeare was a sexist (well, he was), that Tolstoy was a racist (also true), and that T. S. Eliot was an anti-Semite (goes without saying). In this narrative, theory-inflected scholars have torn down the edifice of beauty and truth, which previously bolstered the canon, in favor of hairsplitting over context. But these quibbles are not the real questions. The truly interesting question is, How do we hold the tension between the realities that ugly minds could also produce works of truth and beauty? Mine is a simple observation: some horrible people have produced some truly and utterly sublime work. Now the question is, What possibly do we do with this information?

In attempting to answer the question, critics tend to ignore our dubious inheritance as post-Romantics. We valorize the idea of the individual, of the solitary creative genius whose art is a product and reflection of her soul. In this model, the human is at the center of the humanities, and all prose and poetry are confessional. Thus if there is evidence that a brilliant work was created by an immoral or even terrible human being, it can mean only one of two outcomes—that the work wasn't that brilliant to begin with or that the things that the person did weren't that bad. When neither of these things is true, we must confront that elemental question: How can bad people produce powerful, beautiful, even *sacred* art? And what does it mean when that art moves us?

Recently, there has been a rich discussion on this topic in the popular press. As a result of the #MeToo movement and the Time's Up campaign, there has been a reckoning with the uncomfortable question of what it means to be moved by a monster. The sheer magnitude of revelations ensures that this reckoning can't be ignored. We have to contend with the fact that in many instances, we've been moved to tears and laughter by those who've been cruel, tyrannical, callous, and sadistic. The dilemma isn't about either censorship or exoneration but rather about the far more uncomfortable problem of what it means to see goodness and truth in the work of "Nabokov, Chaplin, Hitchcock, Roth, Updike, Bellow, Mailer, and Picasso" (as listed by scholar Laura Kipnis in a Facebook post). Rather than being a symptom of historical revisionism, this is a grappling with the sheer weight of moral history for what feels like the first time. It's not to argue for turning away from that art—for what good would that do? But it does call for some kind of moral inventory of how it is possible that a perfect sonnet can be penned by a rapist, an immaculate novel written by a murderer, and a profound play crafted by a war criminal.

Among several of the articles emerging in the wake of the #MeToo movement, Claire Dederer provided one of the most nuanced and humane reflections in "What Do We Do with the Art of Monstrous Men?" at the *Paris Review Daily*, which appeared in 2017. Dederer's account of her own engagement with the films of Woody Allen, films that moved her, is wide ranging in the profundity of her questions and devastating in some of her implied conclusions. Asking "What is to be done about monsters? Can and should we love their work? Are all ambitious artists monsters?" Dederer moves beyond simply asking about "Roman Polanski, Woody Allen, Bill Cosby, William Burroughs, Richard Wagner, Sid Vicious, V. S. Naipaul, John Galliano, Norman Mailer, Ezra Pound, Caravaggio, [and] Floyd Mayweather" to a more all-encompassing reflection on Walter Benjamin's astute observation that "at the base of every major work of art is a pile of barbarism." Hers is a method of ethical and aesthetic critique that is shattering because her authorial voice is so humble. She asks, "Which of us is seeing more clearly? The one who had the ability—some might say the privilege—to remain untroubled by the filmmaker's attitudes toward females and history with girls? . . . Or the one who couldn't help but notice the antipathies and urges that seemed to animate the project?" She adds, "I'm really asking." Dederer's analysis probes our own moral culpability while acknowledging that artistic genius is real. She ameliorates neither the monstrousness of her subjects nor the brilliance of their works. Allen isn't a brilliant director who has been maligned with grotesque slander, nor is he a child molester who happens to be a mediocre filmmaker. Rather, she claims, he is a rapist who is also a genius director. Dederer asks her reader to consider what it is that we do with such information.

If we're fumbling awkwardly in response, it's because we're ignoring a sense of the sacred, and I say that whether or not you believe in God, for "God" has little to do with it. We're undergoing such an important sea change in our consciousness, but our language is predictably lagging, which is why our conversations are stalled. When it comes to the dilemma of how we should approach beauty produced by the wicked, we falter. We fall into the same binaries that too often define this conversation. Theology need not supplant the terms, which inadequately define our necessary yet uncomfortable conversations, but it can supplement them. Not just *privilege* but *original sin*; *reparations* but also *reconciliation*. There is need for not just *redistribution* but also *justice*. Our secular ethics are shamefaced about issues of salvation, redemption, and grace, and thus we have no vocabulary to answer necessary questions like the ones asked by Dederer.

As the French philosopher Jean-Pierre Dupuy writes in *The Mark of the Sacred*, the "powerlessness of contemporary rationalism . . . is identical with the denial that lies at its very heart: the refusal to accept that the ways of thinking it authorizes are rooted in our experience of the sacred." I believe that theological language can aid in the clarification of how we're to situate art by immoral artists, albeit by perhaps borrowing a rather obscure term: *Donatism*. Drawing their name from a fourth-century Berber bishop, the Donatists emerged during the brutal suppression of Christians by Emperor Diocletian, when some believers impugned the faith to avoid punishment. These *traditores* included a number of priests, and upon the end of persecution, many of them returned to their former functions within the church. The Donatists, composed largely of working-class North Africans who'd never abandoned Christianity, were appalled that collaborators were now reinstated, and furthermore, the Donatists regarded any sacraments administered by these turncoat clergy as illegitimate. This position, it should be said, makes a certain amount of sense, especially in its fairness. Why should somebody who abjured the church be allowed to administer its sacraments? How could one say that a priest who'd spit on the crucifix, who'd let the Gospels be burned, can now present the Eucharist? How could any sacred transformation take place in the hands of such a sinner? Perhaps you see the nature of my analogy. Today the traditional conduit between the sacred and the profane embodied by the sacraments has dissipated as part of that process of disenchantment initiated by the Reformation. For the secular, these mysteries of church ritual are now empty, and if there is to be any "outward sign of an inward grace," per the official definition of a sacrament from the Roman Catholic Church, it's in being moved by poetry, art, film, or music. Of course, a poem isn't the Eucharist, a play isn't Baptism, and a novel isn't contrition. But in a godless world, they have taken on a sacramental import. People find grace in David Bowie's *Heroes*, the poetry of Kaveh Akbar, or any album by Nina Simone.

As God dies, art will become our new religion. Continuing vagaries of religious extremism belie that prediction, but it is incontrovertible that art has become Western culture's new sacrament. Perhaps the Dionysian enthusiasms of those countercultural Romantics, and Transcendentalists, and Beats who thought that our new liturgy would be poetry were overstated, but to me, it seems undeniable that we are awash with cultural production in a manner unthinkable decades ago. Our new sacraments are offered not by faith but by art. Our churches are filled with laptops and iPhones, our fellowship is the sharing of links, and our scripture the pop culture that sustains us. Providing a more subtle interpretation than that old Romantic wish, scholar Regina Schwartz has analyzed in *Sacramental Poetics at the Dawn of Secularism* how the debates over the sacraments (the Eucharist in particular) during the Reformation resulted in a sublimation of sacred enthusiasm into profane expression, writing that "instead of God leaving the world without a trace, the very sacramental character of religion lent itself to developing the so-called secular forms of culture" and that "these are often thinly disguised sacramental cultural expressions." Humans abhor a vacuum of meaning, and no person is truly an atheist; thus in the disenchanted West, scholar James Simpson can observe in *Under the Hammer* that the "museum ceaselessly replicates the sacred space," where galleries are our cathedrals, song lyrics our scripture, and phone screens the sites of our ecstatic visions.

Such a sacramental model explains why we feel so personally betrayed by heinous creators of beautiful creations. Like the Donatists of old, we too are anxious about partaking in the sacrament of poetry birthed by malignant minds. But our fears are generated by taking art somehow both too seriously and not seriously enough. Too seriously because this distress is the product of that post-Romantic idolatrizing of the individual, of the confessional nature of the poem as an artifact of inner life, where anything produced by a sinner is tainted by that sin. It seems impossible to see premoderns sharing that anxiety—that Caravaggio's fingers were stained with both oil and the blood of men he'd murdered was of no account in recognizing his paintings' beauty. Earlier people cared not a whit about what the anonymous hands that sculpted the *Winged Victory of Samothrace* or the Notre Dame gargoyles were doing when they weren't at work. Such anxiety only develops with the elevation of art to sacrament. But that's where our current moment doesn't take art seriously enough, for we've primitively made the same error that the Donatists did, assuming that sacraments are only legitimate if delivered by immaculate priests. We rightly elevated poetry but stupidly assumed the poet's apotheosis. And thus when we discover that poets, and filmmakers, and novelists are sinners, here in our fallen world, we despair that their art must be fallen as well. We are all Neo-Donatists stumbling about in a land that we pray is Eden but seems to be somewhere very far to the West.

What I suggest is that we reevaluate the relationship between creator and created through the perspective of those who criticized Donatist moral absolutism. For the architects of orthodox Catholicism, flawed and fallen though the mediating priest may be, a sacrament always finds its origin in God. To argue otherwise is to denigrate the sacrament itself. According to the formula advanced by the fourth-century Numidian bishop Saint Optatus—the greatest critic of the Donatists until Saint Augustine—"Sacramenta per se esse sancta, non per homines." That is, sacraments are sanctified, but not because of the humans who perform them. And so it is with great art—a sacrament is sacred regardless of who has performed it, so beautiful, moving art is holy regardless of who brought it into existence.

I'm not requiring us to see poetry as an ideal state save for when an ideal state is a form of holiness. When I claim that the truly transcendent offered by some art is as if a type of sacramental poetics, this is not metaphor or simile. This is my contention. And although biography must be noted, as it would be for a priest who had once abjured the faith, I also believe that a sacrament truly performed is like the very voice of God. What I suggest is embracing an older model of inspiration and creative origins that identifies Cædmon's song not with the singer but with the dream. A literary pantheism that sees the beauties of great art as dispersed and spread among all of us, that celebrates the poetry even, and maybe especially, at the expense of the poet. Often, Roland Barthes's 1967 observation that the "birth of the reader must be ransomed by the death of the Author," in an essay titled after the last five words of that quote, is characterized as the worst type of French theoretical sophistry, as simple postmodern affectation. I don't believe that; I believe that what Barthes speaks of is a type of ancient and sacred wisdom. For in speaking of the "death of the Author," we can preserve the sanctity of poetry despite the poet's cruelty; we can delight in the holiness of prose despite the author's sadism. Barthes's vision is, dare I say it, a profoundly theological one, for whether you declare the "death of the Author" or of God, you've effectively democratized the sacred. Let's abandon that which heightens the poet at the expense of the poetry, and let's gladly grab a few lilacs as we step off the grave of the author. *The Faerie Queene* is too inspiring, too beautiful, too sacred, and too holy to be left only to the man who merely transcribed it onto parchment. True, Spenser was a fundamentally evil man. If there is perdition, then he better be in it. But his poem—his poem is sublime.

15

Interrogating the Interrogative

Quid est veritas?
—Pontius Pilate

From whence did the interrogative arise? In what pool of primordial muck could the first question have been asked?

Certainly, mold asks no questions; lichen presents no queries. At some point in that evolutionary chain, we went from ooze to something that could face the world-which-is-not-us and assault it with inquiry. Gnostic cosmology, in all of its labyrinthine and baroque complexities, posited an originating question at the very beginning, for the initial word wasn't declarative but interrogative. Sophia, the bride of Christ, God's indwelling manifestation of wisdom that was one of the emanations during the creation of reality, is both the producer and product of questions. With an admirable sense of Hebraic parallelism and the rhetorical power of contradiction, the anonymous second-century Gnostic poet of the exhortatory lyric "The Thunder, Perfect Mind," discovered as part of the papyri cache of the Nag Hammadi library preserved in the sunbaked sands of Egypt, writes of Sophia, "I am the first and the last. / I am the honored one and the scorned one."

If there were no questions, then there is a pacific stasis, for questions imply disquiet, they imply imperfection, they imply a lack that is trying to be rectified. When that part of God known as Sophia asks the first question, it's the collapse of the wave function, the ruptured equilibrium, the disrupted symmetry. From those cracks could grow the very weeds of creation, but the process of dialectic begins with a question and continues on until the final answer.

I imagine that in a universe where no questions had ever been asked, perhaps God first asked, "What, then, is this thing called reality?" That schizoid rupture was the Big Bang that inaugurated everything. This is myth, though; it doesn't answer what the actual first question could have been, for the only implicit question that can ever really be asked when reality is stripped naked and we stare at it in all of its sublime, awful, infinite glory is "What exactly is a question?"

The interrogative is a conscious affliction. There aren't really any actual questions when it concerns being; Sophia is forever mute but for in our legends. The world asks of us no questions; the world simply is. If after the heat death of the universe, or the big crunch, when either by fire or by ice the world does put itself to sleep, there will be no more questions, for there shall be nobody left to ask them. If a question is asked by nobody, does it matter? Such inquiries can only occur when a mind comes up against base matter, when those bits of the latter have become sufficiently complex enough so as to wonder about the former. But the universe itself—that soup of quarks and leptons, quasars and black holes—has no questions to ask about itself, for it is not capable of any such reflection. And it's all the more divine because of it. That's why it's God.

So if we're to venture some kind of natural history of questions, we must be aware that they're the unique property of consciousness. This is not to claim that questions are what separate us from those other creatures in the evolutionary great chain of being. It is obvious to me that other animals are able to query their place in reality, that they can pose interrogatives whether in language or not. When I consider my delightful dog, who is both the smartest and cutest canine in the world, I can try to surmise certain things about her experience of the world. To be able to solve that metaphysical conundrum known as the "problem of other minds" is difficult with humans, much less animals, yet it's my intuition that almost all of our furry beast friends (and feathered and scaled ones) are actually smarter than we assume.

Questions arise from subjectivity, from the individual experience of consciousness, but what is the nature of those questions? In his 1974 paper "What Is It like to Be a Bat?" the philosopher Thomas Nagel asks whether it's possible to say with any authority what the subjective experience of our chiropteran friends might be. He argues that "there is no reason to suppose that it is subjectively like anything we experience or imagine." That evolutionarily speaking, bats are conscious, that they have self-awareness, is observable and unassailable. Nagel contends, however, that while we know bats have some kind of inner life, so different are the material circumstances of their existence that it's impossible for us to ever fully intuit what that life must be like with any degree of certainty. A world of spindly flapping flight, of hanging upside down in dark and moist caves, of guano and blood, of seeing with sound.

That bats ask questions also seems clear, at least to me. They're presumably not queries translated into language; they're not grammatically interrogative. But that bats must pursue knowledge of things unknown to them in the moment that are instrumental to their survival seems to simply be a result of the Darwinian imperative. Nagel's argument is well taken, though; that bats are capable of questions and what those questions are remain two very different things. Bulldogs are closer to our experience in all ways than the flapping, scaly *flittermice* are, so I feel more confident in venturing a guess as to what questions they're capable of, even if indeterminacy must still define such a task.

That my dog questions is clear to me, but what variety of questions is she capable of? The existence of animal consciousness is so obvious that to argue otherwise is rank denialism. The great French Renaissance humanist Michel de Montaigne observed in his 1576 *An Apology for Raymond Sebond* that the watchdogs that "we often see growl in their sleep, and then bark outright and wake up with a start, as if they saw some stranger coming" evidence their own inner lives, of thoughts and dreams. Montaigne conjectures that his sleeping dog sees a spectral rabbit, a "hare without fur or bones," which is to say that the canine can imagine that which is not there. And as questions are both the ancestors and progeny of imagination, it seems fair to assume that dogs must have their questions as well, but what form they take I do not know. As Sarah Bakewell writes in her *How to Live: Or a Life of Montaigne in One Question and Twenty Attempts at an Answer*, for the scholar, "it is enough to watch a dog dreaming to see that it must have an inner world just like ours." Montaigne's later countryman René Descartes may have posited that animals were as little mechanical automatons, but anyone who has ever had a pet, regardless of where they fall on that ladder from guppies to lemurs, knows that they have a rich intersubjectivity. As Montaigne himself wondered, "When I am playing with my cat, how do I know she is not playing with me?"

Without getting into the specific nature of those questions ("Where is my food?"), we can think about the variety of questions that either Montaigne's cat or my dog might entertain by examining that old journalistic trope of the "Six Ws"—who, what, where, when, why, and how. Each one of these types of questions implies something about how humans are able to interact with reality; they're born from our senses, and their purpose is to orient us in time and space. For our pets, there is a clear utility to those classes of questions that orient them in a space composed of objects—the what—as well as those that trade in the identities of living beings that are separate from them—the who—and to a lesser degree, those that deal with time—the when. And when it comes to the activities of life, the questions that illuminate how to actually do stuff—the how—all are clearly important.

You can hide food from your puppy or play hide-and-seek with a parrot, so the question of "Where?" is obviously entertained by them. Temporality is a different quality; any pet owner can't help but wonder how clear their animal's sense of time is. Yet all things being relative, our dogs are creatures of habit, waking at certain times and napping at others, an estimably conservative species whose safety relies on routine. Thus "When?" is also within their purview. The analytical acumen of a dog also seems to include the "Who?" and the "What?" for every time a dog barks at the mailman, it's obvious that they can differentiate between people; that they respond to clothes with the scent of their owner and not some other's is evidence enough that they can differentiate the subtle shadings of the "Who?" And that the "How?" is available to our furred, feathered, scaled coanimals need not be doubted; when Jane Goodall observed chimps using sticks to pull ants from a log, it was the needed scientific confirmation of something that any pet owner suspects about animal intelligence. When I was growing up, our

Jack Russell terrier used to drop his toy golf balls in his water bowl when the level was getting low, like one of those unnervingly smart crows from Aesop.

But that last variety of question, the "Why?"—are nonhuman animals capable of that? Because "Why?" is a very particular, very weird type of question. It doesn't orient us in space or time, nor does it necessarily identify an object or another person, or prescribe a way of accomplishing some task. Rather, "Why?" has the gloss of ethics about it, the stench of metaphysics. "Why?" trades in intentionality, in meaning, and that's what's gotten us into all of this trouble. With "Why?" we begin to grapple with fundamentally more abstract things—possibly more illusory ones as well. If one should come across a dead baby rabbit in the tall New England grasses, there can be an approach based on the "What?" (a dead baby rabbit), the "Where?" (the tall New England grasses), the "When?" (early in the morning), the "Who?" (perhaps that basset hound who skulks around), and the "How?" (jaws, teeth), but the "Why?" doesn't quite ultimately fit. No doubt you'll protest, "The why is the predator instinct of the basset hound," but I'd suggest that it's fairer to categorize that as just a more specific subset of the "How?"

As anyone who has ever spent any time with children knows (and I have not, but I take the following claim on faith), it's always possible to find a deeper "Why?" for it is the most recursive of questions. Yes, the basset hound has a predator instinct, but why this rabbit and not another? Why a rabbit and not a squirrel? "Why?" proliferates with beauty, but like Bertrand Russell's turtle shell on which the earth sits, it's turtles all the way down. The who, what, where, when, and how burn themselves out at a certain point, but the why can always be asked of more and more minute answers so that the chimera of meaning always flees from that ever-burning fire.

One can gather a suspicion that "Why?" is an exercise, a certain type of baselessness, because of this inability to ever conclude. That "Why?" is an illusion, since the ability to dilute its results ever further indicates neither rigor nor certainty, but a defect in our linguistic apparatus. At a point, the other types of questions are exhaustible, but "Why?" is inexhaustible. Closely connected to our ability to craft fiction, because "Why?" is grown in the counterfactual's soil, it is planted in potentiality and watered in wonder (no matter how tepid), but the crop proliferates like a weed. The bounty has been all of human philosophy, literature, culture, and religion. With "Why?" being such a late bloomer, it's fair to conjecture as to what other categories of questions may evolve in the future, that which we're not cognitively capable of right now, but through the gift of interrogative synesthesia, we may be able to confuse the what with the how and the when with the where—and perhaps conceive of entirely new types of questions as well.

Maybe some higher-order primates have the capability of "Why?" Goodall has written it is "possible that the chimpanzees are responding to some feeling like awe," and maybe that's evidence of curiosity about ultimate things, about the teleology behind our experiences. There is some point in the evolutionary narrative that *meaning* becomes a possibility, and the "Why?" becomes the tool to try to access it. And in the realm of conscious intentionality, "Why?" certainly has a utility—I wouldn't mean to suggest otherwise. When discussing motivations and meaning, consequences and causality, "Why?" can have a function. But to look at a quark, at a nucleus, at an amino acid, at a cell, at a dead rabbit, at a field, at a sunset, at a star, at a quasar, at a black hole, at a galaxy, at the universe and to force it toward the procrustean bed of "Why?" is a rank category mistake. To fully understand that "Why?" is a *meaningless* question when interrogating *meaning*, for neither word *means* anything, is certainly disorienting. This is not nihilism but its opposite, an attempt to make the world glow again. A divine subtraction until disenchantment becomes its opposite. Because I'd venture to argue that the purpose of all true belief is the exorcism of "Why?"

Zen koans aside, I take it as a given that a dog has Buddha-nature, for though they are capable of all useful questions, they do not fall into the fallacy of "Why?" For them, existence is bare, and it is true enough in its own being. They have, like their fellow creatures, maintained a state that the great faiths think of as enlightenment, the elimination of the unnecessary question, the reduction of the fallacy of intentionality. A creation laid bare that asks no question of "Why?" for it is already its own answer. Existence itself has no questions and poses no answers; such a state is only possible in those bits of matter complicated enough to get into all of that trouble inventing imaginary worlds. A felix culpa, that ability to question. To build a ladder of words, its planks questions and answers, so as to transcend to that realm where the interrogative shall no longer hold dominion, and then with a pause to kick that ladder over.

16

Novel Prognostications; or, What's the Zeitgeist Saying Now?

> He undertakes to write a Chronicle of things before they
> are done, which is an irregular, and a perverse way.
>
> —John Donne, sermon preached at Lincoln's Inn (1620)

Between 1997 and 1998, representatives of His Majesty's government stationed in Constantinople, Rome, Paris, and Moscow wrote a series of diplomatic missives about the chaotic state of the world, later compiled into an anthology titled *Memoirs of the Twentieth Century*. With tongue only slightly in cheek, I say that this anthology was edited earlier than it was written, for that odd volume was anonymously compiled by an Anglo-Irish vicar named Samuel Madden and first saw print in 1733. Inspired by his countryman Jonathan Swift, Madden attempted to pen a romance that would do for time what *Gulliver's Travels* had done for space, presenting a prognostication about the world two and a half centuries in the future with the conceit that a guardian angel (or future time traveler) has delivered a cache of documents to the Irish minister. A sort of temporal WikiLeaks, if you will.

Madden's twentieth century sees a simmering cold war between the great powers, a Russia with expansionist designs on her neighbors, and a Jesuit pope sitting on the throne of Saint Peter. Though Madden's guardian angel is skimpy on the details, the author assures us that medical and communication technology has progressed in ways that would astound an eighteenth-century reader. Other details are less familiar. A George VI sits on a British throne decades after the actual monarch had died; Bourbon heads never rolled in the gutters of Paris, and so a Louis XIX reigns in France. But in other ways, the author of this strange and largely forgotten volume is prescient. Giving a diagnosis of the spiritual maladies of modernity, the editor of this epistolary describes the economic inequities of what we often call late capitalism, where the "luxury of the Nobility and Gentry is increas'd beyond all Bounds, as if they were not only insensible of, but even rejoyc'd in the publick Calamities of their Fellow-Subjects," which, antiquated prose aside, is an apt description of what Naomi Klein has called the shock doctrine.

Memoirs of the Twentieth Century is arguably the first of a type. With only a few minor continental antecedents, Madden's romance is "the earliest example of British futuristic fiction," as Steven Moore writes in *The Novel: An Alternative History, 1600–1800*. Madden makes predictions, but prophecies (using the more popular definition of that term) go back deep into antiquity. From Joseph to John Dee, there have been strategies of interpreting dreams, tea leaves, and the shape of sheep livers, of bibliomancy, rhapsodomancy, cleromancy, and necromancy. Prophetic arts divine have scryed a vision into the future, yet those methods always had a veneer of the occult about them. *Memoirs of the Twentieth Century* uses a guardian angel as its mechanism of communication, making it seem not that far from Joseph and his interpretation of Pharaoh's dreams, but as scholar Paul Alkon makes clear in *Science Fiction Studies*, such a subject as astral messengers wasn't so easily extractable from nascent science during the early eighteenth century. Among other "sciences," Madden writes that he was skilled in "Anthropomantia, or divining of men . . . the Chiromantia by the line of the hand or Palmistry . . . the celestia Astrologia of the Stars . . . not to mention the Corpomantia, as the Greeks calls it, or in plain English, the art of divining from the dung of creature: a matter I wish from my soul the sage inspectors of our close-stools were a little better skilled." Alkon writes that though Madden's novel "had no apparent impact on later 18th-century fiction," he concurs with Moore that it's the first futuristic science fiction text in English—guardian angels notwithstanding. Even more importantly, earlier prognostications rarely had a sense that the distant future would be substantially *different* from the present, and while Madden is in some sense broadly guilty of the same presentism—with a French king still ruling—there are subtle indications that the minister was embracing a new myth of the eighteenth century, a fallacy that is sometimes called "progress."

Madden writes that "few years are past, since we improv'd Astronomy by a true system, verified by demonstration, and founded Philosophy on actual experiments," and as with Francis Bacon in his 1626 *New Atlantis*, the author extrapolates from the scientific and technological shifts of the past generation to conjecture on the inevitable arc of change that could be assumed through the twentieth century. He lists past improvements in navigation, military technology, and printing, stating that "physicians found out either new drugs or specificks, or even the secrets of Anatomy, or the circulation of the blood." He discusses geographic discoveries, when "one half of the earth had found out the other," so that it might be assumed even greater marvels and wonders await: "The small compass of time, which all these great events have happen'd in, seems to promise vast improvements in the growing centuries." As such, "it will not appear surprising, and much less absurd, that such discoveries and improvements are allotted to our posterity."

While Madden made an implied promise of enumerating those discoveries and improvements, he left such conjectures to later prognosticators like Jules Verne and H. G. Wells, with Moore unfairly claiming that Madden "doesn't describe any technological advances or even try to imagine what the 20th century might be like," even while Madden does accurately predict the Suez Canal, Russia's rise to prominence, and the establishment of a Jewish homeland in Israel. Society is Madden's primary concern—*Memoirs of the Twentieth Century* largely functions as anti-Catholic polemic rather than a work of scientific prediction, more an exercise in warning about a Machiavellian Jesuitical pope pulling the levers of power in Rome and Paris, and a fantasy of the Ottoman Empire falling and being replaced with a deism-embracing Tatar aristocracy (for real . . .). Alkon writes that "by any criterion known to me," *Memoirs of the Twentieth Century* is "failed satire." He explains, "Madden's few palpable hits lose their force in a welter of tiresome religious satire and other incoherent attacks . . . miss their mark or hit their target too bluntly," which is why though we still read Swift, we've forgotten his younger contemporary. Regardless of Madden's failures in satire, Alkon emphasizes that *Memoirs of the Twentieth Century* remains exemplary because it is the first in that aforementioned genre—the novel of prognostication that is clearly not written in the prophetic mode and that expresses, however feebly, that those who will come after us will exist in a world different from that which we inhabit today.

Not just the prediction of events as in a Nostradamus, because events are simply *things that happen*, but Madden was able, however subtly and ham-handedly, to prognosticate cultural shifts as well. Arguably a more important task, for predicting that this-or-that person will be king or that this-or-that army will cross this-or-that border is one thing, and something whose exactitude is impressive, but it's also less important than reading the tea leaves of cultural change. The difference between a parlor trick and a policy brief. *Memoirs of the Twentieth Century* predicts our contemporary era as one of increasing authoritarianism and nationalism, and though Madden didn't foresee the eclipse of Christendom, our ideological polarization is credibly as sectarian as the Cold War détente he envisioned between Catholics and Protestants. Madden just extrapolated from his own era into the future; the twentieth and twenty-first centuries are just extensions of the authoritarianism, nationalism, and sectarianism that see their origins in earlier time periods. But that's precisely my point: fiction, particularly the novel, can be a finely wrought mechanism that puts an author's ear to the ground.

Which is what *Memoirs of the Twentieth Century* actually heralds—a new form of divination that might as well be called *novelmancy*. It makes a certain amount of sense that the development of novelmancy requires the development of the novel, and as the eighteenth century is the dawn (with a few antecedents) of that form, it's reasonable to expect that a Madden would sooner or later develop. We can disagree about the aesthetic or critical quality of Madden's book, we can disagree about how accurate any of his predictions are, but in a long line of predictive novels—of texts that are engines of prognostication from Jules Verne's *Paris in the Twentieth Century* to Aldous Huxley's *Brave New World*—*Memoirs of the Twentieth Century* is the first example of novelmancy. While

I'd avoid claiming anything overly occult for novelmancy beyond the occultism that I ascribe to all literary production, I'd imagine what's most fair to say about novelmancy as a methodology is that it's a manner in which authors of a certain sensitivity, awareness, and prescience are able to synthesize either consciously or unconsciously the trends, beliefs, personalities, movements, and shifts of an era to derive conclusions about what a likely future may be. Therefore, if one author can derive a certain understanding of what the future may herald, what would a reading of several texts that make prognostications tell us about what our likely fate may be?

As part of this argument's theoretical scaffolding, it's worth considering briefly what the "history of the future" is, for part of novelmancy's innovation rests on the ways in which the early modern period derived a new understanding of historical progress. If the novel is a modern literary form, emphasizing individuality and interiority in a manner that previous genres could not, then it also largely reflects a differing understanding of the arc of history as well, an understanding that simultaneously developed alongside the novel. Walter Benjamin writes in his 1940 "Theses on the Philosophy of History" that "there is a secret agreement between past generations and the present one. Our coming was expected on earth," and indeed, novelmancy is one clause in that agreement, though one that connects our current generation to future ones. Where novelmancy differs from more antique methods of divination (beyond any claims to its objective empiricism) is that it doesn't merely predict *events*—it's not an issue of Joseph interpreting Pharaoh's dreams of lean and fat cows, of withered grain, and imagining feasts and famines. Rather, novelmancy is *modern*, and as such, it has a modern understanding of time and history. Novelmancy is done with the understanding that the present is fundamentally different from the past and that the future will be different from the present.

So enmeshed are we in ideologies of progress that it can be sobering to consider that such a concept has a history. Consider medieval and Renaissance depictions of biblical scenes, all of those paintings of the crucifixion in which Lombard or Breton aristocracy dwell in the background watching the events of Golgotha. Think of all of those depictions of scenes from the Hebrew Scriptures, Judith wearing the clothing of a Renaissance matron, David depicted as an Italian youth. In the fifteenth-century French painter André d'Ypres's *The Crucifixion*, which hangs in the Getty Museum, the sacrifice at Calvary presents Christ and the two condemned men surrounded not by first-century Jewish mourners dressed for the Levant but by French aristocrats. Longinus upon horseback looks not like a legionnaire with his spear but like a Saracen in rich, gold-threaded robes. Behind the hill is not the sunbaked sandstone of Herod's Temple but a European gothic castle as if from a fairy tale. In medieval tapestry and illuminated manuscript, King Solomon is depicted not as a Judean but as a European monarch; when the Virgin Mary is presented, it's not as a woman of ancient Judea but as a French, or Italian, or German maiden. There are reasons for representing biblical scenes with your contemporaries, ranging from the same reasons why contemporary audiences enjoy hackneyed Shakespeare adaptations to an implicit typological argument that emphasizes divine eternity and the present's inevitable presence in a past where all of time can be collapsed into God's singularity. A more prosaic reason as well—the artists who made those depictions *might not have considered how the past looked different from their present.*

Under the influence of Renaissance humanism in fourteenth- and fifteenth-century Italy, which was to be distilled and dispersed through the rest of Europe in subsequent generations, there was an understanding that developed that the past was a foreign country. Suddenly, there was an awareness that previous generations neither looked like us nor lived like us nor perhaps even thought like us—what the Whiggish historian Herbert Butterfield described in his 1949 *The Origins of Modern Science* as being that the "men of the Renaissance were in a peculiar situation. . . . What they saw behind them . . . were the peaks of classical antiquity . . . the summit of human reason." Such is a perspective on the centuries of the Renaissance derived from the nineteenth-century Swiss historian Jacob Burckhardt's triumphalist view, holding that this was an era in which a rediscovery of pagan and classical learning reinvigorated the present and that this was, in part, made possible by considering all those Greek and Roman antiquities—those monumental ruins, those manuscripts depicting a past so different from the present—and realizing that *things have changed*. We can perhaps question the accuracy of this model. There are good reasons to. But something undeniable that for whatever the reason, women and men began to imagine distant generations as not simply being our partners.

Appropriately enough, considering the theme of this essay, examine Rembrandt's painting *Belshazzar's Feast*, made between 1635 and 1638 and now displayed in the National Gallery of London, which presents the scene from Daniel in which the hand of God writes upon the wall a prophetic warning to the Babylonian king Nebuchadnezzar. When Rembrandt imagines the monarch, he is depicted not as a Low Country burgher but as a Chaldean ruler; Nebuchadnezzar wears not a crown or tiara but a turban. God's hand writes not in Latin letters or in Dutch but rather in Hebrew letters and an Aramaic that Rembrandt learned from his friend Rabbi Menasseh ben Israel. Perhaps there are inaccuracies here; perhaps there is a problematic Orientalism. But Rembrandt's imagining attempts to move beyond Holland in the seventeenth century; whether it falls short or not, he gestures toward verisimilitude. A dispatch from the ongoing Renaissance discovery of the past—a recognition that when we look to previous centuries, there is a heterogeneity of time.

If the Renaissance was the era in which the past was discovered, then the Enlightenment was when the future was found. During the eighteenth century, the heterogeneity of time that had been previously extended to the past was projected into the future. The discovery that the past was radically different from the present was logically extrapolated into the inevitable conclusion that the future would also be different from the present, an understanding that is indicated in Madden's novel. While it's true that *Memoirs of the Twentieth Century* lacks the full imaginative possibility of later speculative fiction, it's the genesis of Anglophone depictions of a future that is still *different* from the present in which it was written, no matter how marginal that difference may be. Such a progressive view of the arc of history, emerging right at the time that the novel developed as a form, inevitably leads to the possibility of novelistic speculative fiction and, thus, the methodology I've called novelmancy. When reading *Memoirs of the Twentieth Century*, what's notable is not the accuracy or the lack thereof. What's notable is that Madden sat down in the early eighteenth century and tried to envision 1997, that he tried to imagine 1998. That in his mind, he attempted to form a picture of *us*, for Madden knew that we would not be like him—at least, not exactly.

Memoirs of the Twentieth Century may be a novel prognostication, but it inaugurated endless examples. I've mentioned antecedents, a notable one being Bacon's *New Atlantis*. Technically a protonovel within the utopian genre, Bacon imagines a perfect island society named Bensalem, where a priesthood of scientists at an institution called Solomon's House derived technologies ranging from synthetic plastics to organ transplants. Though easily categorized as nascent speculative fiction, *New Atlantis* isn't quite the novel of prognostication that *Memoirs of the Twentieth Century* is, even if Bacon's hypotheses about technology are far more prescient, simply because Bacon identifies such innovations not with the future but rather with an imagined land in his own present. Novels of prognostication that followed Madden are numerous, arguably the mainstay of science fiction, with a range of predictions from Mary Shelley's postapocalyptic 1826 *The Last Man* to Verne's 1863 *Paris in the Twentieth Century* (which predicted both alternative energy and the internet) to Edward Bellamy's 1888 utopian socialist *Looking Backward: 2000–1887*—not to speak of the more obvious examples of George Orwell's *1984* and Aldous Huxley's *Brave New World*. These novels are a sampling of thousands of predictive speculative fiction texts, giving a sense of the contradictory visions that motivate the very form.

Imagining the future isn't the only criterion that defines science fiction, but it's perhaps the most obvious. Margaret Atwood observes in her critical anthology *In Other Worlds: SF and the Human Imagination* that "if your writing about the future isn't forecast journalism, it will most likely be something people will call either science fiction or speculative fiction." With a humility concerning science fiction's efficacy as a diagnostic tool, Atwood writes that the "future can never be truly predicted because there are too many variables." And, it might be added, all of these conflicting novels can't all be correct; Bellamy's future utopia can't exist alongside Shelley's apocalyptic one. Not in spite of that fact, but precisely because of it, Atwood holds that "you can . . . dip into the present, which contains the seeds of what might become the future." Atwood is correct—no single novel can accurately predict the future in its totality. She is also right that when we say that these novels contain prognostications, that they are ideally based on a sensitive reading and expansion of the present into the future. Madden's was but one voice, and most of what he predicted was wrong. Still, his was a mind sensitive enough to extrapolate certain trends forward, with at least some accuracy.

What if you didn't rely on one novel but instead took a collection of novels to extrapolate forward what a likely future may be as dependent on a given present? What if you harnessed the collective, crowdsourced popularity of certain futurist narratives in our present? Assuming that there was a particular power in having all of those sensitive, subtle, empathetic authors' predictions pooled together in the same way a bunch of computers can be linked into an array. The contours of this argument are that no particular author has any exact prescience, but if certain literary trends emerge in how we imagine the future, it could be claimed that a wide enough variety of authors are picking up on particular trends; thus we might surmise that if certain conditions in our present continue, we can anticipate particular futures.

Literary critic Franco Moretti in *Distant Reading* conceives of a method of literary critical analysis that doesn't rely on the hermetic exegesis that defines traditional New Critical close reading but rather treats the mass of literary texts as a field to be mathematically analyzed for patterns. He writes that for distant reading, often accomplished through computational analysis, the point is to "focus on units that are much smaller or much larger than the text: devices, themes, tropes—or genres and systems." Using Moretti's logic to think about novels of prognostication, what if a "distant reading" of speculative fiction texts would aid in helping us, in some sense, "predict" the likely future based on our current moment? Where certain divergent book plots can be excluded, but what is important is what the larger number of books that talk about the future happen to be saying about those coming decades and centuries. The pooling of all those creative, empathetic, imaginative resources into a collective act of prognostication. The psychoanalyzing of literature's body communal. The use of our culture's literary corpus as the raw material in calculating an expected teleology.

Such an approach bears a similarity to the mathematical sociology that defines "psychohistory" in Isaac Asimov's Foundation trilogy. In that series of novels, Asimov imagines a science that develops among the scholars of a galactic empire that is able to identify and analyze all cultural and social trends so as to predict the future with exactitude. As a character says in the first book of that series, "Psychohistory is a statistical science and cannot predict the future of a single man with any accuracy," and so it is with novelmancy. Almost a "Mass Algorithmic Zeitgeist Reading," if you will. This is not reading tea leaves but rather guessing at what exactly the zeitgeist of our era might have in store for us. Furthermore, the future is always changing as the arrow of time moves forward, and the year 2050 is not the same in 2000 as it was in 1950—the future looks very different to Madden than it does to Bellamy than it would to Huxley. This is not to say that any were wrong, for the future is a fickle thing. Unlike the past, the future is always shifting, always changing, always mercurial. She is a variable thing, for there is an infinite number of futures. An undulating liquid field of pure potentiality. Which one of those possibilities is the most likely during a given present is always changing, and it's the task of novelmancy to see what vibrations all of those authorial ears to the ground happen to be picking up.

What exactly is the history of our future as it is right now? While not personally privy to the most sophisticated of computational technologies, a bit of fiddling around on the Ngram Viewer program available for free at Google can give you an idea of the occurrence of particular words and combination of words across twenty million books printed between 1500 and 2000, and thus glimmers of what occupied the mass of humanity during particular years. For example, overall instances of the word *utopia* spiked between 1500 and 1550, when utopian romances would have made up a significant percentage of the literature then being produced, with a smaller spike in the mid-seventeenth century, and then an immediate decline only to inch slowly with an upward slope over the course of the following centuries, albeit never gaining those enthusiastic heights that greeted its coinage as a term in the Renaissance. By contrast, instances of the word *apocalypse*, though there are some predictably early modern spikes when millennialism was in theological vogue, actually hits its height of popularity toward the year 2000 and has been climbing ever since. Get out your literary barometer, turn on your novelistic radar. You're not imagining that pressure; the beeping isn't just in your head. Put your ear to the ground and listen to the horseman galloping. Your nightmares of apocalypse aren't just your own; it's something that we've all been dreaming together.

Critic Fredric Jameson wrote in *The Seeds of Time* that it's "easier to imagine the end of the world than the end of capitalism," and as we face ecological calamity brought about by our economic totalism, it's worth considering what anecdotal novelmancy tells us, the ways that literary prognostication seems to herald that apocalypse. Thinking about Jameson's adage, when was the last era that really imagined the possibility of future social arrangements free of capitalist exploitation? When was the socialist moment last embraced by novel prognosticators? Bellamy's utopia seems distant; we've rather traded dreams for nightmares or our authors (with antenna up) have noted the likelihood of the latter rather than the former. The last great utopian work of speculative fiction was the *Star Trek* franchise, the last bit of noncapitalist imagining that sees humanity surviving into a postscarcity world. Otherwise, drawing from Orwell, Huxley, and Atwood, the collective imagination of our speculative fiction writers has not welcomed utopia but warned of dystopia.

If Gene Roddenberry's tea leaves saw something hopeful in the postwar consensus, in the positivism of technological progress celebrated in the mid-twentieth century, then the tea leaves seem to say something different today. More Cormac McCarthy's *The Road*, Robert Kirkman's *The Walking Dead*, and Stephen King's *The Stand* in our discontented age of late capitalism. If there is a causal relationship between literature and reality, some sort of symbiosis whereby novels don't merely predict but in some sense shape, then there becomes a very real concern about what our dreams and nightmares might be. Perhaps the din of ecological apocalypse is too loud, its heat vapors too scorching. If there is any charged potentiality in imagining a better world, if there is any significance in dreaming into reality some forgotten utopian promise, now is the moment for it. Maybe the last juncture when such dreams are even possible, before they're forever precluded in apocalyptic finality. We must dream for our survival, for whether or not it's possible to collectively imagine a better world into existence, we must have the blind faith that prays that we can.

17

Interiority Combustion Engine

> And I'm writing a novel
> because it's never been done before.
> —Father John Misty (2012)

Ann Radcliffe's 1794 best-selling novel *The Mysteries of Udolpho*, containing as it does all of the stereotypical accoutrement of its gothic genre, from perfidious Italian counts to dark castles, also has a scene that indicates the very means by which the book may have found itself commonly read among an enthused eighteenth-century audience. Radcliffe's virtuous and noble protagonist, Emily St. Aubert, reflects on how her suitor, Valancourt, would often read aloud to her from dog-eared books, the author writing that the character "sat and worked, while he conversed or read; and she now well remembered . . . he used to repeat some of the sublimest passages of their favourite authors; how often he would pause to

211

admire with her their excellence, and with what tender delight he would listen to her remarks." For Emily and Valancourt, reading is a social activity that happens between companions, not simply a static, locked-away silence happening between covers.

At times in *The Mysteries of Udolpho*, Emily found herself in domestic situations not dissimilar to that of her literary forerunner, the titular character of Samuel Richardson's 1740 *Pamela; or, Virtue Rewarded*. Both Emily and Pamela are ingenues pursued by worldly men, both are figured as exemplars of feminine virtue, and as the former thrilled at being read aloud to, millions of readers thrilled at reading the story of the latter aloud. The nineteenth-century British astronomer and botanist Sir John Herschel recounted that he'd been told by an inhabitant of Windsor that in 1777, the village blacksmith had "got hold of Richardson's novel . . . and used to read it aloud in the long summer evenings, seated on his anvil, and never failed to have a large and attentive audience."

Scholar Abigail Williams in *The Social Life of Books: Reading Together in the Eighteenth-Century Home* explains how "people shared their literature in very different ways: reading books together as a sedative, a performance, an accompaniment to handiwork, a means of whiling away a journey or a long dark evening." The rise of the vernacular, the proliferation of printed books, and the development of more portable ones are all causes of increased individual reading, but while in the eighteenth century "reading could be about isolation and retreat," it could also still be about "the foundation of sociable interaction." Emily and Valancourt read not just to learn or be entertained, or to meditate and reflect, but rather as something shared audibly and publicly. What must be understood is that such a scene is not Radcliffe's affectation but reportage on how novels were often consumed.

The Mysteries of Udolpho is a youthful example of the "English novel," predated by Daniel Defoe's 1719 *Robinson Crusoe*, or Aphra

Behn's 1688 *Oroonoko*, or even earlier curios such as William Baldwin's bizarre 1561 *Beware the Cat* (with, of course, even earlier continental antecedents). But in England, Richardson's *Pamela* marks the moment when the very literary form became a genuine writerly possibility and not just an experimental mutation of older romances. That doorstop of an epistolary, which for the contemporary reader comes across as exemplifying the dry, slow, boring eighteenth-century affectation of synthesizing Puritan scolding with the poor man's version of titillation (despite Richardson's objective talents), was phenomenally successful when it was serially released.

Pamela is the sort of book with prose best described as purple, where characters can declare that they will "bear any thing you can inflict upon me with Patience, even to the laying down of my Life, to shew my Obedience to you in other Cases; but I cannot be patient, I cannot be passive, when my Virtue is at Stake!" Richardson's prose is a cacophony of exclamation and anaphora. Such language (and narrative) lends itself to a certain sociability, and as urbane twenty-first-century television viewers organized watch parties for the finales of *Breaking Bad* and *Mad Men* (our most novelistic of television entertainments), so too did Richardson's readers approach *Pamela* in a spirit of neighborly communion. Herschel explained that during happy scenes of *Pamela*, its reader's audience was "so delighted as to raise a great shout, and procuring the church keys, actually set the parish bells ringing." We may think of reading novels as exercises in isolation, either where the site of study must be quiet and singular or where the psychological space of imagination is within our mind's interior, but in the eighteenth century, the novel was often as social as ancient Greek drama or a modern Hollywood movie.

Novels had, of course, been written before; there is a tired parlor game of identifying what protracted narrative of prose fiction is "novelish" enough to qualify as the first, be it Miguel de Cervantes's

1605 *Don Quixote*, Murasaki Shikibu's eleventh-century *The Tale of Genji*, or Apuleius's second-century *The Golden Ass*. What's clear is that the Whig historiography that classifies the novel as a firmly early modern invention is woefully inadequate, as Steven Moore writes in his brilliant *The Novel: An Alternative History, Beginnings to 1600*. Most earlier examples of the form, Moore writes, "have been the victims of antiquated nomenclature." Moore provides ample evidence for hundreds, arguably thousands, of texts that are centuries if not millennia older than Cervantes and could be credibly called "novels."

Yet propriety must force us to admit that it was in the seventeenth and eighteenth centuries that the mode moved from the periphery to the center, forever supplanting the epic poem as the most exulted type of "serious literature." Helpful here to keep in mind Raymond Williams's terminology introduced in *Marxism and Literature*, where the critic explicated the difference between the culturally "dominant, residual, and emergent." Moore's examples of Akkadian or Latin prose aside, the novel as a literary form was emergent for a very long time and has been dominant for a few comparatively short centuries, and in the twenty-first century, we're living in its long decline. All of these matters have certain implications, ones that are personal, social, economic, psychological, and even metaphysical and theological.

Because if the reading of novels was social in the era that Williams describes, such an activity is substantially less so in the twenty-first century. Today, the public reading of literature remains that of dramatic performance. Novels are barely read aloud at all, certainly not in their entirety, with the exception of audiobooks, where the discerning listener can encounter Nick Offerman giving a manly take on Mark Twain's *The Adventures of Huckleberry Finn* or Alan Cumming narrating Bram Stoker's *Dracula* in his urbane,

Scottish brogue. Audiobooks may be the descendants of Windsor's Richardson-loving blacksmith, but they lack in the aleatory, participatory element embodied by those earlier performances.

Reading novels aloud is different when experienced through your iPhone rather than in a village square, with contemporary live recitations limited to excerpts as read by the author (where the audience members are normally on their phones, engaged with a different form of social communion) or the performance of books to children. Despite some attempts to revive the lost art of reading novels aloud, such as the New Bedford Whaling Museum's annual marathon for Herman Melville's *Moby-Dick*; Harvard's Houghton Library's marathon of Mary Shelley's *Frankenstein* this past Halloween in honor of that book's two hundredth anniversary; and of course, Dublin's celebrated Bloomsday revels, novels in the twenty-first century are experienced either in the static confines of the audiobook or in that isolating room from which the form has most thrived—that of the individual head.

Public reading in past centuries had several material causes, from the relative rarity and expense of books, to higher rates of illiteracy, to the need to preserve the candles by which books were to be read. Williams's study emphasizes that the transition from an oral to a literate culture was not seamless, and while we'd do well to remember that the novel's ascendance doesn't clearly demark a fluid motion from one age to the next, there is still much truth in acknowledging the conventional perspective that sees the novel's reign as marking a new individualism, a new singularity, a new isolation, a new privacy, and a new interiority. That final concept, related as it is to all of those I listed before it, goes not uncontested. *Interiority* is perhaps a wooly theoretical term, one of those phrases bandied about in graduate seminars with more conviction than definition, and yet it still offers us a helpful way to parse what makes the novel, well, *novel*. Generally, the word is used to mean some nebulous "inwardness" in the mimetic depiction of the characters, the sense that when we read about Madame Bovary or David Copperfield, these are beings that in some mysterious way display an inner life, a subjectivity, a consciousness.

Sometimes it's taken as a critical truism that the novel is the preeminent means of representing personal consciousness, that where the static surface representations of epic poetry and premodern drama display human beings as broad types, it's only with these novel engines of interiority that literature becomes truly capable of displaying individual subjectivity in all of its complexity. Homer's Achilles, in short, seems much less real than Jane Austen's Emma. Erich Auerbach writes in *Mimesis: The Representation of Reality in Western Literature* that the "basic impulse of the Homeric style . . . [is] to represent phenomena in a fully externalized form, visible and palpable in all their parts."

Reading the *Iliad* and the *Odyssey*—or Virgil's *Aeneid*, for that matter—leads one to observe that regarding psychology, "nothing must remain hidden and unexpressed," as the editors of *N+1* write. By way of contrast, they argue that the "novel is unexcelled at one thing only: the creation of interiority, or inwardness. . . . No better instrument than prose fiction was ever developed" for that purpose. Moore's correction of the record concerning the genealogy of the form may be an important one, but even if novels (of a type) have been written into deep antiquity, they didn't become omnipresent until relatively recently, and there are certain conclusions that must be teased out concerning interiority, especially as the novel perhaps once again retreats to the margins.

Interpreted in one way, we could see the public reading depicted in Radcliffe and Richardson as a residual holdover from performative literature, the early modern public not yet fully congruent with the interiority exemplified by the novel as a form. The interiority of the novel cannot be separated from the material conditions that regulated the relationship between the individual and the social during this time period, for if the novel has come to be anything, in both its writing and reading, then it is the form that exemplifies Virginia Woolf's defense of a "room of one's own." Novels are indicative of the architecture of privacy; I'd suggest that it's not a mistake that the novel's ascendance is simultaneous with developments like separate hallways in seventeenth-century homes or the emergence of widespread private bedrooms from that same century. The technology of the printed codex itself facilitated a type of interiority—so much so that it's sometimes unclear when we speak of that term if we mean its representation in literature or its actual existence within human experience.

Critical consensus concerning Renaissance humanism's discovery of the individual waxes and wanes; if you've ever listened to a rightly chagrined medievalist react to Harold Bloom's assertion that William Shakespeare invented the human, you'll get a sense of the regard in which scholars hold that old-fashioned triumphalist view claiming that individualism is a Renaissance development. If novels are both representations of and evidence for interiority, then Moore's point that Apuleius depicts an inner life every bit as complex as those of Gustave Flaubert should disavow us of the fallacy that the ancients were merely sleepwalking through history. But here again, Raymond Williams's critical terminology becomes helpful, for an argument could be proffered that while interiority and intersubjectivity were always phenomenological states humans had access too, they were in many cases only emergent with Renaissance individualism.

The consciousness of the unitary narrator (whether of the first or third person) is thus an aesthetic reflection of René Descartes's

"Cogito"; for that matter, it's an aesthetic reflection of the fact that many people finally had rooms of their own to laugh, cry, sigh, sleep, fart, and fuck in, not to mention to read and write in. Conditions of privacy inculcated conditions of interiority so that psychology could become an internal and not just a social affair, with the novel as both the dominant literary expression of that reality as well as a reciprocal cause of that reality. Our lips were simply still moving for a few centuries before we realized we could actually hear those words on the page within our own heads. In the novel, there is the mimicry of consciousness, an enshrinement of ambiguity, and the rapture of negative capability.

If interiority is a concept long emergent, alongside its fullest expression in the form of the novel, then we can rather easily trace its evolutionary twists and turns. Consider that silent reading was long regarded as an aberration, the idea that words could mysteriously exist in your head without an equivalent speech act stretching the credulity of most people. Observing Ambrose of Milan in the fourth century, and Augustine would write in his *Confessions* that when the saint read, "his eyes ran over the columns of writing and his heart searched out the meaning, but his voice and his tongue were at rest. . . . I have seen him reading silently, never in fact otherwise. I would sit for a long time in silence, not daring to disturb . . . and then go on my way," as translated by Eduard Norden.

Augustine asked himself "why he read in this way." Ambrose, it would seem, had constructed an imaginative kingdom within his own skull, not listening to his mouth murmur words under his own breath but rather reading as anyone on a flight from JFK to Heathrow or on the Q Train ideally does—quietly and internally. Arresting to learn that the ancients, as complex as their thought was, could be flummoxed by something we take as second nature, and hard to conclude that the interiority of the novel's form has nothing to do with our own experience of consciousness, an explanation for the relative dearth of novels before the early modern period. Envision the scriptorium of an Irish monastery during the Middle Ages, the monks copying out those very words from *Confessions*, the stone hall containing the gentle din of dozens of calligraphers mumbling those words aloud to themselves.

Alberto Manguel in *A History of Reading* writes that "until well into the Middle Ages, writers assumed that their readers would hear rather than simply see the text, much as they themselves spoke their word out loud as they composed them." Starting in the seventh century, it was those same Irish monks who grew tired of the *scriptio continua* of transcribing all writing with no concern for the spaces between words (which, incidentally, made silent reading almost impossible, save for the prodigious) and who resuscitated the idea of punctuation from its forgotten origins with an Alexandrian librarian of the third century BCE named Aristophanes. Partially inspired by musical notation, the Middle Ages would see the development of punctuation marks like the *punctus elevatus*, the *punctus versus*, and the question mark's ancestor, the *punctus interrogatives*. Manguel quotes Saint Isaac of Syria, who drew the connection between punctuation and interiority, of the practice of silence. Isaac claims, "I practice silence" in reading so that the verses and prayers "should fill me with delight." He continues by explaining silent, solitary reading "as in a dream, I enter a state when my senses and thoughts are concentrated . . . the turmoil of memories is stilled in my heart, ceaseless waves of joy are sent me by inner thoughts . . . suddenly arising to delight my heart" so that in the sixth century, a monk in Nineveh could describe the rare experience of interior reading that, unless you're declaring this to some startled passenger on a crosstown bus, you're doing right now.

By the fifteenth century, commas, colons, dashes, periods, and a whole host of diacritical marks were invented or evolved to facilitate silent reading, in part because of the invention of the printing press, with the semicolon making a late 1494 appearance in the Venice print shop of the great Aldus Manutius. A different version of this essay spends time arguing, without irony, that the semicolon in and of itself has the pathos of a great novel, a space carved out for a pause in which whole narratives can be implied, punctuation as a microcosm of reality with room enough to contain an entire little universe. Without conjecture as to whether punctuation facilitated interiority or interiority necessitated punctuation, I will simply observe that the development of such "weird little marks," as Cormac McCarthy calls them in a private letter to an editor, evidences that reading was moving from audible to silent, from communal to private, even if sometimes, readers like a certain Windsor blacksmith felt the spirit move them to declare novels aloud.

A whole raft of theorizing remains to be done on the ways in which a consensus on both how to correctly punctuate sentences and how to spell words triggered a transition from medieval Aristotelian scholasticism to Renaissance Platonist humanism, on the ways in which caring about the correct arrangement of letters signals an assault on phonocentrism or a valorization of the idea of written language. Jacques Derrida writes in *Of Grammatology* that there is a historical privileging of oral communication so that writing is commonly understood as a "servile instrument of speech dreaming of its plentitude and its self-presence." I'm curious how much of that sense of speech being privileged over the written word was altered in the era when book printers decided that spelling had to have some uniformity?

Keith Houston explains in *Shady Characters: The Secret Life of Punctuation, Symbols, and Other Typographical Marks* that "before the advent of the printing press, the imprecision of manual copying meant that punctuation evolved as it passed from scribe to scribe," but by 1640, the poet and dramatist Ben Jonson's *English Grammar* built on two centuries of humanism to advocate for punctuation as not just a means of facilitating oratory but, in conveying the proper interpretation of a work based on the author's individual intent, a seeming victory in the battle between speech and writing. Curious, but outside of the scope of this essay, other than to obverse that it was telling that the technology of Johannes Gutenberg's printing press standardized punctuation and eventually orthography, for regardless of its origin, no account of interiority can ignore technology.

Without venturing as to the causal relationships, and always personally loath to reduce explanations to mere material conditions, the emergence of spaces between words, punctuation, and uniform spelling is merely given as evidence for the ascendancy of silent reading and, in turn, the idea that silent reading is evidence of interiority's growing importance, not just in its literary depictions, but in reality as well. Manguel describes this reality, where women and men could "exist in interior space. . . . And the text itself, protected from outsiders by its covers, became the reader's own possession, the reader's intimate knowledge, whether in the busy scriptorium, the market-place or the home."

I'd suggest that a useful vocabulary for talking about the emergence of such subjectivity is something I call the "interiority axis." By this schema, I'd propose that we have to understand that concerning the rise and fall of interiority, there is an intrinsic connection among literary form, the idea of the author, the idea of the narrator, and the idea of the reader. Premodern literature, often oral in both composition and reproduction, favored the poetic over prose, and there has never been a novel written and recited as only oral literature. In such circumstances, the author has little authority, and the work is rather a collaborative social act, just as the consciousness of the narrator is more collective than individual. Such a model of authorship endured well into the early modern period as a type of residual culture, as exemplified in moribund forms such as the commonplace book, a type of individual compendium whereby readers would mix and match unstable texts that moved them, sometimes writing new endings to old stories. Commonplace books didn't necessarily respect the authorial intention of some individual creator; rather, it was a form that relished in the collaborative nature of literature across individuals. Commonplace books were a type of open-source technology.

What the novel signals is the ascension of a form that most fully encapsulates subjectivity and signals the parallel emergence of individualism in all of its glory, excess, and detriment. The novel as a written form of literature fixes in relationship to one another the concept of the author as primogeniture of literature, the authority of the narrative voice, and silent reading. All aspects of the interiority axis are in some way related to one another, so the shift of any one of these concepts from an emergent into a dominant discourse must by necessity affect the rest. Novels are defined not just by length, or form, or subject but by the model of how we understand their creation and consumption, by how we write and read them, and where we identify the voice that narrates them as ultimately coming from. Bards no longer sing epics; rather, disembodied voices within our own heads weave tremendously complex fictions, worlds born from their own imaginative space, creating the ability by which you can experience the individual consciousness of another person and thus marking the novel as the most tremendous engine for empathy yet conceived.

But in inculcating this experience of an atomistic consciousness as well as expressing it, the novel reflects a final category along the interiority axis, which is a theological one. No coincidence in the reality that the author, as complete master of a novel's narrative, bears such a striking resemblance to the emerging Protestant God, with his complete sovereignty and radical freedom at the expense of all of his creatures' individual agencies. Such is my extension of Joseph Bottum's argument in *Books & Culture: A*

Christian Review that the "novel was an art form—*the* art form—of the modern Protestant West." True enough that there are scores of antecedents long before the eighteenth century, and indeed, the book most commonly proffered as the first novel was by a Spanish Catholic (even if occasionally imprisoned by the Inquisition). Yet what shifts the novel as a form from being perennially emergent to finally dominant is a model of individuality in the form of the supremely sovereign Protestant God, who controls everything down to the minutest detail and leaves nothing up to fortune as he uses the writing workshop tool known as double predestination. The novel as a form was ultimately the result of Protestantism and positivism, its actual fathers being John Calvin and Isaac Newton, both independent codevelopers of an orderly universe governed by deterministic rules, the exact model by which the novel understands itself.

Michael McKeon in *The Origins of the English Novel, 1600–1700* notes that the form is "coextensive with the early modern secularization crisis," yet secularization is simply another name for a specific type of Protestant heresy. The novel is a product of the Reformation because every category of the interiority axis for literature produced under its aegis is reciprocal so that an absolute God implies an absolute author implies a solitary narrative voice implies a private reader. The novel's metaphysical basis is such that we conceive of the author as a type of God, in complete control over every detail of plot and character, so that even the multiplicity of voices implied by collaborative writing, by the voice reading the book aloud, is rather eliminated in favor of the single voice of the Lord alone in your head. As Richardson would declare in *Pamela*, "O! what a Godlike power!"

It's as if the social nature of oral literature was a cacophony of pagan gods eliminated in favor of the monotheistic, omnipresent, and omniscient God of the author. Such a metaphysic is, of course, older than Protestantism, being ultimately Hebraic in origin, with Auerbach writing in his study *Mimesis* that in contrast to the Homeric aesthetic, the Jewish ethos was such that God was "not fixed in form and content, and was alone; his lack of form, his lack of local habitation, his singleness, was in the end not only maintained but developed" so that by the time the novel is in its ascendancy, we discover that the third-person omniscient voice narrates the very language of the divine. As the Lord is alone, so is the silent reader, enraptured by the powers of the author.

Such a perspective is glorious in its way, for in privacy, there is the possibility of regenerative self-creation. Humans may be limited by God's sovereignty, but in the creation of a novel, every author is offered the Faustian illusion of being a deity, as is every reader who joins them in the story. In the ersatz Calvinism offered by the novel, both author and reader can experience the consciousness of being God, for though liberty is precluded by that theology, there is the most radical of freedom in the ability to flit between the consciousness of various people, to experience a multitude of minds, to be able to see the world from a potentially infinite number of eyes. In a Calvinist universe, the only freedom is to become God, and the novel was the technology developed to help women and men do this. But there can also be a profound loneliness in this solipsism, a rarefied state that's impossible if you're among that audience listening to a reader intone words aloud.

Bottum writes that as the "main strength of established Protestant Christendom began to fail in the United States in recent decades, so did the cultural importance of the novel." Friedrich Nietzsche killed God in 1882, Roland Barthes killed the author less than a century later in 1967, and now it seems as if the reader is on life support. I come not to burn the novel but to praise her, for it seems that she has become more and more residual. The interiority axis that was dominant for the past few centuries is waning so that though no variety of human consciousness can ever fully dim, our models of subjectivity, privacy, individualism, and agency still seem to be in eclipse. Novels will always be written, of course; after all, somebody is still writing epic poems as well.

Such is the case that the interiority axis is once again altered by material conditions, by technology, as the solitary reader is replaced by the frantic chorus of the internet. The Calvinist-Newtonian God faces deicide by polytheistic collaborations of open-source digital literature, and the novel itself is now a million tweeted fragments. If the metaphysical implications of the novel are privacy, then the emergent forms of our new interiority axis return us, for better and worse, to sitting in a crowd listening to a delivered story—though this time, our shouting at the speaker is instrumental to the development of that plot. This is what Walter Ong in *Rhetoric, Romance, and Technology: Studies in the Interaction of Expression and Culture* referred to as the "secondary orality." In 1971, well before a public internet, Ong was able to describe communication that would depart from the "individualized introversion of the age of writing, print, and rationalism." What new visions may this postsecularity promise, what new enchantments, what rich paganism enabled by technology? What prayers crafted by crowdsource, by algorithm, by artificial intelligence? God is dead, as is the author, as is the reader so that now we are all once again squabbling gods.

18

Jay Gatsby Is Real

It is a truth universally acknowledged that a reader in possession of a novel with a distinctive voice often finds the very substance of her thought affected by that book's characters as if they were real. Yet in my younger and more vulnerable years, an English professor gave me some advice that I've been turning over in my mind ever since. "Whenever you feel like asking if fictional characters are 'real,'" he told me, "just remember that fiction is by definition not real and that the voice of a compelling character is an illusion and no more. Whether formal or historical criticism, all literary theorists must remember this." And if you really want to hear about it, the first thing you'll want to know is if I still agree with that professor, and how lousy literary theory is, and all that Holden Caulfield kind of crap, but I don't feel like going into it.

Well, actually, I do feel a little like going into it. Anyone who has ever been immersed in a novel—still the greatest mechanism for experiencing the subjectivity of another mind that has ever been developed—has experienced the overwhelming sense that fictional characters are in some sense "real." Elizabeth Bennet, Nick Carraway, and Holden Caulfield may just be fictional creations of Jane Austen, F. Scott Fitzgerald, and J. D. Salinger, respectively, but if you've read (and reread) *Pride and Prejudice*, *The Great Gatsby*, and *The Catcher in the Rye*, you can be forgiven your momentary suspension of disbelief, maybe even your protracted suspension of disbelief, in sort of starting to think that those fictional characters are "real." Certain characters get into the very sinews of your body and synapses of your mind, even if they never actually existed as material people.

If you've had the same experience that I often have, dwelling in the interiority of a fictional character whose material existence is simply ink on a page, then you're not alone. A February 14, 2017, article in the *Guardian* reports that researchers at Durham University have discovered that close to a fifth of all readers report experiencing fictional characters as being real in their own lives, including "influencing the style and tone of their thoughts—or even speaking to them directly." Characters like Bennet, Carraway, and Caulfield "cross" into our lives, which includes hearing fictional people talking and imagining what their reactions might be to real events. Some readers even had the sense that these characters "had started to narrate [our] world," as if the reader were Will Ferrell in the 2006 film *Stranger than Fiction*.

Psychologist Charles Fernyhough, who directed the study, includes a wide variety of related phenomena under the term "experiential crossing." These include the hearing of voices and the feeling of other sensory details, readers feeling as if they know characters as friends, as well as the sense that a particularly vivid character has somehow inhabited the reader and that the fictional person is herself experiencing what the reader does. The study found that in turn, this affects the reader's interactions with the world, as if Elizabeth Bennet (who never actually lived) is in some way possessing a real person. An evocative perspective, and one that seems to acknowledge the spooky power of literature that many people seem to intuitively understand.

Not just as avid readers, but those of us who teach literature to students are more than familiar with the phenomenon. If you're a particularly lucky professor, then you might have students who concur with Fernyhough when he says, "Some of my most powerful reading experiences come when I feel that the author has tinkered with the software of my own brain." Certainly anyone who has chosen the not-particularly-lucrative career of the academic study of literature is familiar with Fernyhough's sentiment. And yet overconcentration on that aspect of literature is largely verboten in academic literary criticism, and we often extend that bias to our own students' writing about novels, lest they produce overly subjective reflections on how a novel made them feel, reminding them that questions about what characters "really" thought or what happens to Holden Caulfield after the last page is nonsense, since fiction does not correspond to the actual, objective world of physical reality. And yet we keep hearing those voices in our head.

Strangely, the study reminds me of a concept from Tibetan Buddhism called the *tulpa*. These are thought-created beings who develop an existence independent of their creators. The twentieth-century Belgian Buddhist writer Alexandra David-Néel explored this enigmatic belief in her book *Magic and Mystery in Tibet*, writing that "once the tulpa is endowed with enough vitality to be capable of playing the part of a real being, it tends to free itself from its maker's control." If *tulpas* are a useful concept, then what are Bennet, Carraway, and Caulfield but *tulpas*? And what would it mean if academic literary criticism began its own taxonomy of something as exotic as the *tulpa*?

It's hard to imagine what exactly that might look like, since the unspoken prohibition on focusing too much on the effect that nonexistent characters have on readers does make some sense. In this view, fictional characters don't actually exist, so how is it academically productive to talk about them as if they do? With some exceptions, since the New Critics, most formalist theorists take it as a given that the "intentional and affective fallacies" define the parameters of good literary interpretation. Historicist critics have broadened the sorts of questions we can ask to ones of cultural context. But metaphysics is largely bracketed out; asking in what sense a character is "real" or can interact with us has a bit of the glom of the occult about it—of the *tulpa*.

But maybe that's OK; maybe it's time for a bit of some occult literary criticism. If we lean too much on the text itself or the history surrounding it and view with suspicion questions of not just why people read but what happens when they do, then we threaten to ignore some of the central and most interesting questions that this weird thing called literature presents to us. Human beings are complex, multifaceted things; we're a collection of voices rather than a voice, a dialogue and not a monologue. All of us are choirs, not soloists. Some of these voices aren't even ours; some are the fictional creations of master authors. A reality-shattering book's power does not dissipate once it's closed. So we beat on, books against the current, born back ceaselessly into minds not our own.

19

The Varieties of Metafictional Experience

Whoever is in charge here?
—Daffy Duck, *Merrie Melodies* (1953)

Like all of us, Daffy Duck was perennially put upon by his creator. The sputtering, stuttering, rageful waterfowl's life was a morass of indignity, embarrassment, anxiety, and existential horror. Despite all of the humiliation Daffy had to contend with, the aquatic bird was perfectly willing to shake his wings at the unfair universe. As expertly delivered by voice artist Mel Blanc, Daffy could honk, "Who is responsible for this? I demand that you show yourself!" In animator Chuck Jones's brilliant and classic 1953 episode of *Merrie Melodies* titled "Duck Amuck," he presents Daffy as a veritable Everyduck, a sinner in the hands of a smart-assed illustrator. "Duck Amuck" has remained a canonical episode in the Warner Brothers cartoon catalog, its postmodern, metafictional experimentation heralded for its daring and cheekiness. Any account of what critics very loosely term "postmodern literature"—with its playfulness, its self-referentiality, and its breaking of the fourth wall—that only considers Italo Calvino, Jorge Luis Borges, Vladimir Nabokov, Paul Auster, and not Jones is only telling part of the metafictional story. Not for nothing, but two decades ago, "Duck Amuck" was added to the National Film Registry by the Library of Congress as an enduring piece of American culture.

Throughout the episode, Jones depicts increasingly absurd metafictional scenarios involving Daffy's sublime suffering. Jones first imagines Daffy as a swordsman in a *Three Musketeers* parody, only to have him wander into a shining, white abyss as the French Renaissance background fades away. "Look, Mac," Daffy asks, never one to let ontological terror impinge on his sense of personal justice, "what's going on here?" Jones wrenches the poor bird from the musketeer scenery to the blinding whiteness of the nothing-place, then to a bucolic pastoral, and finally to a paradisiacal Hawaiian beach. Daffy's admirable sense of his own integrity remains intact even throughout his torture. Pushed through multiple parallel universes, wrenched, torn, and jostled through several different realities, Daffy shouts, "All right, wise guy, where am I?"

But eventually, not even his own sense of identity is allowed to continue unaffected, as the God-animator turns him into a country-western singer who can only produce jarring sound effects from his guitar or as a transcendent paintbrush recolors Daffy blue. At one point, the animator's pencil impinges into Daffy's world, erasing him, negating him, making him nothing. Daffy's very being, his continued existence, depends on the whims of a cruel and capricious God; his is the world of Shakespeare's *King Lear*, where the Duke of Gloucester makes his plaintive cry, "As flies are to wanton boys are we to th' gods; / They kill us for their sport." Or at least, they erase us. Finally, like Job before the whirlwind, Daffy implores, "Who is responsible for this? I demand that you show yourself!" As the view pans upward, into that transcendent realm of paper and ink where the animator god dwells, it's revealed to be none other than the trickster par excellence, Bugs Bunny. "Ain't I a stinker?" the Lord saith.

Creation, it should be said, is not accomplished without a certain amount of violence. According to one perspective, we can think of Daffy's tussling with Bugs as being a variation on that venerable old Aristotelian narrative conflict of "man against God." If older literature was focused on the agon (as the Greeks put it) between a human and a deity, and modernist literature concerned itself with the conflict that resulted as people had to confront the reality of no God, then the wisdom goes that our postmodern moment is fascinated with the idea of a fictional character searching out their creator. According to narrative theorists, that branch of literary study that concerns itself with the structure and organization of story and plot (not synonyms, incidentally), such metafictional affectations are technically called *metalepsis.* H. Porter Abbott in his invaluable *The Cambridge Introduction to Narrative* explains that such tales involve a "violation of narrative levels" when a "storyworld" is "invaded by an entity or entities from another narrative level."

Metalepsis can be radical in its execution, as when an "extradiegetic narrator" (that means somebody from outside the story entirely) enters into the narrative, as in those narratives where an "author appears and starts quarreling with one of the characters," Abbott writes. We'll see that there are precedents for that sort of thing, but whether interpreted as gimmick or deep reflection on the idea of literature, the conceit that has a narrator enter into the narrative as if theophany is most often associated with something called, not always helpfully, "postmodernism." Whatever that much-maligned term might mean, in popular parlance, it has an association with self-referentiality, recursiveness, and metafictional playfulness (even if readers might find cleverness such as that exhausting). The term might as well be thought of as referring to our historical preponderance of literature that knows it is literature.

With just a bit of British disdain in his critique, the *New Yorker*'s literary critic James Wood writes in his pithy and helpful *How Fiction Works* that "postmodern novelists . . . like to remind us of the metafictionality of all things." Think of the crop of experimental novelists and short story writers from the 1960s, such as John Barth in his *Lost in the Funhouse*, where one story is to be cut out and turned into an actual Möbius strip; Robert Coover in the classic and disturbing short story "The Babysitter," in which a variety of potential realities and parallel histories exist simultaneously in the most mundane of suburban contexts; and John Fowles in *The French Lieutenant's Woman*, in which the author also supplies multiple "forking paths" to the story, and where the omniscient narrator occasionally appears as a character in the book. Added to this could be works where the actual first-person author themselves becomes a character, such as Auster's *New York Trilogy* or Philip Roth's *Operation Shylock* (among other works where he appears as a character). Not always just as a character, but as the creator, for if the French philosopher Roland Barthes killed off the idea of such a figure in his seminal 1967 essay "The Death of the Author," then much of the period's literature resurrected him. Wood notes that, perhaps in response to Barthes, "a certain kind of postmodern novelist . . . is always lecturing us: 'Remember, this character is just a character. I invented him.'" Metafiction is when fiction thinks about itself.

Confirming Wood's observation, Fowles's narrator writes in *The French Lieutenant's Woman*, "This story I am telling is all imagination.

These characters I create never existed outside my own mind. . . . The novelist stands next to God. He may not know all, yet he tries to pretend that he does." Metafictional literature like this is supposed to interrogate the idea of the author, the idea of the reader, the very idea of narrative. When the first line to Calvino's *If on a Winter's Night a Traveler* is "You are about to begin reading Italo Calvino's new novel, *If on a Winter's Night a Traveler*," it has been signaled that the narrative you're entering is supposed to be different from those weighty tomes of realism that supposedly dominated in previous centuries. If metalepsis is a favored gambit of our experimental novelists, then it's certainly omnipresent in our pop culture as well, beyond just "Duck Amuck."

A list of sitcoms that indulge the conceit would include *30 Rock*, *Community*, *Scrubs*, and *The Fresh Prince of Bel-Air*. The final example—which was, after all, already an experimental narrative about a wholesome rapper from West Philly named Will played by a wholesome rapper from West Philly named Will Smith—was a font of avant-garde fourth wall breaking deserving of Luigi Pirandello or Bertolt Brecht. Prime instances would include the season five episodes "Will's Misery," which depicts Carlton running through the live studio audience, and "Same Game, Next Season," in which Will asks, "If we so rich, why we can't afford no ceiling?" with the camera panning up to show the rafters and lights of the soundstage. Abbot writes that metafiction asks, "To what extent do narrative conventions come between us and the world?" which, in its playfulness, is exactly what *The Fresh Prince of Bel-Air* is doing, forcing its audience to consider how "they act as invisible constructors of what we think is true, shaping the world to match our assumptions."

Sitcoms like these are doing what Barth, Fowles, and Coover are doing—they're asking us to examine the strange artificiality of fiction, this illusion in which we're asked by a hidden author to hallucinate and enter a reality that isn't really there. Both audience and narrator are strange, abstracted constructs; their literal corollaries of reader and writer aren't much more comprehensible. When we read a third-person omniscient narrator, it would be natural to ask, "Who exactly is supposed to be recounting this story?" *Metafiction is that which does ask that question.* It's the same question the writers of *The Office* confront us with when we wonder who exactly is collecting all of that documentary footage over those nine seasons.

Far from being simply a postmodern trick, metalepsis as a conceit, and the metafiction that results has centuries' worth of examples. Interactions between creator and created, and certainly author and audience, have a far more extensive history than both a handful of tony novelists from the middle of the twentieth century and the back catalog of Nick at Nite. For those whose definition of the novel doesn't broach any consideration of that which was written earlier than 1945, it might come as a shock that all of the tricks we associate with metafiction thread so deep into history that realist literature can seem the exception rather than the rule. This is obvious in drama; the aforementioned theater term *breaking the fourth wall* attests to the endurance of metalepsis in literature. As a phrase, it goes back to Molière in the seventeenth century, referring to when characters in a drama acknowledge their audience, when they break the invisible wall that separates the action of the stage from that of the observers in their seats. If Molière coined the term, it's certainly older than even him. In all of those asides in Shakespeare, such as that opening monologue of *Richard III* when the title villain informs all of us who are joining him on his descent into perdition that "now is the winter of our discontent," we're in some sense to understand ourselves as being characters in the action of the play itself.

As unnatural as Shakespearean asides may seem, they don't have the same sheer metaleptic import of metafictional drama from the avant-garde theater of the twentieth century. Pirandello's classic experimental play *Six Characters in Search of an Author* is illustrative here, a high-concept work in which unfinished and unnamed characters arrive at a Pirandello production asking their creator to more fully flesh them out. As a character named the Father explains, the "author who created us alive no longer wished . . . materially to put us into a work of art. And this was a real crime." A real crime because to be a fictional character means that you cannot die, even though "the man, the writer, the instrument of the creation will die, but his creation does not die." An immaculate creation outliving its creator, more blessed than the world that is forever cursed to be ruled over by its God. But first, Pirandello's unfortunates must compel their God to grant them existence; they need a "fecundating matrix, a fantasy which could rise and nourish them: make them live forever!" If this seems abstract, you should know that such metaleptic tricks were staged long before Pirandello—and Shakespeare, for that matter. Henry Medwall's 1497 *Fulgens and Lucrece*, the first secular play in the entire English canon, has two characters initially named "A" and "B" who argue about a play only to have it revealed that the work in question is actually Medwall's, which the audience is currently watching. More than a century later, and metafictional poses were still explored by dramatists, a prime and delightful example being Shakespeare's younger contemporary and sometimes collaborator Francis Beaumont's *The Knight of the Burning Pestle*. In that Jacobean play of 1607, deploying a conceit worthy of Thomas Pynchon's *The Crying of Lot 49*, Beaumont imagines the production of a play within a play entitled *The London Merchant*. In the first act, two characters climb the stage from the audience, one simply called "Citizen" and the other "Wife," who begin to heckle and critique *The London Merchant* and its perceived unfairness to the rapidly ascending commercial class. *The Knight of the Burning Pestle* allows the audience to strike back, the Citizen cheekily telling the actor reading the prologue, "Boy, let my wife and I have a couple of stools / and then begin; and let the grocer do rare / things."

Historical metalepsis can also be seen in what are called "frame tales"—that is, stories within stories that nestle narratives together like Russian dolls. Think of the overreaching narrative of Geoffrey Chaucer's fourteenth-century *The Canterbury Tales*, with its pilgrims telling one another their stories as they make their way to the shrine of Thomas Becket, or of Scheherazade recounting her life-saving anthology to her murderous husband in *One Thousand and One Nights* as compiled from folktales during the Islamic Golden Age between the eighth and fourteenth centuries. Abbot describes frame tales by explaining that "as you move to the outer edges of a narrative, you may find that it is embedded in another narrative." Popular in medieval Europe, and finding their structure from Arabic and Indian sources that go back much further, frame tales are basically unified anthologies where an overreaching narrative supplies its own metastory. Think of Giovanni Boccaccio's fourteenth-century *The Decameron*, in which seven women and three men each tell ten stories to pass the time while they're holed up in a villa outside of Florence to wait for the passage of the Black Death through the city. The hundred resulting stories are ribald, earthy, and sexy, but present through all of their tellings is an awareness of the tellers, this narrative about a group of young Florentines in claustrophobic, if elegant, quarantine. "The power of the pen," one of Boccaccio's characters says on their eighth day in exile, "is far greater than those people suppose who have not proved it by experience," as translated by Wayne Rebhorn. Great enough, it would seem, to create a massive, sprawling world with so many stories in it. "In my father's book," the character would seem to be saying of his creator Boccaccio, "there are many mansions."

As metaleptic as frame tales might be, a reader will note that Chaucer doesn't hitch up for that long slog into Canterbury himself, nor does Boccaccio find himself eating melon and prosciutto while quaffing chianti with his aristocrats in *The Decameron*. But it would be a mistake to assume that older literature lacks examples of the harder forms of metalepsis, that writing before the twentieth century is devoid of the author god appearing to her characters as if God on Sinai. So-called premodern literature is replete with whimsical experimentation that would seem at home in Nabokov or Calvino; audiences directly addressed on stage and books speaking as themselves to their readers, authors appearing in narratives as creators, and fictions announcing their fictionality.

Miguel de Cervantes's seventeenth-century *Don Quixote* plays with issues of representation and artificiality when the titular character and his trusty squire, Sancho Panza, visit a print shop that is producing copies of the very book you are reading, the errant knight and his sidekick then endeavoring to prove that it is an inferior plagiarism of the real thing. Cervantes's narrator reflects at an earlier point in the novel about the novel itself, enthusing that "we now enjoy in this age of ours, so poor in light entertainment, not only the charm of his veracious history, but also of the tales and episodes contained in it which are, in a measure, no less pleasing, ingenious, and truthful, than the history itself." Thus Cervantes can lay claim to being the primogeniture of both realism and metafictionality.

Following *Don Quixote*'s example could be added other metafictional works that long precede postmodernism, including Laurence Sterne's eighteenth-century *The Life and Opinions of Tristram Shandy, Gentleman*, where the physical book takes time to mourn the death of a central character (when an all-black page is printed); the Polish count Jan Potocki's underread, late eighteenth-century *The Manuscript Found in Saragossa*, with not just its fantastic caste of Iberian necromancers, kabbalists, and occultists but its intricate frame structure and forking paths (not least of which include reference to the book that you're reading); James Hogg's

Satanic masterpiece *The Private Memoirs and Confessions of a Justified Sinner*, in which the author himself makes an appearance; and Jane Austen's *Northanger Abbey*, in which the characters remark on how it feels as if they're in a gothic novel (or perhaps a parody of one). Long before Barthes killed the author, writers were conflating themselves as creator with the creator. As Sterne notes, "The thing is this. That of all the several ways of beginning a book which are now in practice throughout the known world, I am confident my own way of doing it is the best—I'm sure it is the most religious—for I begin with writing the first sentence—and trusting to Almighty God for the second."

Sterne's sentiment provides evidence as to why metafiction is so alluring and enduring despite its minimization by some critics who dismiss it as a mere trick while obscuring its long history. What makes metalepsis such an intellectually attractive conceit is not that it makes us question how literature and reality interact but rather what it implies about the author toward whom Sterne gestures—"Almighty God." The author of *Tristram Shandy* understood, as all adept priests of metafiction do (whether explicitly or implicitly), that at its core, metalepsis is theological. In questioning and confusing issues of characters and writers, narrators and readers, actors and audience, metafiction experiments with the very idea of creation. Some metafiction privileges the author as being the supreme god of the fiction, as in *The French Lieutenant's Woman*, and some casts its lot with the characters, as in *The Knight of the Burning Pestle*. Some metafiction is softer in its deployment, allowing the characters within a narrative to give us stories within stories; others are hard in how emphatic they are about the artifice and illusion of fiction, as in Jones's sublime cartoon. What all of them share, however, is an understanding that fiction is a strange thing, an illusion whereby whether we're gods or penitents, we're all privy to a world spun from something as ephemeral as letters and breath. Wood asks, "Is there a way in which all of us are fictional characters, parented by life and written by ourselves?" and the metaphysicians of metafiction answer in the affirmative.

As a final axiom, to join my claim that metafiction is when literature thinks about itself and that metalepsis has a far longer history than is often surmised, I'd finally argue that because all fiction—all literature—is artifice, then all of it is, in some sense, metafiction. What defines fiction, what makes it different from other forms of language, is that quality of metalepsis. Even if not explicitly stated, the different realms of reality implied by the very existence of fiction imply something of the meta. Abbot writes that "world-making is so much a part of most narratives that some narrative scholars have begun to include it as a defining feature of narrative," and with that, I heartily concur. Even our Scripture is metafictional, for what else are we to call the Bible in which Moses is both author and character and where his death itself is depicted? In metafiction, perspective is confused—writer turns to reader, narrator to character, creator to creation. No more apt a description of metafiction, of fiction, of life than that which is offered by Prospero at the conclusion of *The Tempest*: "Our revels now are ended. These our actors, / As I foretold you, were all spirits and / Are melted into air, into thin air." For Prospero, the "great globe itself . . . / all which it inherit, shall dissolve / And, like this insubstantial pageant faded. . . . / We are such stuff / As dreams are made on, and our little life / Is rounded with a sleep." Nothingness before and nothingness after but with everything in between, just like the universe circumscribed by the cover of a book. Metafiction has always defined literature; we've always been characters in a novel that somebody else is writing.

20

The Final Sentence

Every novel is apocalyptic because every novel ends. Narrative is a strange thing, that little circumscribed universe bound between the covers of a book. Unlike life, a novel actually draws to a close. Regarding the former, that whole litany of grimacing philosophers from Epicurious to Seneca, Epictetus to Lucretius, claimed that either there was survival after death or the very definition of extinction implied that it will be an event for which we're not present. Either way, there isn't the finality that there is when we finish a book. Principles of narratology are very different from the course of life; narratives are shaped by story and plot, by *fabula* and *syuzhet*. When reading for narrative—analyzing the implications of why a story has been structured the way that it has and how that structure alters the potential interpretations of a novel, or story, or epic—there is an arsenal of terms that exist to explain how form and shape delineate these little universes we call books. In *anagnorisis*, we have the epiphany whereby our main characters discover something crucial to the narrative; in *eucatastrophe*, we have the moment whereby the protagonist is saved from what had seemed an inevitable tragedy; with *peripeteia*, we have the more general shifting of events in any direction. My favorite is *metalepsis*, the proverbial breaking of the fourth wall, whereby the author herself appears within a fictional narrative; when it occurs in real life, we call *theophany*.

Such vocabulary is adept at explaining how all of the parts of story and plot fit together to construct a narrative, to create a universe. Easy to forget that they're only applicable to our actual lives in the form of metaphor; there is no actual anagnorisis furthering your story toward its inevitable denouement; there is only finding something out that you didn't know before that may or may not be important. There is no eucatastrophe—just events that happen one after the other ad infinitum. Russian formalist critics Vladimir Propp and Viktor Shklovsky divided narrative into the aforementioned *fabula* and *syuzhet*, the first being the literal chronological ordering of events and the later referring to the manner in which the author has organized them. Derrida writes in the anthology *Deconstruction and Criticism* that the "question-of-narrative covers, with a certain modesty, a demand for narrative, a violent putting-to-the-question, an instrument of torture working to wring out the narrative as if it were a terrible secret"; there is a desire to wrench the randomness of *fabula* into the divine design of *syuzhet*. But of course, when it comes to life, there is no need to apply narrative theory to our experiences; there is no foreshadowing, and no deus ex machina is coming. We have no *syuzhet*, only *fabula*.

Inevitably, we see signs of authorial intention in our own lives; the logic of narratology colors how we interpret our experience. We see coincidences as indicating future plot points; we read signifi-cance into the pace, rhythm, and order of events; we hear the scat-tered voice of consciousness as if it were a narrator—and of course, we're the main character. We all imagine ourselves to be characters in a narrative, attaching ourselves to whatever genre is dominant in the period in which we live. Thus perhaps the ancients saw them-selves in the world of myth, as our early modern forebearers under-stood themselves to be in the pages of a novel, and we frequently imagine our lives with the logic of film. Who doesn't envision their lives edited as if on celluloid, see the course of events as filtered through jump cut, montage, and mise-en-scène? As you drive down a winding overlook, don't you feel the camera following you? When your Spotify playlist is running, don't you sometimes imagine that it's a soundtrack? We're not characters in a movie, of course, nor are we in a novel or story—save for one that is perhaps tremendously polyvocal and written by an author who hides her voice incredibly well. When we apply narratology to our lives, we call it providence; when we interpret time with it, that's what we call teleology. But in reality, it's all just one thing right after another.

Which is what makes the construction of a narrative, the crea-tion of that little universe, not an incidental thing but a profoundly *sacred* thing. It's the circumscription of reality into this monad that we call literature that's transcendent, that's noumenal. If life is lack-ing meaning in the objective particulars, then we've been able to impose significance in the realm of invented worlds. In that ritual of creation, whereby authors have generated so many worlds with so many people in them, the first sentence of a narrative is often spoken of with particular reverence, and for good reasons. But the Genesis for the moment of creation implicit in the ex nihilo of the first sentence must be read by the glow of the last sentence's apocalypse, the final words of a narrative like the breaking of the seals or the blasting of Gabriel's trumpet. So much depends on a first sentence, the portal into which a reader enters that new reality, but between it and the last page lays an entire kingdom, and we mustn't obscure the importance of that window through which we leave. Between the first and the last sentence, there is the very world, and in the latter, the intimations of millennium. A concluding line is an eschaton; it is an apocalypse.

I'd posit that a great last sentence is as if a poem—in fact, so is a great first sentence. All that is needed of a transcendent novel are those two parts; everything in between is implied already anyhow and can thus be ingested as pure candy. A perfect last sentence has implicit within it the power of incantatory poetics; it draws the entire creation to a close, like a bubble popping, or a candle being blown out, or Prospero letting the entire great globe itself disappear into gossamer nothingness. In a last sentence, you are deprived of knowing what is in the "after"; we can imagine, we can invent, we can extrapolate, but for the characters of the narrative, their God has deigned to draw on their existence a veil. Such is the literal description as supplied by Salman Rushdie in *Midnight's Children*, its closing page invoking that "yes, they will trample me underfoot . . . reducing me to specks of voiceless dust . . . and be sucked into the annihilating whirlpool of multitudes, and to be unable to live or die in peace." Every last sentence is finally, and with finality, about itself. Every last sentence is about where we choose to end, what we choose to leave out. Every sentence is about annihilation; it sustains itself on the sublime intimations of nothingness.

Foolhardy to attempt any general theory of last sentences, but there are certain themes, tropes, and dare I say it, philosophies implicit within how a lot of writers choose to complete the theurgy that is writing a novel. As with Rushdie's final sentence in *Midnight's Children*, there are not just last words that function to draw the narrative itself to a logical (or open-ended) conclusion but lines that serve to draw attention to the idea of finality itself. This is what Mary Shelley does in *Frankenstein*, depicting her monster as disappearing into the Arctic nothingness, for "he was soon borne away by the waves and lost in darkness and distance." Something so attractive in that nihilistic alliteration at the end, the sense of enveloping blackness erasing the monster as surely as closing *Frankenstein* draws his narrative to a finality.

Joseph Conrad does something similar in *Heart of Darkness*, with Marlow discovering that the "offing was barred by a black bank of clouds, and the tranquil waterway leading to the utmost ends of the earth flowed sombre under an overcast sky—seemed to lead into the heart of an immense blackness." Those plosive consonants in the alliterative "barred by a black bank" do something not unlike what Shelley was doing, sounding nothing so much like the sputtering engine on a boat sailing down the Congo coming to a stop. Note how Conrad conflates both spatial and temporal endings, how easily the "ends of the earth" implies the "End of the Earth." And in the same way that both the end of a novel (where all characters disappear, their invented stories subsumed back into that divine ether) and the end of our lives imply the same "immense blackness," that thick nothingness from which no answers are forthcoming until we're able to sail there ourselves.

Some of the most exemplary of last sentences gesture toward the finality of apocalypse by emphasizing how singular, detached, and endlessly regenerative each eternal second is. Emily Brontë, for example, ends *Wuthering Heights* with the apocalyptic intimations that both the end of a novel and death require, writing, "I lingered round them, under the benign sky; watching the moths fluttering among the heath, and hare-bells; I listened to the soft wind breathing through the grass; and wondered how anyone could imagine unquiet slumbers for the sleepers in the quiet earth." Brontë provides an instance of what I've called elsewhere the "crystalline moment"—that is, that the final lines of *Wuthering Heights* provide access to that singularity that is the present moment, one that expresses a certain sublime infinitude and compels that koan-like sense of what it would feel like to have an eternal perspective, as if you were God. All of the quiet details—the "moths fluttering," the "soft wind breathing through the grass"—supply that sense of timelessness that is hidden within every moment but that only transcendent art can make accessible. Furthermore, Brontë's sentence makes visible how static an end can be, where the "benign sky" is like an event horizon you approach but never reach—the same way that we can never truly experience our own deaths.

As different a writer from Brontë as could be imagined would be Jack Kerouac, there being little correspondence between Regency and Beat literature. When it comes to final sentences, however, *On the Road* does something not unlike *Wuthering Heights* in terms of distilling the calmness implicit within the final moment (while remembering that all sentences, and thus all literature, are fundamentally concerned with the question of moment). On the last page of that novel, Kerouac has Sal Paradise ruminate in a run-on sentence composed in bop prosody and evocative of the expanse of the land itself, writing that "in America when the sun goes down and I sit on the old broken-down river pier watching the long, long skies over New Jersey and sense all that raw land that rolls in one unbelievable huge bulge over the West Coast, and all that road going, all the people dreaming in the immensity of it, and in Iowa I know by now the children must be crying in the land where they let the children cry," for as the appropriately named Paradise does surmise, "the evening star . . . [is] shedding her sparkler dims on the prairie, which . . . darkens all rivers, cups the peaks and folds the final shore in, and nobody, nobody knows what's going to happen to anybody," and so on, and so forth.

Despite the snark that holds that Kerouac was less an author than a typist, the last sentence of *On the Road* does something metaphysically similar to what Brontë's does in *Wuthering Heights*. Does two similar things, in fact: The first is that Kerouac endows this final moment of *On the Road* with a certain enchanted significance, where all things are glowing, and he does this by presenting a vivid portrayal of the crystalline moment. As an example of the crystalline moment, Kerouac's concluding passage is recursive, memories sliding into this particular second and reflecting back upon one another. As Brontë gives us those details that accrue tiny shards of meaning into her moment—the moths and wind rustling the tall grasses—so too does Kerouac imbue his description with the little details that, like paint being applied over and over to a canvas, build up a writerly texture. We have the dipping sun over polluted Jersey, which reminds him of the sparkling sky over an Iowa prairie. If constructing a precise crystalline moment is one manner in which Kerouac does something similar to Brontë, then another is the way in which the last line of the book evokes the end (and thus the destruction) of the narrative in a similar manner, by calling upon the sublimity of nature. *Wuthering Heights* does this by dwelling amid the charged luminescence of the English moors, but in many ways, *On the Road* is among the last Romantic novels, and because it is American, the nature in which it luxuriates is the grandiosity and enormity of the land itself (which is then mimicked in the uncontrolled syntax of Kerouac's sentence).

If final sentences gesture toward extinction—of both the narrative and ultimately all sentient awareness—then the nothingness to which they direct the reader depends on the type of novel that we're reading. As Conrad indicated an inchoate darkness as falling like an infernal dusk upon his narrative, so do American novels, death obsessed as they are, focus on the land of America as a surrogate for both death and God. Critic Leslie Fiedler wrote in *Love and Death in the American Novel*, which stands with D. H. Lawrence's *Classic Studies in American Literature* as among the best books ever written about this land, that "our literature is a gothic fiction, nonrealistic and negative, sadist and melodramatic, a literature of darkness and the grotesque in a land of light and affirmation." Nothing is more American than the novel precisely because it both ends and para-doxically indicates the infinitude that continues beyond the last page.

A novel, the creation of a solitary genius we deign to call the author, is the ultimate product of bootstrapping rugged individualism—the theophany of the writer into a creator god, where she alone decides when the universe is to end with the last page. America's immensity has always been a convenient metaphor-ical locus for that, encompassing both the death of the novel's char-acters as they cease to speak to us and our own deaths as well. In those dreams, a blanketed, undifferentiated, terrifying space of the American continent looms forth toward the dwindling west as rep-resentative of all that which we can never know after we've closed our eyes for the last time. Kerouac was anticipated by another "great American novel" in the form of the closing sentence of F. Scott Fitz-gerald's *The Great Gatsby*, which with its invocation of the "fresh, green breast of the new world" had a similarly westerly scope and transposed the spatial into the temporal with "we beat on, boats against the current, borne back ceaselessly into the past." Before Fitzgerald, Mark Twain did the exact same thing, marking the terra incognita of America as a type of wilderness into which the reader and the narrative could not go, a paradise beyond the comprehen-sion of words, and so the world must finally end with the novel itself. His titular character in *The Adventures of Huckleberry Finn* takes leave of us with "I got to light out for the Territory ahead of the rest, because Aunt Sally she's going to adopt me and sivilize me, and I can't stand it. I been there before."

Then there are books whose endings reveal that they understand there is no true apocalypse, for to be on the other side of the end of the world is still to be in the world. After all, when we close books, *we're still here*, even if the characters aren't anymore. These novels enact the commonsense understanding we all intuit—that the completion of a book isn't the end of anything; that even after the characters are silent, their narration still rings in our head; that after the last page has been turned, we can't help but imagine time's arrow still propelling the story forward, even while the naturally limited author, lacking in omnipotence, is mute on what has happened in that universe. In this way, no novel is actually apocalyptic, because what the narrative presents is not a universe itself but a brief window into a world that we're allowed to view for a little bit before we pass on. These final sentences imply not finality but continuance. We see this in Margaret Mitchell's novel of unrepentant Confederate schmaltz *Gone with the Wind* when she writes, "After all, tomorrow is another day."

We also see it brilliantly in James Joyce's *Finnegans Wake*, a novel that implies both continuation and completeness of a fictional universe when the last sentence, "A lone a last a loved a long the," is completed in the first sentence, which reads, "Riverrun, past Eve and Adam's, from swerve of shore to bend of bay, brings us by a commodius vicus of recirculation back to Howth Castle and Environs." But it's Joyce's countryman Samuel Beckett who penned the most distilled and honest of final sentences, writing in *The Unnamable*, "Where I am, I don't know, I'll never know, in the silence you don't know, you must go on, I can't go on, I'll go on." By dwelling in both the ineffability and the inexplicability, as well as the indefinability and the impossibility of an end, Beckett's final sentence is the last line of all novels—and of all of our stories as well.

Part Three

Greatest of Characters

21

God Created Consciousness in Fiction

Where is the Sumerian Alice Munro? Why is humanity's oldest literature unable to present the interior experience of humans in the way that the realist novel can? Why do characters from *Gilgamesh* to the *Iliad* and *Odyssey* lack the inner life that modern characters do? Do ancient texts reflect a difference in consciousness itself? Gilgamesh, Odysseus, and Achilles are fundamentally flatter than characters such as Don Quixote, Hamlet, Robinson Crusoe, and Elizabeth Bennet. But there is one major exception to the flatness of ancient characters—that in his contradictions, fallibilities, exaltations, subtlety, nuance, grandeur, pettiness, and complexity is capable of introspection—and that character is named "God."

Erich Auerbach's 1946 *Mimesis: The Representation of Reality in Western Literature* was concerned with the depiction of experience. He argued that there are differences between classical and biblical

255

mimesis. For Auerbach, "faith in the truth of language" is central to "an entire human experience." When discussing human consciousness, the term *interiority* is helpful in describing a character's inner life. Ancient epic may express the range of human tragedy and triumph, but it doesn't depict the rich interiority that later writing does. A novel such as Gustave Flaubert's *Madame Bovary* simulates the complex, multifaceted, contradictory, layered, subtle, specific, internal fullness of human consciousness. Same with writers like James Joyce, or Virginia Woolf, or Vladimir Nabokov. And earlier novelists too, Miguel de Cervantes and Daniel Defoe, are able to express inner life fully.

Flaubert wrote that "it wasn't the first time in their lives that they had seen trees, blue sky and lawn, or heard the flowing of water or the rustle of the breeze in the branches, but never before, certainly, had they looked on it all with such wonder: it was as though nature had not existed before." He describes an internal state, one that isn't indicated physically. Now compare Flaubert to a line from the ancient Egyptian masterpiece *Story of Sinuhe*: "He flew to heaven and was united with the sun's disk; the flesh of the god was merged in him, who made him. Then was the Residence hushed . . . the courtiers crouched head on lap; the people grieved." *Story of Sinuhe* explores exile and loss and is beautiful in its evocations. But it's impossible to imagine the sort of language Flaubert uses appearing there. Flaubert's style never appears in cuneiform on some ancient stele.

Why are writers over the past half a millennia—since the rise of the novel as a genre—able to represent their slice of reality, while ancient literature seems incapable of that same sort of interiority? Ancient literature presents complex narratives, ingenious rhetorical conceits, and sophisticated thematic concerns. Yet the inner life of a character like Beowulf, from the relatively late seventh-century titular Anglo-Saxon epic, bears more similarity to a video game character than to Woolf's Mrs. Dalloway. There are exceptions. Virgil arguably expresses deep interiority, and as literary historian Steven Moore has explicated, there are forerunners to the novel long before Cervantes penned *Don Quixote*, from Apuleius's *The Golden Ass* in second-century Rome to Murasaki Shikibu's *The Tale of Genji* in eleventh-century Japan. But modern novels do something that the earliest literature seems incapable of doing—representing conscious subjectivity. Or perhaps the observation is backward—maybe the ancients didn't represent consciousness because the ancients were incapable of consciousness?

A variation of this assertion was proposed in 1976 by psychologist Julian Jaynes in *The Origin of Consciousness in the Breakdown of the Bicameral Mind*. He argued that ancient humans were not "conscious" in the current sense, that they lacked introspection, and that they interpreted their inner monologue as generated by outside beings, such as gods and muses. He wrote, "It is perfectly possible that there could have existed a race of men who spoke, judged, reasoned, solved problems . . . but were not conscious at all." This then explains why the most ancient literature has no depictions of interiority—because there was no interiority to depict.

Jaynes claimed that the first glimmerings of consciousness appeared three millennia ago (a period that the philosopher Karl Jaspers called the "Axial Age") due to a variety of social, cultural, material, and biological reasons. Because of his reliance on poetic evidence, he was feted by literary types (John Updike blurbed the first edition), though his fellow psychologists remain less convinced. And yet, from the perspective of the literary critic, there is something thrilling in Jaynes's conjectures. Jaynes sees a work like Homer's *Iliad* as a late vestige of "bicameralism," explaining that Hector and Achilles were "directed by [auditory] hallucinations" and that they "were not at all like us. They were noble automatons who knew not what they did." Muses, daemons, and gods were real for the Greeks, voices actually heard in the process of inspiration. Auerbach anticipated Jaynes, writing that Homeric style represents "phenomena in a fully externalized form, visible and palpable in all their parts," adding that "nor do psychological processes receive any other treatment . . . nothing must remain hidden and unexpressed." Jaynes would argue that nothing was left hidden or unexpressed because nothing could be hidden or unexpressed.

If Jaynes's hypothesis is valid, then almost two and a half millennia separate the emergence of conscious humans from the emergence of the novel that is commensurate with the inner life. There are, of course, examples before the novel; Aeneas is arguably more "conscious" than Odysseus. Social convention and generic stricture may have preserved a residual resistance to mimetic interiority, but for writers looking for a model of multifaceted consciousness, they had one in the aforementioned first fully self-aware character—that of God in the Bible. He is loving and jealous, merciful and vengeful, confident and surprisingly vulnerable. He is sometimes a god who doubts, he can be petty, he can be capricious. And importantly, in contrast to the pantheon of Greek polytheism, the Jewish God is one who evolves over the course of the narrative. Jack Miles argued in his 1995 critical masterpiece *God: A Biography* that the deity is "an amalgam of several personalities in one character." Monotheism's genius was that one God necessitated the development of a complex psychology to depict him. As the modern psyche can be described as a collection of different characters resulting in one individual consciousness, God incorporated a number of different deities. Of course, this character is sometimes unpleasant, but what complicated person isn't?

The Bible is the story of the Hebrews' transition from polytheism to monotheism. Since the "documentary hypothesis" of nineteenth-century philologists, we've understood how the Bible was edited, which involved the synthesis of disparate personalities into one God. The earliest written portions of that text are by an anonymous Judean poet called the "Yahwist" for her favored term for the deity (scholar Harold Bloom audaciously claimed that these portions were written by a woman in the court of Solomon). Portions that refer to God as Elohim are by the Elohist, who lived in the northern kingdom of Israel (the word *Elohim*, not unimportantly, is grammatically plural). Following an Assyrian invasion, Israelite refugees assimilated with their southern neighbors, which involved the fusion of these national epics into the Torah. What resulted was the first multifaceted character of its kind in literature.

Miles argues that this creates the template for depictions of inner life, writing that the Bible is "far nearer in spirit to *Hamlet* than *Oedipus Rex*." Like Auerbach, Miles agrees that there are two different types of mimesis in Western culture, and it is the model provided to us by the Jewish Bible that more closely mimics consciousness. *Oedipus Rex* presents a monochromatic character whose thoughts are buffeted by forces greater than him. Hamlet is like God, for his "character is contradictory, and he is trapped within those contradictions." With his interiority, he is more reminiscent of modern consciousness than any other ancient character. God has more in common with Don Quixote than he does with Odysseus and has provided a template for the creation of conscious characters—and perhaps conscious readers.

Ancient literature does not depict inner life because there was not yet any inner life to depict. The past was interpreted by different minds. Achilles, according to Jaynes, acts because of what those gods outside of his head tell him to do; the biblical character of God has subsumed all of those gods inside of his own head. In the beginning, man created God, and so God returned the favor.

22

In the Hands of Angry Gods

James Joyce gives his readers a taste of the eternal torments of hell in his 1916 roman à clef *A Portrait of the Artist as a Young Man.* Toward the beginning of the novel, Joyce's adolescent alter ego, Stephen Dedalus, sits through the fiery sermon of the Jesuit Father Arnall, a scene in which the author marshals his literary genius to convey the full terror of damnation. By the priest's description, "Hell is a strait and dark and foul-smelling prison, an abode of demons and lost souls, filled with fire and smoke." So far so good, as that would seem to be the popular depiction of perdition. But with upsetting specificity, Father Arnall remarks that in hell, the condemned are so heaped on top of one another that they have absolutely no liberty of movement: "They are not even able to remove from the eye a worm that gnaws it." In the Jesuit's explication, hell is a place of "foul matter, leprous corruption, nameless suffocating filth."

Moving from sulfury clichés to ever more baroque and intricate descriptions of the infernal hereafter, the priest perseverates before the congregation on this realm that "burns eternally in darkness," that contains all the "filth of the world, all the offal and scum of the world . . . a vast reeking sewer," best described as the foul odor of a "jelly-like mass of liquid corruption . . . of nauseous loathsome decomposition." Hell is a "boundless, shoreless and bottomless" place, where "blood seethes and boils in the veins, the brains are boiling in the skull, the heart in the breast glowing and bursting, the bowels a red-hot mass of burning pulp, the tender eyes flaming like molten balls." These fetid corpses are a "huge and rotting human fungus," where a mere whiff of the decomposing bodies of the sinful "would suffice to infect the whole world." Father Arnall rhetorically asks his charges, including Stephen Dedalus, who is now tortured by his impure thoughts and his even more impure actions, "What name . . . shall we give to the darkness of hell which is to last not for three days alone but for all eternity?"

The question of how we can name a place such as this is at the center of scholar Scott G. Bruce's new anthology *The Penguin Book of Hell*. Joyce's immaculate and terrifying description of the damned in the eternal hereafter isn't included in Bruce's compendium, though much else is. Excerpts from Church Fathers, Scripture, prophetic writings, Dante, William Blake, and even the playlists used to torture those indefinitely detained in American camps during the "War on Terror" are included in Bruce's exploration of how hell has been represented across millennia of history in Jewish, Christian, and pagan contexts. A loss that Father Arnall's homily isn't included for consideration, as few secular modern depictions of hell rival the religious as much as does *Portrait of the Artist as a Young Man*. Joyce matches the terror of the eighteenth-century American theologian Jonathan Edwards, whose 1741 sermon "Sinners in the

Hands of an Angry God" warned his New England audience about a hell where the "flames do now rage and glow" and was delivered with so much abjection that congregants supposedly fainted in the pews.

But if Edwards's disturbing evocation of hell was meant to instill a fear that would lead to conversion, Joyce's talents were arguably commandeered for the opposite purpose. In *Portrait of the Artist as a Young Man*, the reader is to understand Father Arnall's homily as an assault, a cynical but exquisitely adept use of Christianity's traditional rhetoric about punishment in the afterlife designed for social control. An older Dedalus would later argue in *Ulysses* that his native Ireland was dominated by "two masters," the colonial one in London and the ecclesiastical power in Rome, and much of Father Arnall's speech should be read as a variety of studied, affected, gothic Catholicism. But so visceral are Joyce's descriptions that the reader of the novel would be forgiven for reacting by developing a newfound fear of hell (or, through a Dedalus-like guilty conscience, acquiring one for the first time). Protestations of secularity aside, whether in a Joyce novel or elsewhere, hell is a hard place to escape from. Hell's seeming unconquerability, its persistence in our culture, shouldn't be surprising. As Bruce writes in the introduction to his collection, the idea of hell is "arguably the most powerful and persuasive construct of the human imagination in the Western tradition." Perdition is not abolished easily.

Maybe it shouldn't be. Though it's true, as Joyce's novel makes clear and as Bruce reiterates, that hell "has inspired fear and thereby controlled the behavior of countless human beings," for all of the unnecessary guilt, there is something so *evocative*, so *powerful*, so *charged* in the idea of hell that I worry about abandoning the concept too quickly. First, though, let's be clear: the idea of hell hasn't been abandoned by the majority of Americans. According to the Pew Research Center's 2014 *Religious Landscape Study*, 58 percent of Americans believe in a literal hell as a place of punishment and damnation. Interestingly, at 72 percent, even more Americans believe in heaven. Of the 14 percent who believe in heaven but don't believe in hell, presumably there are a variety of theological positions embraced, ranging from the position that the irredeemable sinful cease to exist upon death, to the "heresy" traditionally known as "universalism," which is the belief that everyone will find salvation, regardless of creed or conduct.

That "New Atheists" like Richard Dawkins, Sam Harris, and Daniel Dennett would understand hell as a barbaric and superstitious fable is obvious, but many of the traditionally religious have jettisoned such rhetoric as well. Controversial evangelical pastors like Rob Bell and Carlton Pearson have questioned or outright rejected a cosmology of hell, with the former writing in *Love Wins: A Book about Heaven, Hell, and the Fate of Every Person Who Ever Lived* that belief in hell can be "misguided and toxic and ultimately subverts the . . . message of love, peace, forgiveness, and joy." And I don't disagree with Bell; in fact, I imagine that there is a lot of overlap between those reform-minded evangelicals, atheists, and myself, all admitting that there is something abusive in convincing a child that they're bound for the torments of eternal fire. To defend the rhetoric of hell while ignoring the reality that such beliefs have caused psychological trauma to millions of people throughout history would be dishonest, and it's understandable why the 14 percent of Americans who've embraced heaven without its opposite take part in a venerable and compassionate theology that rejects the idea of hell.

But it's important to avoid the fallacy that assumes that just because the literal belief in hell may not be as popular, it's no longer worth taking seriously. I'd suggest that the brimstone may burn and waft a bit more even among the secular than we might assume. In *Straw Dogs: Thoughts on Humans and Other Animals*, the British philosopher John Gray describes how among some committed philosophers, "it is a matter of pride to be ignorant of theology." Yet this ignorance obscures our own intellectual genealogies, for the "Christian origins of secular humanism are rarely understood." When we criticize unfettered capitalism, we can't help but think of avarice; when we rightly denounce the narcissism of our leaders, we can't but consider pride. And as a result, who among us hasn't thought that hell might be worthy as a punishment for those who do evil? We'd be forgiven for missing hell a bit. More generally, when we pretend that an ideology of "pure" materialism, "pure" scientism, "pure" secularity is even possible, we simply serve to ignore the traces of the transcendent and the relics of religion that are evident in ostensibly "modern" ideologies. That's why, secular though I may feel that I am, I can't escape the heat of hell. We're still haunted by the demons who are imprisoned there.

This essay is no justification for a belief in a literal hell; I don't think that if you drill far enough into the earth, you'll suddenly come upon a legion of devils in subterranean caves. Though it also needs to be made clear that the idea that this is what most of the faithful believe has much more of the snarky New Atheist slander about it than it does any sense of reality as to what most theologies argue. The *Catechism of the Roman Catholic Church* "affirms the existence of hell and its eternity," but it also defines that place rather abstractly as "a state of definitive self-exclusion from communion with God and the blessed." Pope John Paul II explained that "rather than a place, hell indicates the state of those who freely and definitely separate themselves from . . . the source of all life and joy." Father Arnall's gruesome enumeration of the terrors of hell, all stench of decomposition and infinite burn of dark fire, may be poetic, but it should also in some sense be thought of as a metaphorical approximation of that which, by definition, is fundamentally inapproachable, that which is impossible to accurately describe in human language. Sophisticated theodicies have *always* differentiated between hell as a state and hell as a location, so when I wash my hands of the literal belief in perdition as a place, I understand that it's true of normative Christian theology as well. Rather, I want to understand how a skeptic such as myself might get something useful out of the idea of hell.

Because to claim that my own position on hell is perfectly congruent with the arguments of the church, one where I still argue for the importance of hellish language, would be disingenuous. When discussing eternal things—the noumenal, the transcendent—there is a difficulty in language, where the philosopher Ludwig Wittgenstein's declaration in *Tractatus Logico-Philosophicus* that "whereof one cannot speak, thereof one must be silent" can seem the most honest. Both the church and I (and, I suppose, the New Atheists as well) agree that a group of coal miners isn't going to crack some rock and find the gates of hell. That hell is not a literal place, bound by physicality and defined by materiality, is a given except for the most fundamentalist of believers.

When it comes to hell as a "state," then I must confess that my own faith gets mixed up with issues of simile, metaphor, and allegory. If I must make an affirmative confession, I suppose that regarding things-not-of-this-world, I'm basically agnostic, though this is not a mealymouthed type of atheism so much as it is a profound pose toward epistemology, that branch of philosophy concerned with what we know and how we know it. Truer to say that I'm what theologians call an *ignostic*, that I don't even know what I don't even know, and I believe that when it comes to language about ultimate things, we're too often mired in ambiguity and uncertainty to make definite claims. I've generally embraced an understanding that the claims of belief are different from the claims of science and that creedal confessions are more like poetry than they are logical inferences about the objective world. In such a context, I affirm the poetry of perdition, the rhetoric of damnation, the language of hell. I'm not sure what it means to say if hell is "real" or not, but I know that the poetry like Father Arnall's that is used to describe it very much is, and I think we abandon those words at our own peril. If we see the sweetness of heaven without the bitterness of hell, we exorcize one of the most powerful ideas in our metaphorical arsenal.

And we abolish the idea of hell at the very moment when it could be the most pertinent to us. An ironic reality in an era where the world becomes seemingly more hellish, when humanity has developed the ability to enact a type of burning punishment upon the earth itself. Journalist David Wallace-Wells in his terrifying new book about climate change, *The Uninhabitable Earth: Life after Warming*, writes that "it is much, much worse than you think." Wallace-Wells goes on to describe how anthropogenic warming will result in a twenty-first century that sees coastal cities destroyed and refugees forced to migrate for survival, that will see famines across formerly verdant farmlands and the development of new epidemics that will kill millions, that will see wars fought over fresh water and wildfires scorching the wilderness. Climate change implies not just ecological collapse but societal, political, and moral collapse as well. The science has been clear for over a generation; our reliance on fossil fuels has been hastening an industrial apocalypse of our own invention. Wallace-Wells is critical of what he describes as the "eerily banal language of climatology," where the purposefully sober, logical, and rational arguments of empirical science have unintentionally helped obscure the full extent of what some studying climate change now refer to as our coming "century of hell." Better perhaps to have this discussion using the language of Revelation, where the horsemen of pestilence, war, famine, and death are powered by carbon dioxide.

The rhetoric of hell is charged and powerful for metaphorically conveying the full impact of climate change—the language of burning and thirst, immolation and consumption—a tangible reminder of what's existentially at stake. Such rhetoric also has an important moral dimension to it. Hell is not just a symbolic representation of an unpleasant place to which you would not want to go; it's also explicitly a location of punishment. Obscene when fundamentalist preachers claim that this or that natural disaster is the result of individual sin, but in one sense, climate change is the logical conclusion of our society's rapacious greed, slothfulness, and gluttony. Love of the automobile, air-conditioning, meat, cheap airplane flights, and consumer goods transported thousands of miles around the world have all contributed to the dire predicament in which humanity now finds itself. Romans 6:23 claims that the "wages of sin is death"; I know not whether that's metaphysically true, but there is a disquieting resonance when it comes to the effect that oil companies and their consumers have all had on the future of our planet.

We must be careful with such moralizing language, however, for while it's appropriate to castigate the offenders in corporate boardrooms and their government enablers who've brought us to this precipice, and perhaps we must turn an eye toward our own individual complicity in ecological collapse as well, the reality is that the vast majority of people who will suffer because of climate change are not the authors of this calamity. Rising temperatures will disproportionately affect those in developing countries, and it will of course ultimately impact the lives of generations unborn who had no say in who drove a Hummer. We're confronted, then, with a seeming obscenity, the punishments of hell enacted upon those who did nothing wrong. Yet the theological rhetoric of hell already provides a powerful model for thinking about that exact same circumstance.

For when confronting the enormity of climate change, of the innocent punished for our own iniquity, there are worse narratives to orient ourselves toward than that of Christ harrowing hell to liberate the righteous from the confines of limbo. Scriptural precedent, from Job to the prophets, grapples with the reality that suffering is not always equal, that injustice is often a function of human affairs, and that there is a call for humanity to correct its own sinful ways. Meghan O'Gieblyn in an essay from her recent collection *Interior States*, which reflects both on her evangelical youth and this new trendiness in ignoring hell, echoes Bruce when she writes that hell "remains our most resilient metaphor for the evil both around and within us." Hell might make us feel terrible, but it provides a warning and a corrective to the hubris that threatens the world. She states, "It's precisely this acknowledgment of collective guilt that makes it possible for a community to observe the core virtues of the faith: mercy, forgiveness, grace."

For a conflicted, skeptical, doubtful believer such as myself, whose faith is idiosyncratic enough that sometimes I think it's barely honest to call it faith, that's the power of such language. Metaphors should only be abandoned warily and for good reason, and the flames of the hereafter remain too scorching to quench them fully. Hell is a concept by which we can evaluate our iniquities, our capability for evil, the ruin we enact on our world, and maybe the ways in which we can rectify those sins. Faith is a window, but not a clear one that looks unhampered out onto a world of discernable and measurable reality; it exists not to give us a scientific perspective but rather as an expression of how we wish reality would look. Damnation's reality may not frighten me, but I cannot be but terrified by its language. There is wisdom in understanding that we may approach heaven—but only after we've harrowed hell on earth.

23

Breaking the Third Commandment

An Essay on All the Names of God

Thou shalt not take the name of the Lord thy God in vain; for the
Lord will not hold him guiltless that taketh his name in vain.

—Exodus 20:7

All the many names of the Supreme Being—God, Jehovah,
Allah, and so on—they are only man-made labels. There
is a philosophical problem of some difficulty here, which
I do not propose to discuss, but somewhere among all the
possible combinations of letters that can occur are what one
may call the real names of God. By systematic permutation
of letters, we have been trying to list them all.

—Arthur C. Clarke, "The Nine Billion Names of God" (1953)

Past the sandstone, neoclassical facade of the Scottish National
Gallery, on the loft Mound that overlooks both the Old Town and
the New Town of Edinburgh, down a rococo hallway with blood-red

wallpaper, hangs the French impressionist Paul Gauguin's 1888 *Vision after the Sermon*. Painted in that cool and fresh Brittany air, Gauguin imagines a group of contemporary, local, white-bonnet-clad women apprehending a divine vision following the orgiastic ecstasies of collective worship. The women's heads are bowed in prayer and contemplation, their black-clad bodies announcing humble faith, their covered heads a statement of their simple piety. One in the congregation looks up, for beyond a felled tree trunk and across a field the color of clotting blood, she espies a struggle between a man and an entirely other being. Perhaps the sermon that these women have left provided a homiletic gloss on the scene she is watching, the portion from Genesis where the patriarch Jacob encountered a strange, heavenly, supernatural man who "wrestled with him until the breaking of the day." Imagined by Gauguin (and I suppose by the women in *Vision after the Sermon* as well), the celestial being who has arrived unannounced at Jacob's oasis encampment appears as a blue-robed angel, his golden wings spread like a raptor's while he clenches the poor patriarch's neck in a headlock.

The Bible's account of Jacob wrestling with the angel is one of the myriad incidents in the scriptural canon that serve to remind us that it's a book from an incredibly different culture. Apply more recent theological gloss all that we want, try to tame the wild narrative, but Bronze Age myths resist our boring, bourgeois, logical perspectives. Jacob's wrestling with this creature through the entirety of a star-filled Jordanian night—be it man, angel, or the Lord—has not the coherence of an actual event but the sublime truth of a dream. Genesis recounts how the two fought to a draw, with Jacob gaining the advantage and refusing to let the stranger go until the angel blessed him. The father of Israel, you see, wished to know the name of this unknown, undefined, unannounced being. "Why is it that you ask my name?" the anonymous being asks, but Jacob does not answer that question, and the angel does not define his identity. In a story about names, Jacob acquires a new one himself, born from the struggle with this faceless being. The angel declares, "Your name shall no longer be called Jacob, but Israel, for you have striven with God and with men, and have prevailed." Disagreements on the etymology of the name *Israel*, but with the word ending in *El*, the singular for a popular Canaanite mountain god, there would seem to be some accuracy in the supernatural interlocutor's claim that Jacob's renaming announces him as a man capable of struggling with the divine and surviving, what the scholar Melvin Konner explains in *Unsettled: An Anthropology of the Jews* as being the intellectual hallmark of a "whole nation of God wrestlers, striving and undaunted, hurt but not subdued." Certainly, Jacob thinks so, intoning, "I have seen God face to face, and yet my life has been delivered," the interpretive crux of Genesis long fixated on whether Jacob was wrestling with a mere angel, a representative of the Lord, or with God himself.

What exactly does it mean that the Bible has a story where the omnipotent, omnipresent, omniscient creator of the universe gets into a wrestling match with a mere man and basically loses? Why does Jacob have such an obsession with the name of this being, not just with whatever culturally relative descriptor is used to designate him, be it *El* or *God*, but with the actual *name*? The unheard, unknown, unpronounceable designation that the Lord uses to refer to himself, the name only known to angels? Genesis's reasoning is surreal, its pronouncements inscrutable, its story beautifully weird. That's not even taking into account the detail that God dislodged Jacob's hip, giving him permanent sciatica and a lifelong limp, so that "to this day the people of Israel do not eat the sinew of the thigh that is on the hip socket," still true in kosher law. What any of this means has to be parsed with a historical recounting of

Bronze Age culture. There's also a truth accessible with the higher ruminations of a certain cracked transcendence. Where a complete understanding often isn't found is in the much-later conventional accounts of both synagogue and church.

Our later theological imposition of narrative unity and philosophical logic do a disservice to the profoundly beautiful strangeness of the original text. Harold Bloom writes in *The Book of J* of Jacob's "transcendental struggle" that is shot through with ambiguity in his "extraordinary wrestling match with the angel of reality, a nameless one among the Elohim whom the enigmatic J refuses to identify, so that we wonder if this antagonist is Yahweh or the angel of death, or perhaps Yahweh playing the part of the angel of death," for this mystery is not just a literary quality of "J" (what Bloom calls the author of that portion of Genesis), but indeed, it's the entire point of the story. What Jacob's transcendent struggle concerns isn't just man's conflict with the divine but the issue of appearances and reality and the distance between names and the named. As with other narrative orphans of the Bible—from the Bridegroom of Blood whereby Moses's wife Zipporah must smear the foreskin of their child across the feet of a previously enraged Lord, to when God struck down a helpful man named Uzzah for daring to touch the Ark of the Covenant so as to prevent it from toppling down—Jacob's tussle with the divine is an uncomfortable and inscrutable story. It is dreamt, imagined, and communicated in an idiom for which we have no easy cipher.

Maimonides maintained that the being was always simply an angel, an emissary of the Lord rather than the actual deity himself. John Calvin argued that it was a vision, the celebrated literalist turning to allegory and metaphor when the implications of the tale got too weird to consider. Ironically, some atheists are better at approaching the Bible's resplendent literary oddness, with Ernst

Bloch writing in *Atheism in Christianity* that the story is about "a bloodthirsty, vengeful God . . . outdone by cunning human beings to avoid his fury." Bloch's interpretation allows for the obvious but overlooked—Jacob wasn't wrestling with an angel or an idea, not with himself or a concept, but with the actual living God. But while Bloch's honesty on that score is admirable, and he's not wrong to see a bit of the trickster in Jacob's noble draw, it does little to answer the overweening concern with names, both Jacob's desire to know God's designation and the latter's resistance to sharing it. Translator and author Aviya Kushner writes in *The Grammar of God: A Journey into the Words and Worlds of the Bible* that "Jacob didn't just fight with the angel . . . he *overcame* the angel, and so ruled over a creature more powerful than he." For in a narrative that has Jacob being renamed, and thus designating all of his ancestors by this label that emphasizes God as not just a being to worship but one that's crucial to struggle against, names have a central importance. "God," as author Alexander Waugh writes in his book appropriately entitled *God*, "is fussy about names." The focus of the tale isn't the fight, it's not that wrestling match viewed in spectral reverie by the pious maids of Brittany as dreamt by Gauguin, but it's this question: What is God's actual name, the one that he whispers to himself and that generates all of reality?

God's name is a narrative itself. Not a character but the story, that secret code that makes all other stories a possibility. Does this describe any literal state of affairs? Is that "real" or not? That's the wrong question, for no name—not for anything, be it *chair*, *desk*, or *tree*—is actually real either. Take my nominalist affectations with a judicious literalism, for "God" is what we make of it; what's less important than what the name refers to is what the word does. What the tale of Jacob's midnight fight is actually about—at least in the context of the desert-based, patriarchal, Bronze Age culture that produced it—concerns the sublime aura of names. God's unwillingness to tell Jacob his proper name makes more sense when you realize it's because the knowledge of another's identity and designation allows you to do certain things, that in the knowing of a name, there is theurgy, there is magic. God doesn't want Jacob to know his name because then the patriarch would have certain powers over him. Jacob would be able to use the very letters of God's name, whatever it may be, to affect the world, to alter reality. To have such knowledge would be a reduction in God's power; it would allow one of his own creations to use the divine alphabet to alter the world.

For in the Bible, God may be creator, but he's not exactly omnipotent, omnipresent, omniscient—at least, not yet. Konner writes that in Genesis, God may have "had the transcendent power to bless, but the other had the power to demand, even compel, the blessing." Those abstract categories concerning God's agency are a later theological affectation—they have to do with the Rambam and Rashi, Augustine and Aquinas—but the splendor of rabbis and schoolmen was not the perspective of the nomads who had the strange vision. For those authors to know God's name was to tame the wild deity, to have a degree of control over that being who causes us such trouble. Kushner explains that the "Bible itself insists that names matter," none so more than that of God's. For a "Hebrew reader," Kushner writes, "the Bible's names are a big part of its meaning." There is magic in a name, and it's for that reason that the Lord could never tell Jacob what his actually was.

Which is the origin and justification of the third commandment of the Decalogue. The injunction that the Lord's name must not be taken in vain has little to do with blasphemy or heresy as conventionally understood, for the all-powerful deity who evolved in our understanding over the past two and a half millennia surely isn't effected by a "Goddamnit!" uttered after a stubbed toe, but the agent of theophany struggling against Jacob could be bounded in letters had the patriarch known his true name. This command not to take the Lord's name in vain has nothing to with prudishness and decorum. Blasphemy is neither a question of politeness nor an issue of etiquette; rather, as literary critic Roger Shattuck writes in *Forbidden Knowledge: From Prometheus to Pornography*, it's an issue of "forbidden knowledge closely related to unbridled curiosity and imagination." Shattuck asks, "Can anyone look upon the Lord?" Can anyone, for that matter, know the Lord's actual story, the biography he keeps from all of us? Can anyone know his real name? And do we understand that those things are the same and that to know a name is to know a story is to acquire the key to all narratives that have, will, or could be?

Returning to the Bible (as is popular, I've heard, among some denominational upstarts) garners a bit of assistance in ascertaining the name, or at least some names, of God. The deity is referred to by several different terms throughout Scripture, most commonly El (or its plural, Elohim) and YHWH, which is regularly rendered as "Yahweh" even though its proper pronunciation has long been forgotten, since the utterance was limited to only the high priest within the holy of holies upon Yom Kippur when the temple still stood. In English translations, El is commonly rendered as "God," while instances of Yahweh are figured as "Lord," in imitation of the Hebrew word *Adonai*, which Jews read aloud instead of sounding the divine name. YHWH, composed of the Hebrew letters היה, has long been as mysterious as the Godhead himself, especially considering its unpronounceability, the prohibition on even trying, and the absence of any direct translation. Linguist Joel M. Hoffman explains in his book *In the Beginning: A Short History of the Hebrew Language* that "the letters in yhwh were chosen not because of the sounds they represent, but because of their symbolic power in that they were the Hebrews' magic vowel letter that no other culture had." He continues by claiming that the lack of consensus on how to say the word isn't because "the pronunciation was lost but because it never had a pronunciation to begin with." This is the aura associated with the tetragrammaton, the technical designation for God's four-letter name, and found in the gematria of kabbalah and the Rosicrucian enthusiasms of Renaissance Christian mystics alike, an attempt to harness that awesome magic of God's name that was denied to Jacob.

Because there is something unsettling in that vowel-filled howl that is God's proper name, this title more yawp than nomenclature. An understandable obsession for what God's name (or names) may be, in addition to how the tetragrammaton should be pronounced. In such, there is an acknowledgment that there is power, significance, and meaning in what we call things. To believe that God even has a name evidences a faith that language is never arbitrary—at least, not exactly. If not arbitrary, however, then God's names are certainly . . . multiplicitous. In the Bible, in addition to being known as El and Yahweh, God is also referred to as El Shaddai, Eloah, Tzevaot, Jah, Baal, Elah, El Roi, Elyon, HaShem, and the feminine Shekinah, among others. In the Islamic Qur'an, Allah has a similar roster of potential names, with ninety-nine specifically listed, including al-Qahtar for "he who overpowers," al-Qabid for "he who takes away," and al-Ghani for "the abundant and infinite." According to tradition, there was a hundredth secret name known only by the Prophet Muhammad himself.

Then, of course, there are all the names of the pagan gods, which depending on your degree of ecumenicism are either manifestations of the divine absolute, devils that have tricked their worshippers, or completely nonexistent. What's the relationship between that mysterious ground of being, that God from the whirlwind who denied Jacob his answer, and, say, those other father gods, be they gray-locked and bare-chested Jupiter and Zeus, helmeted Odin, or the potbellied druid Dagda? Are these all names of *the God* or more empty signifiers? The Romans were generous enough to include Yahweh within their pantheon upon the conquering of Judea (as was their tradition with all of those people whom they dominated), choosing to refer to the Jewish God as "Iao." If relation to those other characters is not metaphysical, some have suggested that they may be etymological, with Waugh writing in his underread *God* that as concerns the origins of the tetragrammaton, there "have been many attempts to trace the origins of the name. Perhaps it comes from the Graeco-Egyptian divine name Iao. . . . [And] others have claimed that Yahweh is related to the divine name of Jove, the god who was worshiped by the Etruscans and by the Romans as Jupiter."

Occult traditions have exceedingly more esoteric and untranslatable ways of referring to the Lord. The kabbalistic *Alphabet of Rabbi Akiva* from the first or second century after the Common Era lists seventy potential names for the Lord, all derived from numerological methods and including, among other exotic permutations, Ne'urion, Webidirion, Qapaqupuron, Ab'ibib, Lablabib, and Hadirion YHWH of Hosts, Holy, Holy, Holy. Any of these were, perhaps, the name the belligerent wrestler refused to impart to Jacob at Jabbok. Christian Gnostics in texts like the *Holy Book of the Great Invisible Spirit* or *The Hypostasis of the Archons* variously claimed Abraxas, Barbelo, Norea, and Setheus as the names for the various emanations of God or of the demiurge responsible for crafting our fallen world. Waugh explains that the Gnostics "believed that God's name was a secret, but to those who knew it and could shout it out, he would appear," which may go a bit to explaining his reticence after being bested by Jacob. "Whoever could discover God's secret name would thus be in possession of great power," Waugh emphasizes.

What gravitas does mere "God" have in the light of Abraxas; what power does a simple "Lord" have when we're given the option to call the demiurge "Barbelo"? Indeed, the word *God* is another culturally relative, temporally contingent, completely arbitrary referent for something totally beyond our understanding, our knowledge, our experience. To parse the word *God* as much as the word of God is to remember how relative all such terms must by necessity be when we're confronted with the absolute. The word *God* of course appears nowhere in the Hebrew Tanakh or the Greek Septuagint; it doesn't make its appearance in the context of Yahweh until the sixth-century Gothic *Codex Argenteus*, derived from the Proto-Germanic *gudán*, itself theoretically traceable back to the Proto-Indo-European of the Central Asian steppe spoken several millennia ago and possibly having the literal meaning of everything from "invocation" to "libation." In Greek, *God* is designated as "Theos" and in Latin as "Deus," those words still obvious in everything from theology to the divine. Whatever the angel could have answered Jacob with, it would most likely not be in Greek, Latin, German, Proto-Indo-European, or English. Those are languages that God has limited fluency in—the better to believe that it is that unpronounceable matrix of letters or that vowel-heavy shout that most closely mimics the designation that the Lord gives himself.

The better to chant the name of "God" over and over and over until it's drained of all meaning and becomes a sound—defamiliarized as all such words are when they're repeated continually—so that any internal sense is chased off like a demon exorcized from a body. This sort of prayer may actually approach the closest version of what God's name might really sound like, which is nothing at all. God speaks in tautologies and paradoxes; all other statements are mundanely human in their correspondence to mere fact. Syntactically, these utterances are closest to the sound of nothing while containing words that seem to actually be saying something. The greatest of tautologies stated by God was in his own name, one of the ways of designating the Lord that we have yet to consider. Such was the moment in Exodus when Jacob's distant descendant Moses encounters God in the form of the famed burning bush upon Mount Horeb while he was grazing his father-in-law's flock of sheep. Moses converses with the fiery bramble, the deep resonant basso profundo of the Lord emanating between the cracks and flickers of his branches in that flame that lights and heats but does not consume. Naturally, at one point, Moses asks the burning bush, Who shall he say has sent him when he returns to his people with their discussed task? To which the burning bush / creator of the universe enigmatically responds, his proper name is "I am who I am."

Or variously as "I am what I am," or in the future tense as "I will be what I will be." The variability of ancient Hebrew grammar makes it difficult to parse the exact tense of God's evasive response, but what is clear is that he answers in a tautology—that is to say, he gives Moses a statement that seems to offer no actual content, that seems to refer to nothing outside of itself. Yet it would be a mistake to see this name as being a dodge, for what defines God, what defines the very ground of being, more than that for which there can be nothing outside of its existence? With such qualities, a name that is a tautology makes complete sense, for in a tautology (and a paradox), the semantic content is the infinite everything and the deepest nothing. When we use words like *God*, *Theos*, or *Deus*, they're referents that are culturally relative and contingent; they are, at best, rhetorically playacting when it comes to their correspondence for the absolute in the same way that "Jupiter," "Odin," and "Dagda" are as well. God is not a being within existence but being itself, existence itself. God's actual name must transcend mere contingency, a word whose circumference is nowhere and whose center is everywhere. What qualifies more in its pristine and essential simplicity than "I am what I am"?

If God's name as given to Moses has an intrinsic and complete power because it expresses everything and nothing, then it also can be observed that as a complete sentence, it's also a story. God's name is a narrative. How do we parse this short story, clocking in at only five words (three in Hebrew) and thus beating Ernest Hemingway's famed and apocryphal contribution to the genre of microfiction? In "I am what I am," we have a character, the most fundamental one that can exist, who goes by the name "I" and is both the narrator of all third-person omniscient tales as well as the voice you hear in your own skull, and we have a narrative that concerns the continuation of that character in time. The preferable translation for this interpretation would be that God actually says, "I will be that I will be," for in that sense, we have action in an otherwise static narrative and the implication that the Lord's narrative has yet to be told and as such is not a fable but a promise. That sense of future-tense dynamism, of things to come and things to be revealed, seems an appropriate enough name.

A precedent for that reading in that other name, the letters of the cryptic tetragrammaton. Waugh writes that some have considered that the etymology of "Yahweh" may "lie in the third person singular of a rare Hebrew version of the verb 'to be,'" with Hoffman concurring that Exodus derives "God's name from the verb 'to be.'" When considering questions of narratology, no "story" is more basic, more elemental. The verb *to be* is the key and code, the cipher and origin for all stories. "To be" is the most potent and elemental story that can exist; it is literally the form of all narratives, and it is also the actual name of God. The Lord is not something that dwells within stories; the Lord is all stories. Scripture is not about God; God is Scripture. God is not something that exists; rather, God is something that shall exist. The Lord is not a noun; the Lord is a verb. Not a narrative but the possibility of narrative itself, that which is capable of unfolding the world. God's only name is To Be.

24

Another Man's System

On the Science and Art of Engineering Deities

Si Dieu n'existait pas, il faudrait l'inventer.
[If God did not exist, it would be necessary to invent him.]

—Voltaire (1768)

Excavated from the Iraqi desert at Tell Asmar in 1933 by a group of archeologists from the University of Chicago's Oriental Institute were a dozen votive figurines carved during the Sumerian Early Dynastic period, almost five millennia ago. Variously made of alabaster, gypsum, and limestone, with inlays of lapis lazuli and opal, the so-called Tell Asmar Hoard constituted one of the finest discoveries of ancient Mesopotamian liturgical objects.

None of the statues is over three feet tall; the shortest is only eight inches in height, but what they lack in stature they make up for in their startling uncanniness. Representing both female and male worshippers, most of the Tell Asmar artifacts depict their figures as wearing the traditional skirts of the Early Dynastic period; the men have long, pleated beards that bear traces of the bitumen that dyed them black, and the women's heads are framed with coiled braids. Figurines rigidly stand and clasp their hands underneath their chests, disquieting thin-lipped smiles on their standardized faces. One of their discoverers, the Dutch scholar Henri Frankfort, accurately—if soberly—described them by saying that they approached "bold simplifications which approximate, in a varying degree, the ultimate limit, namely purely geometrical bodies." Whether gods or humans, the figurines convey the unsettling sense that often accompanies those sojourns into the divine, that realm of the not-quite-human. What strikes a viewer the most is not their stature, or their bodily positioning, or their features, save for two—the massive, wide-eyed, unworldly, inhuman eyes that still stare out some five thousand years later.

At some Sumerian sites—whether dedicated to the fertility god Abu (as is the case at Tell Asmar), the god of the air Enlil, or the mysterious queen of heaven and goddess of love, fertility, and sex who goes by the name Inanna—the votive figurines have some variation in the creepy ocular details. Some figurines have lapis lazuli pressed into their sockets to give the statues a wide, blue-eyed appearance; others have black obsidian in lieu of more human orbs. Many have lost their eyes entirely, now only in possession of the darker-than-dark color that is pure absence.

Art historian Jean M. Evans (the current chief curator and deputy director of the Oriental Institute) writes in *The Lives of Sumerian Sculpture: An Archeology of the Early Dynastic Temple* that the "eerie effect of the enlarged eyes . . . has often arisen as a question. These eyes are perplexing." Several hypotheses have been tendered over the decades as to why the Tell Asmar figurines, and other Sumerian votive statues, have this distinctive characteristic. Wide eyes, especially those absurdly large ones on these idols, could convey an emotion of surprise, or of ecstasy, or of pupil-engorged intoxication. Evans gives several examples of modern interactions viewers have had with the figurines, quoting the American painter Willem de Kooning, who commented that the Metropolitan Museum of Art had a cache of Sumerian statues with "huge staring goggle eyes" that were "wild-eyed," and the psychologist George Frankl writing in *The Social History of the Unconsciousness* that these spheres of obsidian and opal convey a "sense of awe and apprehension which obviously indicated the anxiety those people felt in the presence of the gods." Regardless of the intent (or multiple purposes) of the statues' creators, Evans makes the point that the artworks have become "the subjects and objects of gaze." Consider the first of these functions when deciding why the creatures' pupils are so wide—*it's because they're looking at you.*

When a creature with eyes like that looks at you, it's impossible not to sense sentience, a consciousness, a vitality, a life. It reminds me of the line from the seventeenth-century poet Fulke Greville when he wrote of "the eye a watch so inward sense plac'd, / Not seeing, yet still having power of sight." That's the fundamental paradox of iconoclasm, because if you smashed something like that votive figurine, you're acknowledging its power—that it's alive. Controversial but invaluable psychoanalyst Julian Jaynes writes in *The Origin of Consciousness in the Breakdown of the Bicameral Mind* about the Tell Asmar Hoard's "huge globular eyes hypnotically staring out of the unrecorded past of 5000 years ago with defiant authority." Figurines such as these were central to his audacious hypothesis that "consciousness," in the modern sense of there being a sort of interior monologue intrinsic to individuality, is a shockingly recent development, with the majority of human history being dominated by quasi-schizophrenic people who would attribute such intrinsic thoughts to external sources, to being the very voices of the gods.

Such an argument—as hard to prove as it is almost certainly accurate—has profound theological implications concerning individuality, the atomism of the soul, and the unity of God. As an empirical argument, Jaynes's claims are hard to falsify and are thus beyond the purview of science, despite his protestations. Yet Jaynes does defer to evidence, albeit anecdotal, not least of which are those striking eyes of Tell Asmar. Analyzing those strange figures, Jaynes writes that "you are more likely to feel a superior's authority when you and he are staring straight into each other's eyes." Part of Tell Asmar's uncanniness is to make the viewer feel viewed, to make us feel judged. Jaynes writes, "There is a kind of stress, an unresolvedness about the experience, and withal something of a diminution of consciousness, so that, were such a relationship mimicked in a statue, it would enhance the hallucination of divine speech."

The people who carved such figures, who used them in worship, would have actually heard them *speak*, Jaynes would argue, or they would have at least mistaken their own thoughts for the voices of those gods. Consequently, that's how I imagine the idols that populated the Sumerian workshop of Terah, the father of the biblical patriarch Abraham, of whom it was said in Joshua 24:2 that he had "served other gods" and who was famed for the quality of his statues throughout the land of Ur. The Bible is scant on the details of Terah's disreputable profession, but the narrative is filled in by other sources. In the third century of the Common Era, Rabbi Ḥiyya bar Abba records a defiant act of iconoclastic fury that Abraham committed against his father. Writing in the midrash *Genesis Rabba* that Abram (as he was known before his friendship with God) waited until Terah left his workshop, he then "took a stick, broke the idols, and put the stick in the largest idol's hand. When Terah returned, he demanded that Abram explain what he'd done. Abram told his father that the idols fought among themselves and the largest broke the others with the stick." And thus Rabbi Ḥiyya records the genesis of Jewish humor, *because that story is hilarious.* As recounted in the midrash, an enraged Terah demanded to know why he was being mocked, screaming that the idols had no knowledge. Like a Zen master, young Abram imparted to his father the satori whereby the latter would understand the deaf, dumb muteness of his inert shapes of limestone and gypsum.

Except the story must by necessity be more complicated than that, for if we're to understand that idols are stupid things incapable of making anything happen, then the narrative tells the exact opposite tale. Were Terah's statues simply inert, they'd pose no threat to his son. Furthermore, by inspiring such a violent act, the idols were literally able to compel action; they were able to make something happen. Writing of far more recent bouts of iconoclasm, albeit ones that drew inspiration and justification from examples such as that of Abram's, literary scholar James Simpson in *Under the Hammer: Iconoclasm in the Anglo-American Tradition* speaks of the "numinous power of images" and of how iconoclasm only makes sense as a practice, since those who advocated for it "feel the moving power of idols."

As a representative example, the scholar John Dominic Crossan writes in his *In Search of Paul: How Jesus' Apostle Opposed Empire with God's Kingdom* about the defaced representations of the mostly forgotten disciple Saint Thecla, a (celibate) consort of Paul who was celebrated by women of the early Christian church as one especially touched by the Lord. Crossan describes a particular act of vandalism against a Byzantine fresco depicting Thecla, who was subsequently erased from Christian history, explaining that "some later person scratched out the eyes and erased the upraised hand of Thecla." Crossan explains that there are profound implications to this selective destruction, for "if the eyes of both images had been disfigured," that would have been characteristic of the eighth-century iconoclastic controversy within the Orthodox Church. Instead, Crossan writes, "here only Thecla's eyes and her authoritative hand are destroyed" as an attempt to blind and silence Thecla. This is done not as a demonstration of the error in ascribing supernatural powers to idols and icons—*it's done to neutralize those very same powers*. An iconoclast betrays himself, for in his nervous smashing, he belies the faith in which he holds the idol. Abram may have been laughing, but it was an anxious laugh.

Abraham's father was a designer of gods, an engineer of deities, an adept in that science and art that could perhaps be called *deopoesis*—the invention of gods. Arguably, that might make his son the first critic. Terah's deities were made of lapis lazuli bonded with bitumen to alabaster, but Abraham's mental god of pure abstracted thought was no less an act of deopoesis. As an approach to the ineffable—whether concrete or abstract, limestone or poetry—any such encapsulation of the infinite has about it a bit of the idolatrous, which is to say that it has at its core the aesthetic. A mistake to assume that the creation of gods isn't an art like any other, and not just in the literal sense that Terah or the sculptors of Tell Asmar are artists making representations of gods. Rather, we create gods themselves, and they are a medium of creative expression as surely as gypsum and obsidian. There is the ineffable, but the nature of such a thing is that there is an eternal gulf between its reality and the myopia of our understanding; everything else in faith is a question of deopoesis. We do not discover facts about God but rather invent narrative details about her; it is an act of creation.

As Michel de Montaigne infamously wrote in one of his sixteenth-century essays, "Man is certainly insane; he can't make a worm, and yet he makes gods by the dozens." But who would want a worm when you could have a god? Though Montaigne surely meant to castigate human hubris, there is an admirable challenge in the idea of literally designing gods, of creating and compiling the attributes of a deity as a creative act, and then willing it to faith. Literary critics speak of mythopoesis—that is, the creation of realistic-sounding mythological systems—in writers as varied (and as famous) as J. R. R. Tolkien or H. P. Lovecraft. Deopoesis is something different, rarer, and all the more remarkable: it's the conscious willing of a god into existence and then having faith in that very same creation. This isn't an obscure issue of only hermetic import—indeed, in the humid days of the Anthropocene, the invention of new gods and new judgments may be an issue of collective salvation.

There are certainly examples of this in history, more remarkable deopoesis than simply the carving of a statue (though often, those activities are inextricably bound). Pantheons perhaps evolve organically, but there have been audacious examples of creatures becoming the creator, of gods themselves birthed from the minds of mere humans. Pharaoh Amenhotep IV was such a figure of singular genius, who in the thirteenth century before the Common Era looked upon the multitude of scarab-headed and jackal-faced Egyptian deities and eliminated them entirely in favor of his own invented god, Aten—the sun disk. Centering his new cult in the priestly city of Amarna, Amenhotep IV took the name Akhenaten in honor of this god of his own creation and, in the process, abolished millennia of profoundly conservative Egyptian religious culture. Under the rule of Akhenaten, there was a reform of religion and representation, whereby this newly invented god would supplant those previous anthropomorphic monsters in favor of an entirely abstract disk.

Art of the Amarna period, as this solar interregnum in Egyptian history has been remembered, frequently depicts Akhenaten with his distended paunch and his thin limbs prostrate with his beautiful wife Nefertiti before the glowing infinite circle of the dazzling sun. In *Akhenaten and the Origins of Monotheism*, James K. Hoffmeier describes Atenism as a religion of "poetic beauty and . . . theological profundity," a system fully conceived of by Akhenaten and then, for a brief period, willed into existence. The first and perhaps greatest of the "Godbuilders," in Akhenaten's "Great Hymn to Aten," he writes of his deity, "O sole god, like whom there is no other! / Thou didst create the world according to thy desire, / Whilst thou wert alone," an apt description of Akhenaten's own process of singular creation as well. The Amarna revolution supposedly couldn't last, and reactionaries pushed Egypt back to the old gods upon the ascension of Akhenaten's son the boy king Tutankhamen. A bit of that solar energy remained, however, absorbed into the blackness of subsequent literature, hot to the touch even if clouds have obscured Aten in the meantime. When Akhenaten worshipped Aten in his hymn by marveling at "how many are your deeds . . . you alone / All peoples, herds, and flocks," a later poet in a different language would borrow identical language (indeed, paralleled throughout the entire extent of the lyric), imploring, "How manifold are your works . . . you have made them all; the earth is full of your creatures." That later poem is commonly attributed to a different ruler, King David, and it's remembered as Psalm 104, as Aten was traded for Adonai.

The elevation of Yahweh into the one true God was perhaps the ultimate example of God-Building, if not the only one. Some historians have seen traces of Akhenaten's monotheism within the Hebrew version, not least of whom was Sigmund Freud in his idiosyncratic 1939 study *Moses and Monotheism*. In that odd book, the psychoanalyst argues that "Moses is an Egyptian of noble origin whom the myth transforms into a Jew," a renegade priest of Atenism who melded the once-again-forbidden Egyptian monotheism with the henotheism of the enslaved Hebrews, later leading them on their exodus. Even if Freud's hypothesis is dubious (though, it should be charitably said, not completely so), philology demonstrates that the ultimate God of the Bible is the product of a particular type of construction, that the being we associate with the monotheistic Lord of Scripture was the result of melding together several different Near Eastern deities into a new one. Such is obvious from the various names with which God is referenced in the Bible, from "Yahweh" to the (plural) "Elohim."

That these were the appropriated names of different Canaanite gods is crucial in understanding such audacious God-Building, as is the reality that within the Torah, the portions in which he is referred to as Yahweh were most likely first made by a scribe in the southern kingdom of Judea, and the section where he is called Elohim were penned by a poet in the northern kingdom of Israel. These slightly different figures would be melded together into the unified books of Genesis, Exodus, Leviticus, Deuteronomy, and Numbers during the eighth century before the Common Era, when following the Assyrian invasion of the northern kingdom, Israelite refugees arrived in Jerusalem, and there was a political need to synthesize the national epics of the two Hebrew nations into a singular text. Consequently, the God who we've come to worship was constructed because of political expediency and as facilitated through an aesthetic act. Jack Miles explains in *God: A Biography* that the Lord "arose as a fusion. . . . The inner contradictions that were the result of the fusion took shape, quite early on, as a finite set of inner contradictions. It was the biblical writers' common intellectual grasp of this nest of contradictions . . . that permitted them, working over centuries, to contribute to the drawing of a single character." It should be said a character of tremendous subtlety, nuance, and complexity exhibiting a psychologically rich interiority—the result of Hebrew God-Building. The nonreconciliation of those contradictions gives God a psychological verisimilitude lacking in most polytheistic gods and certainly in the flat sunny disk of Aten as well. Call him the Lord of redaction, a deity of editing.

There were other conscious acts of political God-Building that followed that of Yahweh/Elohim in antiquity, such as the syncretic Greco-Egyptian god Serapis. Commissioned to be an invented deity by the ethnically Macedonian ruler Ptolemy in the third century before the Common Era, Serapis was meant to meld together the traditions of both Greece and Egypt into a god suitable for worship by both. Serapis was clearly and obviously designed and created, the engineering of a god as an artistic act, with the new deity combining the biography of Osiris with the anthropomorphic appearance of a Greek god. Edwyn Bevan writes in *The House of Ptolemy* that the dynasty was "marked by one new creation, destined to have a future in the Greek world—the creation of a new cult. A deity whose name had hitherto been unknown to the Greeks outside Egypt became of the great gods of later Paganism—Serapis." Like Aten, Serapis was the result of state planning, a god constructed by bureaucracy but facilitated through ritualistic poetry. Worship of Serapis may strain our credulity, trained as we all are in the Protestant heresy of atheism, for his cult begs the question of why anyone would give due reverence to an entity they knew wasn't real.

But the reality or unreality of Serapis is to miss the point—he is not theory, hypothesis, thesis, postulate, axiom, or theorem. Serapis is a creative act. That he was invented is precisely the reason why he is worthy of worship. Deopoesis is nothing if not an acknowledgment that reverence is found not in logic but in aesthetics. French philosopher Paul Veyne writes in his invaluable study *Did Greeks Believe Their Myths?* that "truths are already products of the imagination and that the imagination has always governed. It is imagination that rules, not reality, reason, or the ongoing work of the negative." Veyne makes clear that gods were not considered "real" by the ancient Greeks in the sense that we think of material objects as being "real" or in the sense that since the Reformation we've defined God as being "real" (reducing the almighty to the level of a chair or a bench whose existence can be easily affirmed or denied). As such, a god was nearer in ontological import to a fictional character, and thus the invention of a being like Serapis would be viewed as no more of a swindle, hoax, lie, or fabrication than would the creation of characters with names like Hamlet or Huck Finn.

As both gods and God became viewed more as hypotheses about objective reality and thus privy to empirical falsification, the idea of there being virtue in the invention of deities would have become largely nonsensical, though not entirely anathema. There have been movements, even in modern times, that have tried to do what Akhenaten did with Aten or Ptolemy with Serapis—to invent gods. Consider the multitude of vying cults born out of the anti-clericalism of the French Revolution, one being the Cult of Reason, founded by, among others, Antoine-François Momoro and Joseph Fouché, and the other being Maximilien Robespierre's more conventionally theistic Cult of the Supreme Being, both established in 1794. There is also Theophilanthropy, which was conceived in part by Thomas Paine in 1797. As Robespierre would describe his invented religion in an official declaration, it would exist to "detest bad faith and despotism, to punish tyrants and traitors, to assist the unfortunate, to respect the weak, to defend the oppressed, to do all the good one can to one's neighbor, and to behave with justice towards all men." The Cult of Reason saw Notre Dame and other cathedrals deconsecrated in favor of the worship of pure rationality, with girls adorned as if they were Athena, having tricolor streamers set in their hair while robed in sashes with "Liberty, Equality, Fraternity" stitched onto them. Robespierre's more traditional Cult of the Supreme Being replaced the atheism of Momoro and Fouché's cult with a sort of reserved deism, but both consciously constructed new aesthetic experiences of a type of divinity, an exercise in the invention of transcendent and noumenal technologies. Nothing more amply demonstrates the manner in which the Enlightenment was simply a form of secularized religion than the ways in which the Cult of Reason and the Cult of the Supreme Being were invented to turn rationality into its own form of ritualized metaphysic.

Revolutionaries were still in the business of inventing deities two centuries later, when a contingent of the Bolsheviks advocated for what they called "God-Building." One of the strangest (and least theorized) aspects of the Russian Revolution, the practice of deopoetic God-Building establishes how fundamentally theological the Marxist project actually was, in a similar manner to how Robespierre's and Momoro and Fouché's projects revealed the sacred core at the center of the French Revolution. Drawing inspiration directly from those earlier projects, the writer Anatoly Lunacharsky advocated for creating a new faith to supplant Orthodoxy in the same way that the Cult of Reason had been intended to supplant Catholicism (and Atenism supplanted Egyptian polytheism). Elaborating on the practice of God-Building in *Religion and Socialism*, Lunacharsky wrote that "scientific socialism, is the most religious of all religions, and the true Social Democrat is the most deeply religious of all human beings." Rejecting the materialism of the most vulgar forms of Marxism, Lunacharsky sought in his role as the People's Commissariat for Education to orient Bolshevism on a secure theological footing. For Lunacharsky, Soviet Communism had to grapple with the religious dimensions implicit within the teleological and eschatological faith of Marxism (despite its protestations toward being science), and he saw in God-Building a manner of reconciling the faith of the mass of Russian people with the rationality of socialism.

Drawing inspiration from sources as varied as Ernst Mach, Friedrich Nietzsche, and the Eleusinian mystery cults of ancient Greece, Lunacharsky claimed his role as the Peoples' Commissariat of Education, writing in *Religion and Socialism* that that political and economic system "unites secular and religious ideological groups in the struggle for the proletariat. Any action aiming to merge socialism with religious fanaticism, or militant atheism, are actions aimed at splitting the proletarian class and have the formula of 'divide and rule,' which plays into the hands of the bourgeois dictatorship." Vladimir Lenin, it should be said, vociferously disagreed with Lunacharsky, even as the latter's minority position exerted some influence on Bolsheviks who sought the melding of politics and the transcendent into a new faith. Important to understand that the God-Builders were not cynically advocating the co-option of religion for political aims but rather genuinely trying to invent a new religion. British philosopher John Gray explains in *The Immortalization Commission: Science and the Strange Quest to Cheat Death* that in Russia, "science and the occult were not separate, but mingled in a current of thought that aimed to create a substitute for religion," with the God-Builders like Lunacharsky maintaining that eventually, the "dead could be technologically resurrected." God-Building had as its dominating metaphysic a radical materialism elevated to the level of the noumenal, with Lunacharsky commanding, "You must love and deify matter above everything else, the corporal nature of the life of your body as the primary cause of things, as existence without a beginning or end, which has been and forever will be." Regardless of one's thoughts on the theology, that God-Building is a theology is obvious.

What all of these case studies demonstrate—Atenism, Serapis, Enlightenment cults, God-Building, and even Abrahamic monotheism itself—is that there are aesthetic ruptures within religious history that countenance the practice of deopoesis, of inventing gods. These moments are constrained, circumscribed, defined activities, religious movements separate from the inchoate stream of religious evolutionary development as well as revolutionary prophetic movements led by figures operating under less conscious intentionality. To borrow the language of the cultural studies theorist Raymond Williams in *Marxism and Literature*, deopoesis is normally a residual phenomenon, despite occasionally being emergent. Such a practice, to invent gods, is never the dominant schema of a culture, even while there are venerable examples of aesthetic approaches to conceiving of the divine. I would propose that if we are to trace the dominant paradigms of how divinity has been conceived over the course of the last several millennia, we can divide history into five major epochs, each of which is named after the primary means of discussing, thinking about, and conceiving of the transcendent within that era. That's not to say that other methods of thinking are precluded during those eras, only that they must by necessity be either residual or emergent. Broadly, I argue that as more complex, abstract, and universalizing religious conceptions emerged from polytheistic practices during the Axial Age, the history of humanity's relationship with the idea of God can be divided into (1) an Ethical Age, (2) a Metaphysical Age, (3) a Logical Age, (4) an Epistemological Age, and finally, (5) a coming Aesthetic Age.

The Ethical Age is equivalent to the era a half millennia before the Common Era first called the Axial Age by the German philosopher Karl Jaspers. He identified that era with the arrival of several disparate religious and philosophical movements defined by both abstraction and universalism, seeing in Greek philosophy, Hebrew monotheism, the Hindu Upanishads and Buddhism, and Chinese Taoism and Confucianism diverse approaches to conceiving of a religious, philosophical, and ethical realm that is transcendent of immediate circumstance. Not uncoincidentally, during the same period in which Jaynes sees interiority developing, Jaspers explains that the Axial Age was "an interregnum between two ages of great empire, a pause for liberty, a deep breath bringing the most lucid consciousness." In my schema, I see the Axial Age as equivalent to an Ethical Age because the most pressing way of talking about God ceased to be ritualistic and became an issue of elucidating correct conduct, morality, and practice. Rather than defining God's attributes, as would be a later philosophical concern, the sages of the Ethical Age sought to define humanity's relationship to God and to one another. As Jaspers correctly saw the Axial Age as defined by universality and abstraction, so could it be added that works as varied as Leviticus, Plato's *The Republic*, and Confucius's *Analects* took as their primary concern an orthopraxic ethical dimension. A preeminent example of the Ethical Age would be formulations of what's often called the "Golden Rule," seemingly universal axioms like Confucius's "What you do not wish for yourself, do not do to others" or Leviticus's "Love your neighbor as yourself."

The Metaphysical Age comes into fruition shortly after the beginning of the Common Era, and while marked by the destruction of the temple in Jerusalem and the concurrent rise of Christianity and rabbinic Judaism, it doesn't easily map onto either. As a dominant paradigm during the Metaphysical Age, there is a concern with the proper definition of God's actual qualities, the development of a kind of divine cosmology that is ever complicated and baroque. In late antiquity, this becomes abundantly clear in the ornate arguments of the seven ecumenical church councils held over the course of the fifth through eighth centuries and convened variously at Nicaea, Constantinople, Ephesus, and Chalcedon. Ethical conduct was a secondary concern for the bishops meeting at these synods; rather, attention was paid to the complex inner workings of divinity and the imposition of a difficult philosophical framework onto the experience of the transcendent. Representative would be the decision arrived at in Chalcedon in 451, whereby the assembled bishops confessed, "One and the same Son, our Lord Jesus Christ, the same perfect in Godhead and also perfect in manhood; truly God and truly man, or a reasonable soul and body; consubstantial with the Father according to the Godhead, and consubstantial with us according to the Manhood; in all things like unto us, without sin; begotten before all ages of the Father according to the Godhead," and so on and so forth. There is no doubt concerning the existence of God; rather, divinity is discussed as if the intricate workings of God can be ascertained through definition. Lest the Metaphysical Age be read as primarily Christian and thus court the ugliness of supersessionism, it should be said that equivalent developments existed with the beginnings of Jewish kabbalah and the academies of Julian the Apostate's theological neo-paganism.

By the end of the first millennium, the Metaphysical Age transitions into the Logical Age, as the councils' definitions of God promulgated by fiat seek to justify themselves on a firmer rational basis, in part by recourse to complex syllogistic argumentation. Broadly concurrent with the Middle Ages, and especially the Aristotelian scholasticism of the High Middle Ages as exemplified by Jewish thinkers such as Maimonides and Rashi, Christian theologians like Aquinas and Peter Abelard, and Islamic philosophers such as Averroes and Avicenna, the Logical Age was a liminal period between the intellectual certainties of the Metaphysical Age and the skepticism of the coming Epistemological Age. Though all serious religious doubts are still emergent, the Logical Age speaks of God in a manner unthinkable during the Metaphysical Age, arguing not about the details of divine definition but rather about how they can be placed on a firm rational basis. This is the era of the great proofs of God's existence. A representative example is the immaculate syllogism of a thinker like Anselm, who in his eleventh-century *Proslogion* conceived of the ontological proof of God's existence. Anselm maintains that God's existence can be concluded rationally, in M. J. Charlesworth's translation, that since "therefore, Lord . . . we believe that you are something than which nothing greater can be thought," and as a manner of logical necessity, it must hold that God himself exists. Regardless of how convincing one finds the syllogism (and attitudes have varied), what makes Anselm's proof representative of the Logical Age is that it exists at all. Despite the example of pre-Socratic and Socratic proofs of God's existence, during the church councils of the previous millennium, the assembled weren't interested in proving God's existence, which was felt, intuited, believed, and lived as a matter of principle, content rather to define the attributes of that being whom they knew to be real. By Anselm's era, a logical proof of God's existence indicates not actual doubt—the monk never wavered in his faith, and he wrote the syllogism to glorify a God that he believed in—but the theoretical possibility of doubt.

The Logical Age thus transitions into the Epistemological Age with the arrival of early modernity. By the Renaissance, Reformation, and later Enlightenment, the rationality of the previous era had descended into doubts and skepticisms, as the primary issue of proving God's existence to glorify a being whom you never doubted transformed into a central question of whether God actually exists at all. Lucien Febvre writes in his classic of Annales school historiography *The Problem of Unbelief in the Sixteenth Century: The Religion of Rabelais* that in the age before modernity, "every activity of the day . . . was saturated with religious beliefs and institutions" so that there were "conceptual difficulties" with even conceiving of religious skepticism. The options of skepticism, agnosticism, and atheism were intellectual impossibilities even during the Logical Age, but by the Epistemological Age, religious uncertainty became a possibility; thus the Reformation sees the valorization and redefinition of faith as the assent toward unproven axioms. Seventeenth-century proofs of God's existence from figures like René Descartes, and Immanuel Kant's eighteenth-century disparagement of the validity for such a project, speak to an anxious new status quo.

By the Age of Epistemology, however, atheism itself becomes viable and the flip side of the new dominant, doubting faith. First with the hedging agnosticism of the sixteenth and seventeenth centuries, and then the transitory atheisms of the eighteenth century and the full-throated atheism of the nineteenth century, epistemology became the dominant schema through which God was understood. If the Ethical Age asked "How does God wish us to act?" then the Metaphysical Age asked "How do we define God?" and the Logical Age asked "How do we prove those definitions of God?" then the Epistemological Age asked "Can we prove God?" What then shall be the dominant question of the Aesthetic Age? Those previous ruptures in history give us a clue, those emergent discourses that in the coming millennium shall be dominant. No longer are we concerned with defining God or proving his existence. Rather, the new question will be, How do we make God beautiful? How do we design God to be sublime? How do we invent a God who moves us? What creating creatures shall we create? The operative mode of the Aesthetic Age will be deopoesis, as the preeminent task of culture will be to invent God. In the upcoming era, new gods shall be born again.

25

Binding the Ghost

On the Physicality of Literature

Homer on parchment pages!
The Iliad and all the adventures
Of Ulysses, for of Priam's kingdom,
All locked within a piece of skin
Folded into several little sheets!

—Martial, *Epigrammata* (ca. 86–103)

A good book is the precious life-blood of a master spirit,
embalmed and treasured up on purpose to a life beyond life.

—John Milton, *Aeropagitica* (1644)

At Piazza Maurizio Bufalini 1 in Cesena, Italy, there is a stately sandstone building of buttressed reading rooms, Venetian windows, and extravagant masonry that holds slightly under a half million volumes, including manuscripts, codices, incunabula, and print. Commissioned by the Malatesta Novello in the fifteenth century, the Malatestiana Library opened its intricately carved walnut door to readers in 1454, at the height of the Italian Renaissance. The nobleman who funded the library had his architects borrow from ecclesiastical design: the columns of its rooms evoke temples, its seats the pews that would later line cathedrals, its high ceilings as if in monasteries.

Committed humanist that he was, Novello organized the volumes of his collection through an idiosyncratic system of classification that owed more to the occultism of Neoplatonist philosophers like Marsilio Ficino, who wrote in nearby Florence, or Giovanni Pico della Mirandola, who would be born shortly after its opening, than he did by the arid categorization of something like our contemporary Dewey decimal system. For those aforementioned philosophers, microcosm and macrocosm were forever nestled into and reflecting one another across the long line of the great chain of being, and so Novello's library was organized in a manner that evoked the connections of both the human mind in contemplation as well as the universe that was to be contemplated itself. Such is the sanctuary described by Matthew Battles in *The Library: An Unquiet History*, where a reader can lift a book and test their heft, can appraise "the fall of letterforms on the title page, scrutinizing marks left by other readers . . . startled into a recognition of the world's materiality by the sheer number of bound volumes; by the sound of pages turning, covers rubbing; by the rank smell of books gathered together in vast numbers."

An awkward-looking yet somehow still-elegant carved elephant serves as the keystone above one door's lintel, and he serves as the modern library's logo. Perhaps the elephant is a descendant of one of Hannibal's pachyderms who thundered over the Alps more than fifteen centuries before, or maybe he's the grandfather of Hanno, Pope Leo X's pet gifted to him by the king of Portugal and who would make the Vatican his home in less than five decades. Like the Renaissance German painter Albrecht Dürer's celebrated engraving of a rhinoceros, the exotic and distant elephant speaks to the concerns of this institution—curiosity, cosmopolitanism, and commonwealth.

It's the last quality that makes the Malatestiana Library so significant. There were libraries that celebrated curiosity before, like the one at Alexandria whose scholars demanded that the original of every book brought to port be deposited within while a reproduction would be returned to the owner. And there were collections that embodied cosmopolitanism, such as that in the Villa of the Papyri owned by Lucius Calpurnius Piso Caesoninus, the uncle of Julius Caesar, which excavators discovered in the ash of Herculaneum and that included sophisticated philosophical and poetic treatises by Epicurus and the Stoic Chrysopsis. But what made the Malatestiana so remarkable wasn't its collections per se (though they are); rather, it was built not for the singular benefit of the Malatesta family or for a religious community, and unlike in monastic libraries, its books were not rendered into place by a heavy chain. The Malatestiana Library was the first of a type—a library for the public.

If the Malatestiana was to be like a map of the human mind, then it would be an open-source mind, a collective brain to which we'd all be invited as individual cells. Novello amended the utopian promise of complete knowledge as embodied by Alexandria into something wholly more democratic. Now not only would an assemblage of humanity's curiosity be gathered into one temple, but that palace would be as a commonwealth for the betterment of all citizens. From that hilly Umbrian town, you can draw a line of descent to the Library Company of Philadelphia founded by Benjamin Franklin, the annotated works of Plato and John

Locke owned by Thomas Jefferson and housed in a glass cube at the Library of Congress, the reading rooms of the British Museum where Karl Marx penned *Das Kapital* (that collection having since moved closer to King's Cross Station), the Boston Public Library in Copley Square with its chiseled names of local worthies like Ralph Waldo Emerson and Henry David Thoreau ringing its colonnade, and the regal stone lions who stand guard on Fifth Avenue in front of the Main Branch of the New York Public Library.

More importantly, the Malatestiana is the progenitor of millions of local public libraries from Bombay to Budapest. In the United States, the public library arguably endures as one of the last truly democratic institutions. In libraries, there are not just the books collectively owned by a community but the toy exchanges for children, the book clubs and discussion groups, the 12 Step meetings in basements, and the respite from winter cold for the indigent. For all of their varied purposes, and even with the tyrannical ascending reign of modern technology, the library is still focused on the idea of the *book*. Sometimes the techno-utopians malign the concerns of us partisans of the physical book as being merely a species of fetishism, the desire to turn crinkled pages labeled an affectation, the pleasure drawn from the heft of a hardback dismissed as misplaced nostalgia. Yet there are indomitably pragmatic defenses of the book as physical object—now more than ever.

For one, a physical book is safe from the Orwellian deletions of Amazon and the electronic surveillance of the NSA. A physical book, in being unconnected to the internet, can be as a closed-off monastery from the distraction and dwindling attention span engendered by push notifications and smartphone apps. The book as object allows for a true degree of interiority, of genuine privacy that cannot be ensured on any electronic device. To penetrate the sovereignty of the Kingdom of the Book requires the lo-fi method of looking over a reader's shoulder. A physical book is inviolate in the face of power outages, and it cannot short-circuit. There is no rainbow pinwheel of death when you open a book.

But if I can cop to some of what the critics of us Luddites impugn us with, there is something crucial about the weight of a book. So much does depend on a cracked spine and a coffee-stained page. There is an "incarnational poetics" to the very physical reality of a book that can't be replicated on a greasy touch screen. John Milton wrote in his 1644 *Aeropagitica*, still among one of the most potent defenses of free speech written, that "books are not absolutely dead things, but do contain a potency of life in them to be as active as that soul whose progeny they are." This is not just simply metaphor; in some sense, we must understand books as being alive, and just as it's impossible to extricate the soul of a person from their very sinews and nerves, bones and flesh, so to can we not divorce the text from the smooth sheen of velum, the warp and weft of paper, the glow of the screen. Geoffrey Chaucer or William Shakespeare must be interpreted differently depending on how they're read. The medium, to echo media theorist Marshall McLuhan, has always very much been the message.

This embodied poetics is, by its sheer sensual physicality, directly related to the commonwealth that is the library. Battles argues that "the experience of the physicality of the book is strongest in large libraries," and stand among the glass cube at the center of the British Library, the stacks upon stacks in Harvard's Widener Library, or the domed portico of the Library of Congress and tell me any differently. In sharing books that have been read by hundreds before we're privy to other minds in a communal manner, from the barely erased penciled marginalia in a beaten copy of *The Merchant of Venice*, to the dog-ears in *Leaves of Grass*.

What I wish to sing of, then, is the physicality of the book, its immanence, its embodiment, its very incarnational poetics. Writing about these "contraptions of paper, ink, cardboard, and glue,"

Keith Houston in *The Book: A Cover-to-Cover Exploration of the Most Powerful Object of Our Time* challenges us to grab the closest volume and to "open it and hear the rustle of paper and the crackle of glue. Smell it! Flip through the pages and feel the breeze on your face." The exquisite physicality of *matter* defines the arid abstractions of this thing we call literature, even as we forget the basic fact that writing may originate in the brain and may be uttered by the larynx, but it's preserved on clay, papyrus, paper, and patterns of electrons. In twentieth-century literary theory, we've taken to calling anything written a "text," which endlessly confuses our students, who themselves are privy to call anything printed a "novel" (regardless of whether or not it's fictional). The text, however, is a ghost. Literature is the spookiest of arts, leaving not the Ozymandian monuments of architectural ruins, words rather grooved into the very electric synapses of our squishy brains.

Not just our brains, though, for *Gilgamesh* is dried in the rich, baked soil of the Euphrates; Socrates's denunciation of the written word from Plato's *Phaedrus* was wrapped in the fibrous reeds grown alongside the Nile; Beowulf forever slaughters Grendel upon the taut, tanned skin of some English lamb; Prospero contemplates his magic books among the rendered rags of Renaissance paper pressed into the quarto of *The Tempest*; and Emily Dickinson's scraps of envelope from the wood pulp of trees grown in the Berkshires forever entomb her divine dashes. Ask a cuneiform scholar, a papyrologist, a codicologist, a bibliographer. The spirit is strong, but so is the flesh; books can never be separated from the circumstances of those bodies that house their souls. In *A History of Reading*, Alberto Manguel confesses as much, writing that "I judge a book by its cover; I judge a book by its shape."

Perhaps this seems an obvious contention, and the analysis of material conditions, from the economics of printing and distribution to the physical properties of the book as an object, has been a mainstay of some literary study for the past two generations. This is as it should be, for a history of literature could be written not in titles and authors but from the mediums on which that literature was preserved, from the clay tablets of Mesopotamia to the copper filaments and fiber-optic cables that convey the internet. Grappling with the physicality of the latest medium is particularly important, because we've been able to delude ourselves into thinking that there is something purely unembodied about electronic literature, falling into that Cartesian delusion that strictly separates the mind from the flesh.

Such a clean divorce was impossible in earthier times. Examine the smooth vellum of a medieval manuscript and notice that occasionally, small hairs from the slaughtered animals still cling to William Langland's *Piers Plowman* or Dante's *The Divine Comedy*. Houston explains that "a sheet of parchment is the end product of a bloody, protracted, and physical process that begins with the death of a calf, lamb, or kid, and proceeds thereafter through a series of grimly anatomical steps until parchment emerges at the other end," where holding up to the light one of these volumes can sometimes reveal "the delicate tracery of veins—which, if the animal was not properly bled upon its slaughter, are darker and more obvious." Important to remember the sacred reality that all of medieval literature that survives is but the stained flesh of dead animals.

Nor did the arrival of Johannes Gutenberg's printing press make writing any less physical, even if was less bloody. Medieval literature was born from the marriage of flesh and stain, but early modern writing was culled from the fusion of paper, ink, and metal. John Man in *The Gutenberg Revolution: How Printing Changed the Course of History* describes how the eponymous inventor had to "use linseed oil, soot and amber as basic ingredients" in the composition of ink, where the "oil for the varnish had to be of just the right consistency," and the soot that was used in its composition "was best derived from burnt oil and resin," having had to be "degreased by careful roasting." Battles writes in *Palimpsest: A History of the Written Word* that printing is a trade that bears the "marks of the metalsmith, the punch cutter, the machinist." The Bible may be the word of God, but Gutenberg printed it onto stripped and rendered rags with keys "at 82 percent lead, with tin making up a further 9 percent, the soft, metallic element antimony 6 percent, and trace amounts of copper among the remainder," as Houston reminds us. Scripture preached of heaven but was made possible through the very minerals of the earth.

Medieval scriptoriums were dominated by scribes, calligraphers, and clerics; Gutenberg was none of these; rather, he was a member of the goldsmith's guild. His innovation was one we can ascribe as a victory to that abstract realm of literature, but fundamentally, it was derived from the metallurgical knowledge of how to "combine the supple softness of lead with the durability of tin," as Battles writes, a process that allowed him to forge the letter matrices that fit into his movable printing press. We may think of the handwritten manuscripts of medieval monasteries as expressing a certain uniqueness—but physicality was just as preserved in the printed book—and also of "letters carved in word or punched and chased in silver, embroidered in tapestry and needlepoint, wrought in iron and worked into paintings, a world in which words are things."

We'd do well not to separate the embodied poetics of this thing we've elected to call the text from a proper interpretation of said text. Books are not written by angels in a medium of pure spirit; they're recorded upon wood pulp, and we should remember that. The seventeenth-century philosopher René Descartes claimed in his *Discourse on the Method* that the spirit interacted with the body through the pineal gland, the "principal seat of the soul," as translated by John Cottingham. Books, of course, have no pineal gland, but we act as if the text is a thing of pure spirit, excluding it from the gritty matter upon which it's actually constituted. Now more than ever we see the internet as a disembodied realm, the heaven promised by theologians but delivered by Silicon Valley. Our libraries are now composed of ghosts in the machine. Houston reminds us that this is an illusion, for even as you read this article on your phone, recall that it is delivered by "copper wire and fiber optics, solder and silicon, and the farther ends of the electromagnetic spectrum."

Far from disenchanting the spooky theurgy of literature, an embrace of the materiality of reading and writing only illuminates how powerful this strange art is. By staring at a gradation of light upon dark in abstracted symbols, upon whatever medium it is recorded, an individual is capable of hallucinating the most exquisite visions; they are able to even experience the subjectivity of another person's mind. The medieval English librarian Richard de Bury wrote in his fourteenth-century *Philobiblon* that "in books I find the dead as if they were alive. . . . All things are corrupted and decay in time; Saturn ceases not to devour the children that he generates; all the glory of the world would be buried in oblivion, unless God had provided mortals with the remedy of books."

If books are marked by their materiality, then they in turn mark us; literature "contrived to take up space in the head *and* in the world of things," as Battles writes. The neuroplasticity of our mind is set by the words that we read, our fingers cut from turned pages and our eyes strained from looking at screens. We are made of words as much as words are preserved on things, we're as if those Egyptian mummies who were swaddled in papyrus printed with lost works of Plato and Euripides, we're as if the figure in the Italian Renaissance painter Giuseppe Arcimboldo's 1566 *The Librarian*, perhaps inspired by those stacks of the Malatestiana. In that uncanny and beautiful portrait, Arcimboldo presents an anatomy built from a pile of books, the skin of his figure the tanned red and green leather of a volume's cover, the cacophony of hair a quarto whose pages are falling open. In the rough materiality of the book, we see our very bodies reflected back to us in the skin of the cover, the organs of the pages, the blood of ink. Be forewarned: to read a book as separate from the physicality that defines it is to scarcely read at all.

Acknowledgments

I must acknowledge the numerous editors and publishers whose support, guidance, and insight made the writing of these essays possible, particularly Adam Boretz and Lydia Kiesling at the *Millions*. I must also express my gratitude for the hard work of my editor at Broadleaf, Emily King, as well as the project's book manager, Elvis Ramirez. Finally, the indefatigable and loving support of my wife, Meg, makes not only my writing possible but all things beautiful.

Appendix

Punic Encomium—a Style Guide

> Purple is a homage to nature and to what human
> ingenuity can do with nature's givens.
>
> —Paul West, "In Defense of Purple Prose" (1985)

> The "less is more" idea may soon become so entrenched in the
> culture that future readers will pick Dan Brown over Milton or
> Melville. That, in truth, is a very grim future. And every writer,
> including myself, should aim to prevent this from happening.
>
> —Chigozie Obioma, *The Millions* (2015)

For those partisans of parsimony, those sycophants of simplicity,
those who penned the canonical style guides that have long done
abuse to twentieth-century composition, men like William Strunk,
E. B. White, and George Orwell (among others), there would not be
much to recommend in the sentences of the greatest prose essayist

in the English language, the seventeenth-century physician Sir Thomas Browne. His is a style that relishes the texture, flavor, and odor of words; that delights in combining phrases and clauses in new and ingenious ways; that conceives of language not merely as a vehicle to deliver meaning but as the very thing in itself. It's a style known for convoluted verbosity and an attraction to the wondrous word wrought delightfully (or, if you're not a fan, exhaustingly). Even Dr. Johnson, who was a fan, described Browne's prose as "a tissue of many languages; a mixture of heterogeneous words, brought together from distant regions, with terms originally appropriated to one art, and drawn by violence into the service of another." And yet Dr. Johnson also admitted that Browne "had uncommon sentiments, and was not content to express, in many words, that idea for which any language could supply a single term," which by necessity must remain the defense of that style of writing, regardless of what the advocates of concision and minimalism might thunder as decree by fiat. In his brilliant defense of ornate prose, author Paul West writes that "it takes a certain amount of sass to speak up for prose that's rich, succulent and full of novelty." Let's be sassy then.

Decreed by fiat the partisans of parsimony have, and despite new editions of Browne's specimens of rare excellence—such as his digressive and aphoristic account on faith, 1643's *Religio Medici*, or his extended reflection on the intersections of archeology and mortality, 1658's *Hydrotaphia*—the good doctor remains mostly read only by specialists. That's despite having advocates of the caliber of Herman Melville, who called Browne a "crack'd archangel," or Virginia Woolf, who in an essay wrote that "few people love the writings of Sir Thomas Browne, but those that do are the salt of the earth." That few people even read the writings of Browne, much less love them, is a certainty; those who were his most enthused defenders are late Romantics like Melville or wordy modernists of a particular caliber such as Woolf, for the long lines and complex sentence structure of Browne haven't been celebrated for a century. There have been periods of retrenchment in this war of attrition between the Attic and the Asiatic, with the latter being seemingly victorious in the nineteenth century, for certainly no one would accuse an Edward Bulwer-Lytton of being a minimalist. Flipping through the works of Charles Dickens or George Eliot will corroborate that the nineteenth century was an era of mauve ascendency, but with writers like Browne in mind, West argues that it makes more sense to think of the mode as "Elizabethan or Jacobean: fine language, all the way from articulate frenzy to garish excess." But though our most esteemed of canonical writers, from Richardson to Austen to Dickens to Hawthorne, wrote with such Punic adornment, the mavens of MFA programs and the nabobs of newsrooms have long pushed the ornate out of style. Author Ben Masters explains in "A Short Defense of Literary Excess" that "embellished prose is treated with suspicion, if not dismissed outright as overwritten, pretentious or self-indulgent." And not just overwritten, pretentious, and self-indulgent but, in a word, *purple*.

Purple being an error is not, however, a law of physics or a mitzvah of the Hebraic covenant; rather, it is a *suggestion*, and the first thing you must consider about the plain style is that like anything in culture, it has a history and its own biases. That's the central ideological problem with all such authoritative style guides: they precisely confuse issues of style with absolute dictate. Journalist Mark Dery astutely observes in "Strunk and White's Macho Grammar Club" that "Strunkian style embraces the cultural logic of the Machine Age." Any good Marxist can tell you that the culture of superstructure is built upon the material considerations of the base, and as the prose of Milton sounds different from that of Samuel Richardson, who reads differently from Oscar Wilde, who scans alternatively from Ernest Hemingway, so too do all styles reflect something of their own age. The virile, masculine simplicity of contemporary plain style thus evinces nothing so much as the concerns, methods, and goals of neoliberal capitalism, with 140 characters the ultimate culmination of style guides that advocate for brevity and simplicity over all else.

There is a long genealogy that takes us from the plain style of Puritan preachers to Twitter, but viewing that history clear-eyed will perhaps remove the aura of infallibility from *The Elements of Style* and "Politics and the English Language." As a caveat, I should confess that I believe all those writers to be geniuses; we should be forever grateful to Orwell for *1984*, which, clichéd references aside, remains profound (albeit not always for the reasons its advocates assume), and White's *New Yorker* essays are masters of form. My truck is not with their actual writing; my criticism stems from their prescriptions for everyone else. Nevertheless, a historical survey of the plain style's ascendancy can make problematic its claims to exceptionality by placing it in a context in which the subjective idiosyncrasies of its development can demonstrate that it's as artificial as the purplest of prose. Second, a meditation on purple prose's unique powers can exhibit the strength and sublimity of a much-maligned style—a mode that in embracing the very idea of artifice demonstrates how all language is artificial and is thus paradoxically more honest than plain style, which makes colonial claims upon the province of truth.

"Objectivity" is always the costume that any status quo wears, but plain style did not generate sui generis from the void, emerging from the chaos of too many clauses to produce lean, muscular, and tight syntax. If the plain style is associated with the feigned humility of democracy, the efficiency of capitalism, the logic of science, and the iconoclasm of Protestantism, then it's because the apotheosis of the mode is a direct result of the Reformation, bolstered by all of the results of that event, both positive and negative. Browne wasn't a Catholic, but he was a via media latitudinarian High Church Anglican, which for many Puritans might as well be the same thing. And his figurative rhetoric and the poetry of his prose mimic more closely the Latinate excesses of the Catholic Douay–Rheims translation of the Bible than the rightly celebrated King James. Browne's prose styling is baroque, for like some olive-skinned Mediterranean, he delights in language itself, seeing it not as a necessary means to an end but the end in itself—language not simply conveying meaning but enjoyed on its own terms. By contrast, the partisan of parsimony sees prose as a vehicle for meaning and nothing more, even if their feigned rhetoric-of-no-rhetoric is in reality one of the oldest rhetorical gambits there is.

Browne is honest about this artificiality, reminding us that "all things are artificial, for nature is the art of God," and he glories in that profundity as surely as one would an immaculate Hilliard miniature or a Purcell concerto, writing that we "carry with us the wonders, we seek without us: There is all *Africa*, and her prodigies in us; we are that bold and adventurous piece of nature." Furthermore, it was not a foregone conclusion that the maximalists and the advocates of the Asiatic would be pushed to the Anglophone periphery, for the greatest sermonizer of the seventeenth century was Launcelot Andrews (incidentally, one of the translators of the KJV, albeit of the High Church contingent), who could gather a poesy of rhetorical flowers with the best of them, and he was joined in his stature with the preaching of John Donne and the scientific writing of a Robert Burton or a Browne, but by the end of his century, the straight lines and the clean surfaces of the Puritan plain style were dominant in homiletics, as logical and rectilinear as a Shaker quilt, and secular English prose has imitated that voice in gratitude ever since. The plain style was thus the ultimate victory of those same idol smashers who stripped altars, threw bricks through monastic stained glass windows, and burned relics in bonfires of the vanities in front of medieval chapels. The same impulse that takes a hammer to the Virgin is that which would have us strike out adjective and adverb in livid red ink.

Nothing as utopian as Browne's contention that "art is the perfection of nature" has marked the mainstream canon of Anglo-American essayists. Rather, writers like White and Orwell have placed "artifice" and "nature" in erroneous conflict, positioning themselves as the stolid defenders of an illusory ethos of *saying it like you mean it*. This is in marked contrast to the linguistic playfulness of the great essayists in the Latin Catholic tradition, writers like Umberto Eco, Jorge Luis Borges, Italo Calvino, and so on, who have no fear of "mannerisms, tricks, adornments." For the Anglophone world, this trepidation about tricks, this miserliness about metalepsis, and this reluctance against rosiness have been to our detriment—avoiding, as it were, the complexity, the genre ambiguity, and most of all, the playfulness of a Borges essay or a Calvino story. As West in his excellent defense of the purple wrote, "A writer who is afraid of mind, which English-speaking writers tend to be, unlike their continental counterparts, is a lion afraid of meat." Whatever the specifics of the battle across history, at least in Britain and America, Generals Strunk, White, and Orwell authored the contours of our governing accord, the purple rather reserved to rule in Latin America or Italy. When prose is purple in the United States, we call it "genre fiction" and rope it off away from literature, lest the latter be contaminated; in Portugal or Brazil or Mexico, they call it "magical realism," and they give it prizes, and they're the better for it.

And so Strunk, White, and Orwell conceived of a pernicious binary opposition: where purple prose is effeminate, the plain exhibits machismo; where the purple is erudite, decadent, soft, and spoken with a suspicious accent, simple prose is humble, direct, and enunciated with perfect Anglo-Saxon consonants; where the purple is exotic and oriental with the whiff of incense and the feel of oil, the plain style is stiff-upper-lipped and English, with no desire for anything that can stain the cushions, *thankyouverymuch*. And where purple prose is as Catholic as a cleric hiding in some priest-hole fingering rosaries, scapular, and a crucifix, plain style is as unadorned and honest as a stalwart Puritan minister.

There is a valorization of meaning and a shunning of artifice, with Orwell's very designation of condemnation in the word *decadence* signaling what exactly he thinks of all those who use more than two commas per sentence. West explains that for the advocates of simplicity, "purple is immoral, undemocratic and insincere; at best artsy, at worst the exterminating angel of depravity." Rather, as I've written earlier, the Puritans of prose wish style to be lean, tight, and muscular. Is there something sexual in those adjectives? It's not a mistake. The plain style has always presented itself as robustly masculine as Papa Hemingway (just don't examine the particulars of that heterosexuality too closely). Purple prose is as flaming as the adjective that describes it, as decadent as Wilde's scarlet ascot. Mandarin style is complex, affected, showy, bloated, and baroque. Purple is the prose of an H. P. Lovecraft, who writes in "The Call of Cthulu" that "we live on a placid island of ignorance in the midst of black seas of infinity, and it was not meant that we should voyage far . . . up such terrifying vistas of reality, and of our frightful position therein, that we shall either go mad from the revelation or flee from the light into the peace and safety of a new dark age," with its seemingly never-ending pile of words upon words, each abstract and soaked with their overdetermination—an Orwell perhaps arguing that such ornamentation serves to obscure truth in that very ignorance of the "black seas of infinity." Better to write in that lean, muscular, virile, and most of all, masculine style of Hemingway, a man of the Keys and the plains, and not a Providence dandy like the schlock-writer Lovecraft. Hemingway, who treated adjectives as if they were ungrammatical and in the next quotation has nary a single comma, adhering as close as possible to Cormac McCarthy's war of attrition against all punctuation as being nothing more than "queer little marks," could observe, "What a business. You go along your whole life and they seem as though they mean something and they always end up not meaning anything."

Ironically, Hemingway's passage from *For Whom the Bell Tolls* is an apt diagnosis of the pitfalls of the plain style. Not its occasional aesthetic excellence (which in the hands of a master like Hemingway is unassailable) but rather the epistemological and ethical claims of its most vociferous advocates in the form of Strunk, White, and Orwell. That is to say, if the ideological crux of all defenses of the plain over the purple disingenuously claims that concision and clearness are paths to truth, then like Robert Jordan, you will ultimately realize that such prose can also "end up not meaning anything." To paraphrase both West and Obioma, sometimes it's not that less is more but rather that less is actually less. Plain style serves not necessarily truth but rather Mammon, emphasizing those stalwart capitalist principles of efficiency, budgeting, and austerity. Dery explains that "Strunk's is a prose for an age of standardized widgets and standardized workers," but let us not be standard, and let us not be workers. Let us rather be lovers and take pleasure in that which we've produced. For as revolution is an act of love, so too does purple prose stand in opposition to the formulations of style that support the status quo.

The purple is not just a style for those who would be labeled by our Anglo-Saxon rulers as being mere inhabitants of sundry lands but rather one with a venerable tradition within English as well, one that can be mined for inspiration in our contemporary moment. Browne's prose, as with that of the other great masters of a seventeenth-century style including Burton, Andrews, and Donne, rambled on in grand branching rhizomes of multifarious meaning, adverbs tumbling upon adverbs, and adjectives plucking upon adjectives, a tumult of clauses, commas, and semicolons. Certainly the twentieth century has its share of verbose authors, its William Faulkners, and David Foster Wallaces, and Vladimir Nabokovs, and James Joyces, and Woolfs (in sheep's clothing and otherwise). But the standard that is taught in classrooms and emphasized in newsrooms is austere minimalism, exemplified by Orwell's advice in 1946's "Politics and the English Language" that one should "never use a long word where a short one will do," a tall order if directed toward Browne, who, after all, titled his perhaps greatest piece with the cumbersome, Latinate tongue twister *Hydrotaphia*. Orwell continues by telling the dutiful student to, if possible, "always cut [an extra word] out" and to never "use a foreign phrase, a scientific word, or a jargon word if you can think of an everyday English equivalent." Orwell doesn't mention his countryman Browne in that essay, though he does celebrate the English of Browne's near contemporaries, the team of translators behind the admittedly immaculate King James Version of the Bible. But when Orwell writes that the "inflated style is itself a kind of euphemism. A mass of Latin words falls upon the facts like soft snow, blurring the outlines and covering up the details," one would be forgiven for going to Browne as a representative example, though one should also be further forgiven for wondering what Orwell's problem is with fresh snow.

For the advocate of contemporary plain style, the convoluted sentences of a Browne and those in his stead serve to confuse or obscure some actual truth, where the mandarin rather delights in the sensuous and sonorous qualities of language to the detriment of fact. Strunk's *The Elements of Style*, now celebrating its centenary (though fully revised and published by his student White in 1935), argues that "vigorous writing is concise." Labeled as "Rule 17," as if this claim were a sacrosanct law chiseled by fire onto stone tablets at Sinai, Strunk and White argue that an author must "omit needless words." They needlessly continue by claiming that a "sentence should contain no unnecessary words, a paragraph no unnecessary sentences, for the same reason that a drawing should have no unnecessary lines and a machine no unnecessary parts," though, of course, whither the sketches of Durer and the lamps of Tiffany? But I digress. By comparison, a representative sentence of Dr. Browne's from *Religio Medici* reads as follows: "I can look a whole day with delight upon a handsome picture, though it be but of a horse. It is my temper, & I like it the better, to affect all harmony, and sure there is music even in the beauty, and the silent note which *Cupid* strikes, far sweeter than the sound of an instrument. For there is a music wherever there is a harmony, order or proportion; and thus far we may maintain the music of the spheres." For Browne's sake, he better have hoped that drawing of a horse didn't contain too many lines! Because from the perspective of a Strunk, or a White, or an Orwell, or any of the other authors of style guides that have ruled ascendant like Pharaoh over the hearts and minds of contemporary writers, Browne's sentence certainly contained too many words.

Strunk and White, consigning not just Browne but Dickens, Eliot, and Melville to the deleted files bin, write that the immature author sees style as a "garnish for the meat of prose, a sauce by which a dull dish is made palatable." But sometimes sauce is delicious. Who wishes to eat spaghetti with no gravy? Only an Englishman would think that a meal of butter and egg noodles was in any way adequate. Strunk and White write that one should turn "resolutely away from all devices that are popularly believed to indicate style—all mannerisms, tricks, adornments. The approach to style is by way of plainness, simplicity, orderliness, sincerity." They denigrate rhetorical figures all while composing the previous quote with two instances of that classic trope of asyndeton (or did they think I wouldn't notice those deleted conjunctions?). But those conceits, those figures that are sometimes called the "flowers of rhetoric," are the very substance of constructed beauty. Who wishes to visit a greenhouse devoid of plants? When it comes to prose, better to let a million flowers bloom.

In rejecting mannerisms, tricks, and adornments, those guides ironically trick their readers, for no such rejection of adornment necessarily implies sincerity. That's always been the first of the great mendacities of the partisans of parsimony—that simplicity and honesty are equivalent. Better to distrust the rhetorical Greek bearing rhetorical horses of simple craft. Their construction is all straight lines and simple joists, with no decoration to be seen, pretending that such carpentry is any less constructed than a rococo chair. Orwell wrote, "The decadence of our language is probably curable," which presumes that decadence is a disease in need of pharmaceutical, supplied by the author of the style guide, of course. The second of their deceits is White and Strunk's contention that complex writing is "to put on airs, as though you were inviting the reader to join you in a select society of those who know better." But who doesn't yearn for such an invitation, and why would one reject the generosity of the writer who offered one to you? Strunk, White, and Orwell came to demolish the baroque style, and that will simply not do. For as Masters writes, "The novelists I find myself attracted to are those who cannot resist the extra adjective, the additional image, the scale-tipping clause. It feels necessary to assert and celebrate this, for we are living in puritanical times."

Yes, give me Hemingway, but give me Arundhati Roy too; read White, but do not ignore Kiran Desai; celebrate Strunk, but do not neglect Orhan Pamuk. Nigerian author Chigozie Obioma argues that "the essential work of art is to magnify the ordinary, to make that which is banal glorious through artistic exploration," and this obsession with the plain style has wrought too many identical sentences, too many short and prosaic lines, too many nickel words when what is called for are phrases purchased with quarters, half-dollars, ten-dollar bills. Obioma continues with the unassailable claim that it is not the plain style in and of itself that must be attacked; rather, "it is its blind adoption in most contemporary novels as the only viable style in the literary universe that must be questioned, if we are to keep the literary culture healthy." For all prose could be translated easily into plain style—better to simply impart narrative or meaning without the decoration lest we be accused of being verbose, decadent, and baroque—so that Browne's reverie "Man is a Noble Animal, splendid in ashes, and pompous in the grave, solemnizing Nativities and Deaths with equal lustre, nor omitting Ceremonies of Bravery, in the infamy of his nature. Life is a pure flame, and we live by an invisible Sun within us" would better be translated as "People are all right."

The argument that the plain style is the best vehicle for conveying the truth and that decorative language is wasteful is not only unsubstantiated in its particulars; it assumes that the primary function of language must be the conveyance of truth and not the celebration of language itself. Purple luxuriates in the pleasures of language, that which separates man from beast, giving it its due diligence, and is perhaps best explored with the introduction of a certain counter–style guide that acts as a manifesto in its advocacy against all modernist upstarts who'd rather have us eliminate the space bar and comma key in favor of only the delete key. Writing can't approach the thing-in-itself, and anyone who says otherwise is lying. But what it can do is gild the lily and let us enjoy the natures of our own creation a bit. Not only Strunk, White, Orwell but also their inheritors who penned less famous composition handbooks, as well as their adherents in the classroom (ironically including myself in dozens of classes that I've taught), present the plain style as evidently correct. Simple is always better, and one must slash, burn, and "kill your darlings," as F. Scott Fitzgerald once said of editing and revision.

The disingenuousness of such staked objectivity was aptly critiqued by Theodor Adorno, who was himself never shy about being obscure, allusive, or ornate and, as a result, was one of the most cognoscente critics of the Kulturkampf, minimalists who rule behind their stylistic penal codes. In Adorno's 1956 "Punctuation Marks," he reminds us that "lucidity, objectivity, and precision" are simply their own constructed ideologies under the mask of impartiality, and that as regards their helpfully enumerated lists, "writers cannot trust in the rules, which are often rigid and crude." Though the stylistic iconoclasts would have wanted nothing less than to circle and eliminate superfluous words and phrases as surely as some emissary working in the Ministry of Truth, I come not to bury Hemingway nor to abolish the plain style. I would no sooner throw out the pristine simplicities of the King James Bible, the elegant classicism of the Declaration of Independence, or the sublime minimalism of John Cheever than I would denounce my beloved maximalisms. But what I do come to denounce is the philistinism of injunctions from Strunk and White, like "Avoid fancy words" (rule 14) or "Prefer the standard to the offbeat" (rule 21), and bourgeoisie sentiments of that colonial son Orwell when he wrote, "Never use a foreign phrase"—as grotesque a bit of Anglophilic xenophobia as I've ever read. (Oh, I'm sorry, I mean "English-love other-hate.")

Dery calls this predisposition against the complicated I've just parodied exactly what it is: another form of naked ideology. He writes, "The Anglo-American article of faith that clarity can only be achieved through words of one syllable and sentences fit for a telegram is pure dogma. *The Elements of Style* is as ideological, in its bow-tied, wire-rimmed way, as any manifesto." Well then, not to supplant those previous manifestos (as they'd supplant me), I rather offer a countermanifesto, a new style guide for those who'd choose the gnomic over the obvious, the esoteric over the mundane, the allegorical over the literal. And as the scaffold on which I shall build this edifice, I shamelessly borrow from and subvert Henry and Francis Fowler's 1906 *The King's English* (as indeed Orwell did as well, though just as easily as he could name names of his comrades to the Foreign Office, he apparently couldn't as easily properly attribute something).

My rules are as follows:

1.

Prefer the far-fetched word to the familiar, luxuriate in the whiff of exotic nomenclature, feel the tactile sensations of their multisyllabic overdetermination, choose words not just for what they mean but for how they sound. Raid dictionaries and distant archaisms for novel words, ones you don't see in Madison Avenue ads, or on the editorial page of the *Wall Street Journal*, or WRITTEN IN ALL CAPS ON THE INTERNET!!!! Choose the unusual word, the idiosyncratic word, the strange word, the unique word. Language does not just facilitate reading; rather, language is the warm Caribbean water in which we may draw that most primitive pleasure of ecstasy, which, as Obioma reminds us, "can hardly be achieved with sparse, strewn-down prose that mimics silence."

2.

Prefer not the short word for its brevity, but rather, choose the appropriate word. Remember that every word with its etymology, its history both spoken and hidden, its network of correspondences both seen and unseen, its branching central nervous system of dendritic connection to the rest of language is the very empire of connotation. There are no synonyms, and the short word does not always express what you mean to express. Flatten not language in the interests of mere word count. Recall West, who writes, "It says life is infinitely more complex and magical than we will ever know unless we stop trying to pin down feeling in pat little formulas or sentences so understated as to be vacant, their only defense the lamebrain cop-out that, because they say so little, they imply volumes."

3.

Decide whether it is appropriate to cut a word out; sometimes an author must pile on words because mere meaning can't be conveyed in the literalism of letters but must also be imparted with the rhythm, meter, music, and poetry of clauses, fragments, run-ons, and continental-sized sentences. Sometimes repetition is required, for all melodies are conveyed in repetition—and more importantly, meanings as well. Do I repeat myself? Very well then, I repeat myself. The lesson is large; it contains multitudes. Kill not your darlings but only your enemies—the crux is being able to distinguish the two. Masters explains, "Above all else, language should be generous and liberating, and these writers remind us of the pure pleasure to be found in the free play and musicality of words. Their sentences sing rather than grumble or shout, and we are all the richer for them."

4.

Fear not the passive, for sometimes we lack agency, and it is only honest to admit such. Do not have the sentiment of the disciplinary colonist who would mark in red the literature of science, or medicine, or technology when it eschews the active simply because English majors have declared that voice to be anemic. Be not a linguistic prescriptivist; acknowledge that all things in language (even the ungrammatical) have evolved, for they are useful to some purpose of expression somewhere, and the passive is no different.

5.

Reject the Trumps of style; fear not the foreign, the scientific, or the jargon. Adorno informs us that it "avails nothing aesthetically to avoid all technical expressions, all allusions to spheres of culture. . . . The logic of the day, which makes so much of its clarity, has naively adopted this perverted notion of everyday speech." Jargon and scientific terms have developed for the same reason that anything has—their evolution accomplishes something that previously couldn't be accomplished. Arguing against jargon should be a faux pas, like saying we should cut our legs off because the viewer happens to find them visually unpleasing (never mind that in both cases, it's now impossible to get around). An even richer vein than jargon, however, is the foreign word, where one can find *le mot juste*. By vice of English's colonial past, we speak one of the most hybridized tongues on earth, an endlessly regenerative dialect for whom that quality is perhaps that which is most recommendable. A mishmash of Anglo-Saxon, Latin, Welsh, Frisian, Norman French, Scotts, Wolof, Igbo, Algonquin, Spanish, Hindi, and God-knows-what-else, English is built from concrete supplied by other languages. The modus operandi of style guides that would have you ignore this in favor of the "purely Anglo-Saxon" conjure not just an obviously racist understanding of language but an impossible one as well. (For which Anglo-Saxon? The Angle, the Saxon, the Frisian, or the Jute?) In the nineteenth century, some plain style aficionados not in keeping with the linguistic zeitgeist of that era planned to replace all Greek and Latinate words with Tolkienesque Anglo-Saxonisms, where you'd be reading this in a "word-hoard" rather than a "library." I plainly reject that as so much kitsch. But as a mea culpa, where much of our past linguistic loanwords were acquired through imperialism, slavery, invasion, and the exploitation of immigrants, our new acquiring of words must be generous, loving, and reciprocal. We must chart dictionaries as benevolent explorers and thesauruses as reverse missionaries, discovering the language we currently don't have but desperately need. For all of us luftmenschen out there, let us borrow words like Yaghan's melancholic *mamihlapinatapai*, Inuit's anxious *iktsuarpok*, Thai's empathetic *Greng-jai*, Tagalog's adorable *gigil*, Ulwa's spooky *yuputka*, or Arabic's heartbreaking *ya'arburnee*. Linguistic communication is but the smallest portion of language, and every subtlety, nuance, and degree in temperature for human experience could have a word that divides and categorizes that emotion in ever finer grades, ever more specific definitions. Why limit ourselves to Anglo-Saxon only? For that matter, why not invent our own Adamic nomenclature, as John Koenig has at *The Dictionary of Obscure Sorrows,* from *Sonder* ("the realization that each random passerby is living a life as vivid and complex as your own") to *monachopsis* ("the subtle but persistent feeling of being out of place").

6.
Break any of these rules sooner than say anything outright barbarous.

———————————

I've ridden Orwell pretty hard in this essay, but when he writes in "Politics and the English Language" that "if thought corrupts language, language can also corrupt thought," he is unequivocally accurate. We've no need for the contention that language doesn't shape the minds of humans, for words are not just our medium but the very substance of our identity itself. It's not just turtles all the way down, it's definitions too. And Orwell is correct that the words we choose and the permutations and combinations of those words are the theurgy that animates our very lives. The linguist Edward Sapir wrote in *The Status of Linguistics as a Science* that "the worlds in which different societies live are distinct worlds, not merely the same world with different labels attached"; that being our reality, why would we ever limit ourselves to not just our own house but, indeed, only the foyer of our own house? Sometimes the reality on the ground calls for that simple, clear, lean language, and in those circumstances, taking a scalpel to the fat of prose might be necessary so that we may more obviously see the outlines of the beast's skeleton. But sometimes—in an unadorned world, in a plain world, in an ugly world—what is called for is the construction of beautiful castles in the sky. The result of the less-is-more dicta, of the style guides, of the fetishizing of the plain style is nothing less than uniformity of thought, conformity of behavior, and confinement of the spirit. If, at its best, it gives us Hemingway, then good; but at its worst, it gives us writers who all sound identical, a mass of literature that reads as if it were written by the same straight, white, male person.

West writes that "purple prose reminds us of things we do ill to forget," including "the arbitrary, derivative and fictional nature of language . . . its sheer mystery . . . its affinities with pleasure and luxury; its capacity for hitting the mind's eye—the mind's ear, the mind's very membranes—with what isn't there, with what is impossible and (until the very moment of its investiture in words) unthinkable." For West, the purple serves the purpose not just of informing but also of making the "world written up," where our mundane existence is "intensified and made pleasurably palpable" so that we may "suggest the impetuous abundance of Creation" and become partners with God in uttering that first *Bereshit* in the formless void, that we may also "add to it by showing" as if we were the archangels. When Orwell writes that "good prose is like a windowpane," he's not wrong, but he's not giving the full account, and he's not right in exactly the way that he thinks he is. *All writing is like a window.* Both good and bad writing, purple and plain, are varieties of windows, for all language is not the *thing* we're looking at itself but rather that which we use to look out onto and examine the *thing* itself. Crucial that his simile compares the simple style to a window, for a window is still an artifice, a construction of humans made of wood and nails and set into a house. And a simple window, it should be said, can be a useful thing. One can more clearly see the approach of storm clouds or the arrival of a missed friend. What is disingenuous is to pretend that the simple window isn't sometimes itself warped, or mussy with a bit of dirt or a tint that alters the color of sunlight that streams in. The risk, the fallacy, is in assuming that the simple window only ever and always ever gives you the unvarnished, accurate portrait of whatever field it is that you look out onto.

Sometimes our souls call out not for a pane of glass but for a mosaic of painted ones. Sometimes we want a stained glass window, a rose window. We desire a register of red, we have a yearning for yellow and for a panoply of purple. Plain windows have their function, but throw not a brick through stained glass, for reverence and the sacred are emotions that can't be easily edited or revised. Do not fear embroidery, or decoration, or ornamentation. Embrace allusion, and if content should escape you, find a goddamn encyclopedia! Embrace connotation, for true synonyms are like absolute zero, an abstraction with no reality! And most of all, let the dreamy filament of language's lush rhythms and resonances thrum in the stony cavern of your skull! Let us trade in the ascetic for the excessive, the arid for the lush, the parched for the quenched, and the straight line for the curved. Where plain style is reactionary, purple can be radical; where simplicity is capitalism incarnate, complexity can be anarchic celebration; where with all of the sociopathic bravado of toxic masculinity we are told to "kill our darlings," we must rather let a thousand mauve flowers bloom—we must let the purple reign! Simple prose can be for the expression of things, but let the purple be for their very invention. Where the plain style is for work, let us affirm that the mandarin is for play. Let us pray in the simple, white, clapboard Puritan church, for sure; but let us have no fear in supplicating before the altar of a gothic cathedral either.